75 Ways for Managers to Hire, Develop, and Keep Great Employees

75 Ways for Managers to Hire, Develop, and Keep Great Employees

LCCC LIBRARY

Paul Falcone

AMACOM

American Management Association

New York • Atlanta • Brussels • Chicago • Mexico City
San Francisco • Shanghai • Tokyo • Toronto • Washington, D.C.

Bulk discounts available. For details visit:
www.amacombooks.org/go/specialsales
Or contact special sales:
Phone: 800-250-5308
Email: specialsls@amanet.org
View all the AMACOM titles at: www.amacombooks.org
American Management Association: www.amanet.org

This publication is designed to provide accurate and authoritative information in regard to the subject matter covered. It is sold with the understanding that the publisher is not engaged in rendering legal, accounting, or other professional service. If legal advice or other expert assistance is required, the services of a competent professional person should be sought.

AMACOM makes every effort to properly identify trademarked terms and uses them for editorial purposes only, with no intention of trademark violation.

Library of Congress Cataloging-in-Publication Data

Names: Falcone, Paul, author.
Title: 75 ways for managers to hire, develop, and keep great employees / Paul Falcone.
Other titles: Seventy five ways for managers to hire, develop, and keep great employees
Description: New York : American Management Association, [2016] | Includes bibliographical references and index.
Identifiers: LCCN 2015042137 (print) | LCCN 2015045222 (ebook) | ISBN 9780814436691 (pbk.) | ISBN 9780814436707 (e-book)
Subjects: LCSH: Employee selection. | Employee retention. | Personnel management. | Leadership.
Classification: LCC HF5549.5.S38 F36 2016 (print) | LCC HF5549.5.S38 (ebook) | DDC 658.3—dc23
LC record available at http://lccn.loc.gov/2015042137

About AMA
American Management Association (www.amanet.org) is a world leader in talent development, advancing the skills of individuals to drive business success. Our mission is to support the goals of individuals and organizations through a complete range of products and services, including classroom and virtual seminars, webcasts, webinars, podcasts, conferences, corporate and government solutions, business books, and research. AMA's approach to improving performance combines experiential learning—learning through doing—with opportunities for ongoing professional growth at every step of one's career journey.

Printing number

10 9 8 7 6 5 4 3 2 1

To my wonderful wife and best friend, Janet —
Thank you for giving me the time, encouragement,
and loving support to create this very special book.

Contents

CHAPTER 4:
Avoiding Litigation Land Mines   165

CHAPTER 6:
Putting It All Together   254

Acknowledgments

To my wonderful friends and professional associates who are experts in the fields of hiring, talent development, and employment law and who were so giving of their time in reviewing select portions of this manuscript as it made its way through the editing process:

Dr. Jacqueline Hart, Global CEO of Starlight Children's Foundation in Century City, California.

Former employment law litigator, consultant, and award winning author, Jathan Janove, principal of Janove Organization Solutions in Portland, Oregon.

Kim Congdon, Managing Director and Chief Human Resources Officer, Academy of Motion Picture Arts and Sciences in Beverly Hills, California.

Heather D. Rider, retired HR executive and former head of human resources at City of Hope Cancer Center and Intuitive Surgical, Inc., as well as current board member at large, San Diego, California.

Delonna Eyer Kaiser, human resource consultant and employment expert in Austin, Texas.

Rich Falcone, shareholder and employment litigation partner at the Littler Mendelson office in Irvine, California.

Sharon Bauman, Partner in the Employment and Labor Practice Group at Manatt, Phelps & Phillips, LLP, in San Francisco, California.

Richard Kennedy, Human Resources Advisor at HROnline.ie in Dublin, Ireland.

Alison Germain, Organization Development Consultant and former Organization Development Director at Comcast NBC Universal International in London, England.

With special thanks to Stephen S. Power, senior acquisitions editor at AMACOM Books and Barbara Chernow and her staff at Chernow Editorial Services in New York City—what a pleasure it's been working together with you on this book project!

Permissions

The following materials were taken from articles written by Paul Falcone:

Question 15: From "Managers as Mediators," *HR Magazine,* December 1999. Copyright ©1999 by the Society for Human Resource Management. Used by permission of the publisher. All rights reserved.

Question 16: From "The Bearer of Bad News: Use These Tools to Deliver Bad News Up the Line and Up to You." *HR Magazine,* August 2003. Copyright ©2003 by by the Society for Human Resource Management. Used by permission of the publisher. All rights reserved.

Question 19: From "A Talk for All Seasons: How to Address Bad Hair Days, Bad Breath, and Other Uncomfortable Workplace Matters." *HR Magazine,* June 2002. Copyright ©2002 by the Society for Human Resource Management. Used by permission of the publisher. All rights reserved.

Questions 35 and 44: From AMA Playbook: "Executive Coaching: How Do You 'Coach to Normal'?" With permission of the American Management Association.

Question 55: From "Motivating Staff without Money." *HR Magazine,* August 2002. Copyright ©2002 by the Society for Human Resource Management. Used by permission of the publisher. All rights reserved.

Question 56: From "Preserving Restless Top Performers." *HR Magazine,* March 2006. Copyright ©2006 by the Society for Human Resource Management. Used by permission of the publisher. All rights reserved.

Question 57: AMA Playbook: "Stay Interviews: 6 Practical Questions for Key Employee Retention." With permission of the American Management Association.

Question 58: From "How to Make a Counteroffer." *HR Magazine,* November 2003. Copyright ©2003 by the Society for Human Resource Management. Used by permission of the publisher. All rights reserved.

Question 60: From "After They're Gone: Communicating About Employee Departures with Remaining Staff is Critical." *HR Magazine,* October 2013. Copyright ©2013 by the Society for Human Resource Management. Used by permission of the publisher. All rights reserved.

Question 61: From "In the Face of Adversity: When Facing a Mass Layoff that Includes You, Set Aside Any Bitterness and Choose to Lead Your Team." *HR Magazine,* September 2006. Copyright ©2006 by the Society for Human Resource Management. Used by permission of the publisher. All rights reserved.

Question 64: From "Lessons from the HR Trenches: Avoid Workplace Landmines with These Strategies." *HR Magazine,* May 2013. Copyright ©2013 by the Society for Human Resource Management. Used by permission of the publisher. All rights reserved.

Question 65: From "Reporting for SOX Duty: Review Your Sarbanes-Oxley Responsibilities and Brush Up on Other Ethical Practices." *HR Magazine,* June 2006. Copyright ©2006 by the Society for Human Resource Management. Used by permission of the publisher. All rights reserved.

Question 68: From "Inheriting a New Team: When Your Team Expands Suddenly, Here are Ways to Cope with the Change." *HR Magazine*, December 2006. Copyright ©2006 by the Society for Human Resource Management. Used by permission of the publisher. All rights reserved.

Question 70: From "Dealing with Employees in Crisis: Recognize and Deal with Extreme Behaviors Before They Turn Violent." *HR Magazine*, May 2003. Copyright ©2003 by the Society for Human Resource Management. Used by permission of the publisher. All rights reserved.

Figure 3.1: From Paul Falcone and Winston Tan's *The Performance Appraisal Tool Kit: Redesigning Your Performance Review Template to Drive Individual and Organizational Change* (AMACOM Books, 2013). With permission of the American Management Association.

Introduction

HUMAN RESOURCES starts with managers—frontline, in-the-trenches leaders who oversee the work of their teams day in and day out, through good markets and bad, and through new change initiatives that seem to be never ending in today's business environment.

The challenges are daunting, but there have also never been more opportunities to grow and develop leadership careers. Think about the challenges that companies face at the onset of the third millennium—evolutionary change at revolutionary speed, the explosion of new technologies, intense global competition, mergers, integration, and a host of other challenges for keeping up competition-wise at a break-neck pace. Yes, it sounds exhausting, and in many ways it is, but the opportunities for strong leaders to stand out among their peers and build stronger companies have never been greater.

What's the dividing line between great companies and merely good companies, between stellar individual careers and those who struggle to meet minimum expectations, and between effective teams and lackluster teams? The answer is, the leadership edge. The strongest leaders enjoy the opportunities that come along with challenging and changing times—career progression and compensation rewards

1

(individuals), higher revenue and profit margins (companies), and greater group performance and sustainable engagement (teams).

The question for any organization is, How do you get there? Most executives realize that what keeps them up at night is typically related to human capital performance in one aspect or another. If sales numbers aren't being hit, if costs are spiraling through the roof, or if systems implementations aren't rolling out smoothly, then people performance issues are usually at the core of the problem. If excessive turnover or intermittent Family and Medical Leave Act (FMLA) leaves of absence are crippling your ability to provide consistent customer service and are leading to unexpected and unwanted client turnover or sky-high labor costs, then people issues are clearly a problem. On the flip side, if workers are engaged, committed, and self-motivated, then all problems simply appear to melt away, and your organizational focus shifts toward rewards and creative expression as opposed to maintenance and defense.

How Can This Book Help?

75 Ways for Managers to Hire, Develop, and Keep Great Employees is a consultant-in-a-box to walk you through the challenges and opportunities that stem from leading employees effectively. Its purpose is to provide a handy guide and a guiding hand through some of the toughest employee relations challenges that corporate leaders face every day—whether they have an HR team in place to help them or not. The examples and stories provided are replete with real-life scenarios that are common across all industries and geographies because people are people, and most will respond in a predictable fashion under particular sets of circumstances. The focus of this book is on creating the right type of environment—both verbally and in writing—to maximize relationships, foster high performance and productivity, and, when necessary, protect the company legally.

Getting every one of your company's leaders on the same page philosophically, culturally, and mentally is no easy feat. Creating a starting point where organizational leaders—from team leaders to supervisors to managers, directors, vice presidents, and above—are all in harmony when it comes to certain basic premises about work and, more specifically, about working in your organization and for your team, will always be a challenge.

But wouldn't it be tremendously helpful if everyone agreed on one operational field manual that addresses how to lead effectively, how to practice the fine art of employment offense and defense, and how to treat people respectfully so that employees could find new ways of motivating and reinventing themselves in light of your company's changing needs? If so, that one field book would not only have to cover the basics of effective hiring, performance management, and leadership development, but it would also have to jump into the trenches alongside your leaders to provide them with on-the-spot guidance for managing some of the trickiest employment and employee relations situations that may come their way on a day-to-day basis.

At last, *75 Ways for Managers to Hire, Develop, and Keep Great Employees* is truly that field guide, outlining what every senior HR executive wished their departmental and divisional leaders knew about communicating openly and honestly, holding people appropriately accountable, building a spirit of teamwork and camaraderie, and making it safe for workers to find new ways of re-engaging and reinventing themselves so they're part of the solution, not part of the problem. Structured according to the lifecycle of effective employee relations—from hiring to communication, from teambuilding and motivation to tough conversations and, when necessary, documented corrective action—this book can be read cover to cover or picked up at any place in between, depending on your immediate needs.

Of course, no one field guide can perfectly align with all the ideas and beliefs that you hold for your company and for your teams. However, this book creates an important baseline and foundation to draw from. It's okay to disagree with certain "best practices" as outlined in the text because leadership is like parenting—there's no one right way to do this that's always going to work. Situations and personalities differ, and circumstances may limit the options you have available. What's important, though, is that you're talking to your leaders about what you agree with and what you'd want to see done differently at your organization. This book is intended to set the foundation for addressing issues that plague even the strongest managers and the best organizations from time to time.

The goal of this book is to help you harmonize employee relations, hire the best and brightest, communicate effectively so that small problems don't become major impediments, motivate and engage your workers so that they can perform their very best work every day, and, when necessary, know when to trust your gut and practice "defensive HR" strategies so that you don't inadvertently step on land mines that may be awaiting you.

It's leadership offense and defense in the workplace, but it's much more than that. This book teaches workplace *wisdom*—not just rules and compliance, and not just niceness without connection to productivity. It's about fostering a culture where workers want to expend discretionary effort, where contagious energy begets excitement and goodwill, and where the potential for worker burnout is more than offset by the opportunities to find new ways of adding value and feeling recognized and appreciated.

Productivity, loyalty, and performance are not things of the past. They're still attainable in this day and age. But it all begins with the caliber of your frontline leaders and their ability to motivate teams and instill a strong sense of accountability for concrete results. Join us now as we walk you through the key areas of leadership excellence in this all-in-one book covering what every company wants from a great HR department—a standard setter in terms of effective hiring, successful communication and motivation, and the ability to employ progressive discipline and to structure terminations that will withstand legal scrutiny. It's all part of the same continuum, and it's all about management with a heart, selfless leadership, and getting teams to deliver 110 percent because they want to, not because they have to.

Managers who use this guidebook to lead effectively and manage their own careers will see employee engagement and retention soar. People will enjoy work more. This book is intended as a one-stop resource for building effective leadership teams whose members listen to their workers, engage and challenge employees, and get everyone aligned with the strategic leadership values and vision that apply to every workplace. What could be better than helping people prosper in their careers, find new ways of creating value in your organization, and receiving the appropriate recognition and acknowledgement for their efforts? You hold the key to it all. Master the fine art of leadership in the workplace, and touch everyone's life and career as their favorite boss, mentor, and coach. You be the gift. You set the standard for others to follow. Teach what you choose to learn, and fall in love with the idea of helping others build their careers and realize their ambitions. Simply stated, you can give your company no greater benefit than the gift of a motivated, energized, and engaged workforce.

1 **Effective Hiring and Selection**

ONE OF THE MOST IMPORTANT and significant responsibilities and opportunities that comes along with leadership lies in hiring the right people for the jobs in your company. Think about it: whether you're an executive vice president or a first-time supervisor, your individual performance is a direct reflection of your team's productivity. Hire the right people who are self-motivated, have a high level of self-awareness, and who hold themselves accountable for bottom-line results, and your career sails happily along while building and growing the careers of those following in your footsteps. Conversely, hire the wrong people, and you'll end up spending considerable time counseling and disciplining workers who struggle just to meet minimum expectations. Often, you will be forced to do the work yourself—at the expense of your family time, your social life, and your sleep.

Self-motivated new hires find new ways of handling the work flow, assume broader responsibilities beyond their basic job description, and do their best work every day—with little need for your intervention. And you recognize these workers when you see them; they typically stand out from their peers in terms of their willingness to assume additional responsibilities, take creative approaches to their work based on their natural, healthy sense of curiosity, and they appreciate the opportunity you've given them and they behave with gratitude. If you can find these kinds of hires for every job opening, you'll be well ahead of your peers and develop a reputation as a team builder and people developer.

Unfortunately, many leaders in corporate America have become jaded over the course of their careers. They reason that finding exceptional hires is more a matter of chance than planned strategy, and they're so busy doing their day-to-day work that they often don't pay enough attention to the open positions they're responsible for filling. Then again, that becomes a self-fulfilling prophecy of downward spiraling because if you don't take the time to fill the open positions on your team, then you and the rest of your group become overburdened making up for the talent shortage and often plunge into a tailspin that will soon lead to burnout.

So let's make a decision at the beginning of this book to change all that. I'll commit to you that there's a way to partner with your in-house or external recruiter in such a way that making outstanding hires can become the consistent norm—rather than the occasional exception—in terms of the fresh talent that you bring aboard. On the flip side, you'll need to commit to making effective interviewing and hiring your top priority from this point forward in your career. My part of the bargain as the author of this book is actually easier than you think; a few tweaks to your interview questioning techniques and reference checking activities will go a long way in helping you land motivated and engaged new hires who are looking to make their mark in your organization as top-notch performers. Your part of the bargain is a bit more complex; focusing on effective hiring remains challenging when you've got so many other responsibilities that demand your immediate attention.

Our goal, then, in this chapter, is to change your perspective on the hiring and selection process. To achieve this, you'll need to make a leap of faith with me on two critical fronts: First, with the chapter tools in hand that you're about to access, you must believe that you can catapult your candidate evaluation skills to new heights and become a magnet for top-notch talent. Second, no matter what exigencies lie before you at any given time, you have to commit to filling openings on your team as your top-most priority under all circumstances. To do anything less isn't fair to you or the other members of your team. In short, you're only as good as the people you hire. Let's venture together now and determine what new approaches and tools for recruitment and hiring are available to you as you address this critical leadership responsibility head on.

1   Establishing Your Brand: Social Network Outreach, Recruitment Brochures, and Adding New Life to Your Recruitment Advertising Campaigns

Up to the early 1990s, the business world ran ads in newspapers to attract candidates. Recruitment ads were short and almost cryptic because newspapers charged by the word. In large-city newspapers, you could easily end up paying $800 to $1,000 for an ad that barely stretched the length of your thumb, so needless to say, there was very little fluff about the company or its culture and vision, and the entire message was dedicated to the job's critical requirements. Around the year 2000, Monster and other online job boards were established, providing much more room for the hiring organization to be creative and express its true spirit. Job applicants uploaded their résumés online, and both internal recruiters and headhunters had volumes of résumés to choose from at the click of a button.

Flash forward to today's job market, and LinkedIn and other social media sites have clearly overtaken the larger online job boards in capturing talent. Researchers will tell you that employers and recruiters today are looking to the "Big 5" social media locations to source top talent:

Websites Where Employers Are Searching for New Talent

Website or Type of Site	Percent of Employers Using the Website
LinkedIn	94
Facebook	65
Twitter	55
Blogs	20
You Tube	15

Source: Jobvite Social Recruitment Survey, 2013.

In similar fashion, job candidates are defining their résumés by searchable key words, creating a comprehensive social media presence, and identifying which social media platforms are optimal for their target audience.

Where does this massive change in such a short time leave you? You guessed it: investing in and beefing up your online presence to compete and attract the best and brightest talent that your industry and local job market have to offer. It's nothing less than critical that your company—large or small, public or private, international or domestic, union or nonunion—invest heavily in creating and developing your online brand across multiple platforms such as the Big 5 listed above. Ask yourself:

> What are you doing to create visibility and credibility to attract highly qualified applicants?
>
> Would someone looking at the career page on your website, your company's LinkedIn or Facebook pages, or your You Tube presence be over- or underwhelmed by your message? Likewise, when was the last time you made a significant change to your online presence?
>
> Are you engaging in best practices in terms of maintaining your online persona, and are you aware of the ROI (return on investment) of social media in terms of your recruitment brand?

If you are unsure of the answer to any of these questions, you're probably missing out on one of the most fascinating and creative times in recruitment history! Enlist the services of an external consultant for a short-term project to spruce up your online profile and tell your organization's story. Understand that applicants will access your company's website on Google first and foremost, but LinkedIn, Facebook, Glassdoor, and similar sites will also be accessed. The Internet has made so much possible in terms of company intelligence gathering that it would be very shortsighted of an organization to fail to establish a compelling presence on the Internet that describes its company's vision, values, and achievements. Be sure you make your Internet presence especially friendly to mobile devices, where so much initial access and research take place.

Next, create a recruitment/marketing brochure that can be downloaded from your website's career page or otherwise emailed to candidates once they're selected for interview. (Your applicant tracking system should be able to automatically email a brochure once an individual's résumé is moved to the interviewing bin.) Your marketing and communications department or a recent new hire who just graduated from college and has solid writing or graphic arts skills can create a recruitment brochure. Sections of a typical recruitment brochure might include:

A brief company history (year founded, founder's mission and vision, annual revenue, number of employees, stock market ticker symbol, locations, corporate governance structure, customers served, market niche, and the like).

The hiring process, including the fact that your organization conducts background checks and drug screens as well as reference checks before someone can begin working. You can also use this as an opportunity to clarify in writing that you generally expect new hires to provide you with copies of recent performance evaluations to demonstrate their strengths and areas for self-development.

Starting salaries and performance reviews: Clarify that merit increases occur either on employee anniversary dates or on specific dates for the whole company (e.g., the second payroll period in January) and that first-year merit increases are typically prorated based on the number of months served up to that point. Likewise, address whether new-hire evaluations include salary increases or are used strictly to provide initial feedback after 60 or 90 days.

Benefits: Take this opportunity to sell the value of your company's benefits programs! Benefits and paid-time-off privileges are typically worth 30 to 40 percent of a full-time employee's base salary at many organizations, so be sure to highlight the value of your programs that will attract new talent. Defined-benefit pension plans are rare these days, but if your company offers one, be sure to explain how it works and how employees will benefit.

Do the same for tuition reimbursement, wellness programs, generous paid-time-off (PTO) policies, and the like.

Miscellaneous information that employees normally might not learn about unless they ask: parking options and costs, mandatory versus voluntary union membership, employee services (e.g., gymnasium, on-site childcare, movie discounts, and ride-share public transportation subsidies). Casual dress days on Friday can serve as a positive inducement for strong candidates choosing among multiple offers.

Likewise, consider creating and posting a video in your company website's career page or on You Tube that introduces prospective candidates to your current employees. Companies are even creating online avatars so that prospective employees can walk through the online hiring experience and learn first hand what it's like to work for you. The various ways and means of developing your online presence and your website career page go beyond the scope of this book because Internet technology changes so quickly, but the point is simple: The recruitment process has become highly automated and digitized, and your investment in developing a best-in-class online experience will pay considerable dividends.

Similarly, consider drafting a freestanding document titled "What to Expect When You First Come to Work for Us" if you're hiring large volumes of entry-level employees who may not have prior industry experience. Such expectations flyers can serve as a one-sheet handout for applicants who want a clearer understanding of the job they're applying for, and, better yet, they can be used as a tool during the interviewing process to discuss the challenges of the position. A typical expectations flyer might include:

- The particular challenges of customer service in your organization
- Work schedule demands, including weekend work, shift structure, and last-minute overtime
- The physical demands of the job, especially if they include anything out of the ordinary (like standing for eight hours or spending excessive amounts of time in a warehouse freezer)

- An emphasis on internal audits and compliance
- Excessive travel demands, on-call requirements, and the like

The point is not to let these workplace requirements surprise the new hires in their first few weeks on the job. Such transparency will not only be appreciated but will likely cut down on employee turnover in the first ninety days.

Finally, when adding new life to your recruitment advertising campaigns, remember two basic rules: First, candidates are generally more attracted to the organization than to the job, so sell your company aggressively. Outline what makes your organization stand out from the competition, what you value, what achievements you're proudest of, and where your vision and priorities lie. Second, don't underestimate the value of career websites that invite worker feedback regarding working conditions, pay, benefits, and opportunities for growth. Glassdoor (www.Glassdoor.com), CareerLeak (www.CareerLeak.com), PayScale (www.Payscale.com), and other websites invite employee feedback. And while there's no way to validate salary information that's volunteered, for example, the overall tone of the feedback that workers share online is exceptionally important for your branding. Therefore, whenever someone is promoted internally or receives some form of an award or formal recognition, consider encouraging them to log onto a site like Glassdoor to share their experiences. Building that shadow presence may take some time but could pay off handsomely over the long run.

2 _Becoming an Employer of Choice: An Investment Worth Considering_

"Employer of choice" has become a bit of a buzzword in many organizational lexicons. What exactly does that mean? It means that you value competitive pay, promotion from within, ongoing learning, corporate social responsibility, and work–life balance. But the formal "employer of choice" programs that I'm recommending here come from a source outside your company; magazines like _Forbes, Fortune,_ and *Inc.* have made a big business of identifying companies that stand out among their competitors in some way, and it may be worth your investment to dedicate resources to becoming a member of these elite listings.

Why? Simply put, the high brand name recognition that your company garners in being identified on these honor roles can serve as a significant swing factor in helping to convince prospective new hires to join your organization rather than go elsewhere. In addition, think of the tremendous value you get from being identified as a leader within your industry. Unions typically won't bother attempting to organize a company that's ranked and recognized at the top of its pier group. It's too much of an uphill battle, and it's much easier for unions to pursue lower-hanging fruit where they know that workers may be disgruntled and frustrated.

Let's look at an example: If you're part of a large multinational company, then the Fortune Data Store (www.FortuneDatsStore.com) alone offers these prestigious lists that your organization can belong to:

Fortune 500

Fortune 1000

Fortune Global 500

100 Best Companies to Work For

But what if you're not that large? The good news is that the proliferation of these types of company recognition programs is staggering, and it might be easier than you think to pursue a ranking that helps you stand out among your competition. For example, review the following listings and see if any of them strike you as a designation you might want to pursue:

- America's Fastest-Growing Companies

  Fortune: "Fastest-Growing Companies in the *Fortune 1000* by Revenue"
  http://money.cnn.com/gallery/news/companies/2013/05/06/500-fastest-growing-revenue.fortune/index.html

Fortune's Fastest-Growing Companies
http://money.cnn.com/magazines/fortune/fastest-growing/2012/full_list/index.html

Inc.: "Inc. 5000—America's Fastest-Growing Companies"
http://www.inc.com/inc5000

Fortune's 100 Fastest-Growing Companies
http://money.cnn.com/magazines/fortune/fastest-growing/index.html?iid=bc_sp_toprr

- Global and Internationally Based Organizations

Fortune: "Global 500"
http://money.cnn.com/magazines/fortune/global500/2012/snapshots/6388.html?iid=bc_sp_toprr

Forbes: "The International 500"
http://www.forbes.com/2003/07/07/internationaland.html

Bloomberg Businessweek: "Top 100 Global Brands Scoreboard"
http://www.businessweek.com/interactive_reports/top_brands.html

Bloomberg Businessweek: "The Global 1000"
http://www.businessweek.com/stories/2004-07-25/the-global-1000

- America's Most Respected Companies

Forbes: "America's Most Promising Companies"
http://www.forbes.com/most-promising-companies/

Fortune: "World's Most Admired Companies"
http://money.cnn.com/magazines/fortune/most-admired/

Forbes: "America's Best Small Companies"
http://www.forbes.com/best-small-companies/list/

- Best Companies to Work For

Fortune: "100 Best Companies to Work For"
http://money.cnn.com/magazines/fortune/best-companies/?iid=F500_sp_toprr

AARP: "Best Employers for Workers Over 50"
http://www.aarp.org/work/on-the-job/info-06-2013/aarp
-best-employers-winners-2013.html

Working Mother: "100 Best Companies for Working Mothers"
http://www.workingmother.com/best-companies/2012
-working-mother-100-best-companies

Working Mother: "Best Companies for Hourly Workers"
http://www.workingmother.com/best-company-list/138503

Working Mother: "Best Companies for Multicultural Women"
http://www.workingmother.com/best-company-list/140533

Glassdoor.com: "Best Places to Work"
http://www.glassdoor.com/Best-Places-to-Work-LST_KQ0,19.
htm

- Specialty Designations

Forbes: "The World's Most Innovative Companies"
http://www.forbes.com/innovative-companies/list/

Fast Company: "The World's Most Innovative Companies"
http://www.fastcompany.com/section/most-innovative
-companies-2013

CNNMoney: "25 Top Companies for Leaders"
http://money.cnn.com/galleries/2011/news/companies/
1111/gallery.top_companies_leaders.fortune/

Fortune: "Inner City 100"
http://www.money.cnn.com/magazines/fortune/innercity
100/

Flexible *Fortune 500* Jobs—Best Companies List
http://www.flexjobs.com/company-guide/fortune-500

The Daily Beast: "The World's Greenest Companies"
http://www.thedailybeast.com/newsweek/features/2012/
newsweek-green-rankings.html

Inc.com: "The Green 50"
http://www.inc.com/green/

Business Insider: "The 25 Best Companies to Work For If You Want to Get Promoted Quickly"
http://www.businessinsider.com/best-companies-for-advancing-your-career-2012-9?op=1

Forbes: "The World's Most Ethical Companies"
http://www.forbes.com/sites/jacquelynsmith/2013/03/06/the-worlds-most-ethical-companies-in-2013/

This list is by no means exhaustive. But could it be worth the effort to have an employee look into pursuing designations as the most ethical, the greenest, the most flexible, or the best type of company for working moms or hourly employees? How about pursuing a designation as one of the most promising and admired corporations? What about being one of the best-inner city employers or one of the best companies that focus on workers over 50? As you can see, these corporate recognition publications have become a big business.

Just think of the kudos you would garner and the pride your employees might feel in being part of an organization that's formally recognized for these types of attributes. Now *that's* something to write home about, and to add to the top of your LinkedIn page and résumé if you're fortunate enough to be a member of a prestigious organization like that. Nothing will add more spark and pep to your company's self-image and your recruitment-advertising platform than garnering these types of credentials, and they're mostly free (except for a nominal application fee). This may be one of the easier "low-hanging fruits" that mark a major achievement for your organization in the upcoming year.

3   *Direct Sourcing: Alternatives and Options for Proactive Candidate Outreach*

While professional networking tools like LinkedIn allow employers to proactively identify and source "passive" candidates (i.e., those not necessarily in job search mode at the time of contact), there's a lot to be said about the advantages of approaching potential job candidates by phone rather than electronically. Initiating a limited networking campaign to spread the word about job openings in your organization and occasionally generating interviews from "outreach" telephone calls used to be the exclusive domain of headhunters, but you can be empowered as well to become a "shoulder tapper" to potential talent.

The advantages are that you'll access a potential pool of talented workers who may not be looking for a new job but may be open to hearing about new opportunities, you'll reduce your hiring costs if your outreach efforts succeed, and you'll gain an opportunity to network with individuals at competitor firms. Furthermore, you'll generate a sense of self-sufficiency as you develop the skills necessary to proactively reach out to and develop talent that ultimately helps you build your business team and shift the competitive advantage in your favor.

But there also may be disadvantages to this strategy. Many companies opt not to directly "source" candidates from competitor or peer firms for reasons of propriety. After all, if you're perceived as "stealing" from the competition, the competition will feel free to steal from you. In addition, industry relationships could be compromised if old friends at competitor firms find out that your company is raiding theirs.

In general, therefore, it's best to leave headhunting to headhunters. After having done executive search work myself, I can confidently state that there may be too many risks that employers run in terms of damaging industry relationships and being perceived as overly aggressive if they directly source candidates themselves. It's not uncommon that companies will strictly forbid any form of direct sourcing from the competition. Still, on a limited outreach basis, it may make sense for line managers to carefully develop their own network of recruiting sources, so let's discuss how you can pursue this option.

Let's assume you're a vice president of finance looking to fill a director of finance position in your department. You would typically post the job internally, run online ads, scour LinkedIn using a keyword search for qualified individuals in your industry or location, and possibly engage the services of a headhunter. Before engaging that headhunter, though, you might want to first try a limited telephone outreach to other organizations in your industry or geographical area.

After all, headhunters' fees typically approximate one-third of a new hire's base salary (or total cash compensation), so engaging a headhunter is expensive.

Your first step would be to make a list of companies that compete directly with yours. For example, if your organization is a plastics manufacturer with 200 employees and $50 million in revenue, you'd identify other plastics manufacturers of similar size in your geographic area. Let's assume there are ten companies in your city. You'd then contact those companies and ask the person answering the phone for the name of either the manager, director, or the vice president of finance.

At this juncture you'll have to decide if you want to directly recruit the candidate (manager or director) or instead network with the individual one or two tiers above the targeted candidate (vice president). You'll then ask to be connected to that individual. The receptionist, acting as a "screener" or "gatekeeper," will ask about the purpose of your call. Simply state that you work for XYZ Company, a competitor organization, and you've got a networking question for the manager, director, or vice president of finance. That should get your call through. Feel free to leave your name and telephone number if the individual isn't available at the time of your call. (Just be sure to write the person's name down so that when your call is returned, you'll remember where you left off!)

Let's look at how these calls would differ. First, let's call the vice president from an indirect networking standpoint. When the vice president picks up the phone, introduce yourself and your company, and state the purpose of your call:

> Judy, I'm the vice president of finance at XYZ Company, and we're not far from you in Tarrytown, New York. I'm calling you because we haven't had a chance to meet before, and I could really use your help. Is this a good time to talk? [It is.]
>
> Great! We're a plastics manufacturer headquartered in Germany, and we're privately held. We've got about 200 employees and $50 million in revenue, and we specialize in manufacturing plastics primarily for the automotive parts industry. Our director of finance is leaving the company after three years because his wife has just gotten a great job offer in Phoenix, and we're looking to

fill that position. We need someone with a strong background in finance, especially budgeting and forecasting, and ideally an MBA or CPA. The base salary range is around $125,000 to $150,000, and the candidate would be bonus-eligible after the first year. The bonus target would probably fall in the 15 to 20 percent range. Is there anyone in your network who you could recommend, Judy, either because they're in career transition right now or otherwise feeling "boxed in" in their current job? I'd be happy to return the favor in the future.

That's a respectful telephone call, and it's certainly to the point. Rarely will others be offended by such an open and communicative approach. The added benefit is that the call will help you build goodwill relations with others in your industry. Remember, by calling the vice president—one tier above the director-level candidate that you're trying to recruit—there's nothing intrusive or threatening about the phone call. It really is little more than a goodwill outreach. And don't be surprised if this individual calls you in the future for a similar networking purpose. Who knows—you might even want to get together for lunch!

Although such networking calls are fairly simple to make, they're typically not as effective as "direct sourcing" calls. In the latter case, you'd be calling the manager- or director-level candidates directly and asking about their interest in exploring opportunities with your company. Here's how that type of call might sound:

Travis, I'm the vice president of finance at XYZ Company, and we're not far from you in Tarrytown, New York. I'm calling you because we haven't had a chance to meet before, and I could really use your help. Is this a good time to talk?

[It is.]

Great! We're privately held and headquartered in Germany with about 200 employees and $50 million in revenue, and we specialize in manufacturing plastics primarily for the automotive parts industry. Our director of finance is leaving the company after three years because his wife has just gotten a great job offer in Phoenix, and we're looking to fill that position. We need someone with a strong background in finance, especially budgeting and forecasting, and ideally an MBA or CPA.

I don't know if my timing is right or if you're currently looking to explore other career opportunities right now. However, as the manager of finance at

Global Plastics, this might potentially be a good move in career progression for you. I guess my question to you is, Would you consider sitting down with our organization for an hour or so to see if we could build a career path or develop a compensation package for you that might be more progressive than your current situation?

And there you have it—a direct recruitment call to a targeted candidate that is nonthreatening and casual in tone. After all, it is somewhat enticing to spend an hour with a competitor to see if a stronger career path or compensation package could be at hand, isn't it? Even the most satisfied employees might have their curiosity piqued enough to meet with you or at least want to hear more about the opportunity you're offering.

A few final tips when it comes to direct sourcing phone calls: Don't mention salary or bonus specifics during a direct sourcing call until you know the candidate's current compensation package. If the candidate asks about pay, simply say, "Travis, I'll tell you all the specifics in a moment, but if you wouldn't mind, tell me about the current compensation package of the person that you have in mind. I don't like shooting in the dark or answering these types of questions in a vacuum, and I may have some flexibility in the salary or bonus depending on the person's background. Who do you have in mind?" Once you have the individual's salary information, feel free to give the compensation specifics of your package or, if you need to go back to the drawing board for additional compensation, you can always call the candidate back at a later time.

Close the call by saying, "Please make me part of your network. If you have any openings and care to run them by me, I'd be happy to return the favor and refer you to the candidates who we weren't able to hire for whatever reason. And if you ever feel like there might be a better time to explore other career opportunities in the future, just give me a call or email me your résumé. I'd be happy to help."

Likewise, expect candidates to ask you how you got their name. There's no mystery to these phone calls; they will only work if you're open and honest about your approach to networking with competitors: "Travis, I can't say that I knew your name before initiating the call. I'm aware of your company's reputation, and I respect the work your organization does. I figured that a manager of finance at Global Plastics might be interested in a director-level job at our firm, so I simply called the company and asked who the finance manager was. They gave me your name and transferred the call. That's how I got your name." Or you could state that you looked up Global Plastics on the company's website or on LinkedIn and got his name from there.

If you got the name from an individual at another company, be sure that the person is comfortable allowing you to use her name: "Travis, I got your name from Heather Hand at the Chamber of Commerce. She told me that you might consider possibly exploring other opportunities with new companies, and she thought that networking with you would make sense. She said if you weren't interested yourself, you might be in a position to refer others who were either in career transition or otherwise feeling boxed in on their current jobs. Does that explain it?"

If five to ten outreach calls to competitor firms in your area generate one or two exploratory interviews, congratulations, you've done well! If your preliminary networking outreach is not successful, then be sure to tell the headhunter you later retain which organizations you've already contacted. This way, you'll make the best use of the headhunter's time and allow him or her to then generate the additional 100+ calls to indirect competitors that are often necessary to generate qualified candidates with industry-specific background or with functional line experience (as finance professionals in this case). That's a smart way to maximize your relationship with a search firm and simultaneously develop a reputation as a progressive employer looking to find the best and brightest talent for your organization.

4 Effective Telephone Screening Calls: An Incredible Time Saver for Initial Contact

Hiring managers who use telephone screening for first rounds of interviews save themselves considerable time in that they bring in only those candidates who fit both the technical requirements of the role and the personality and business style of your corporate culture. Most managers will tell you that they screen out between 40 and 60 percent of candidates over the phone, which saves them tremendous amounts of time in terms of personal introductions, small talk, and formal interviewing.

Telephone screening calls should generally last ten to twenty minutes and cover the basics in terms of what candidates have done, what their key accomplishments look like, why they're considering leaving their current company, and, very importantly, whether joining your organization can fill those needs. You'll also want to include initial salary discussions at this initial stage, because there's no point in scheduling an in-person interview with someone who's earning $50,000 more than your position is paying unless salary expectations are discussed upfront and the pay cut is justified.

Telephone-screening interviews are never meant to replace full-fledged, in-person interviews. But by the time you're ready to commit to an in-person interview, the initial screening and salary review discussions should have already taken place. An exception, of course, may be made for geographically remote candidates if you're not yet sure, for whatever reason, that you want to go to the expense of flying them in for a formal round of interviews. But formal interviews should always be done in person, because there is considerable information you need that telephone interviews cannot provide, such as the candidate's body language, energy level, ability to make eye contact, and so on. Also, a telephone call can rarely tell you is there is a personality match, so be sure to conduct the formal interviews in person whenever possible.

Your strategy for handling telephone interviews, similar to in-person meetings, is twofold: (1) employ the questioning matrix in Figure 1.1 to gather adequate information regarding a candidate's suitability; (2) after you've completed your initial questioning, sell your company to the candidate. You'll also want to garner information that isn't readily available from a cursory résumé review: ask candidates to describe their company's market niche or size as well as their own straight- and dotted-line reporting relationships. This way you have a contextual framework around which to evaluate the individual more fully.

There are three major segments of the candidate telephone screening: (1) company and job specifics, (2) the candidate's success profile,

Figure 1.1. Telephone screen interviewing guide.

Telephone Screen Interviewing Guide	
Candidate Name	
Date	
Position Title and Location:	
I. Current or Last Company and Role	
Progression indicator: "Walk me through your progression in your career leading me up to how you landed in your current role at your present company."	
Company demographics analysis (size in terms of revenue and number of employees; market niche; primary product markets; specialty areas)	
Current salary and future salary expectations; distinguish base salary from bonus or overtime for total cash compensation (TCC)	
Direct supervisors (numbers and titles, straight-line versus dotted-line reporting relationships)	
Direct reports (numbers and titles) and candidate's immediate org-chart structure	
Budget under control	
Technical systems (basic, intermediate, or advanced knowledge)	

(*continued*)

Figure 1.1. (cont.)

II. Success Profile	
Greatest career accomplishment (in terms of increased revenues, decreased expenses, or saved time)	
"What was the score on your most recent performance review? Do you feel it was justified as an accurate reflection of your work?"	
Reason for leaving current company (qualify circumstances)	

III. Self-Assessment of Candidate's Needs	
"What are the three criteria you're using in selecting your next company or position?"	
"What would the ideal opportunity look like in terms of the industry, company, and role you're pursuing?"	
Counteroffer prep: "What would be your next logical move in progression if you remained with your current employer? How long would it take for you to get there? What would have to change at your present company for you to continue working there?"	
"Generally speaking, are you far along with any other organizations in terms of the interviewing process, and if so, do you have any specific time limitations?"	

and (3) your assessment of the candidate's needs. All three are critical because any one area could raise the candidate's appeal or knock him or her out of contention. Furthermore, the information you develop in advance will go a long way toward further preparing for the in-person meeting still to come. Therefore, simply make copies of the matrix in Figure 1.1 and attach it to the résumés (if available) of prospective telephone interviewees. Once you've completed a full round of telephone interviews and gained critical insights into the candidates' success profiles and career needs, you'll be better positioned to call back the finalists and arrange in-person meetings.

As I outlined in my book *96 Great Interview Questions to Ask Before You Hire* (AMACOM Books, 2009), the candidates' current level of responsibilities, technical knowledge, achievement profile, and company niche will help you quickly determine whether their experience matches your company's way of doing business. Generally speaking, the closer the match between a candidate's present employer (the company's demographics and market specialty) and your firm's operations, the better the chances of a successful hire.

Screening for salary history and salary expectations is probably the most significant part of the telephone interview. If candidates are unwilling to tell you about their current salary or future compensation expectations, it's usually for one of two reasons: they think they're underpaid currently and want to be evaluated based solely on their potential rather than on their current salary, or they're concerned that they're way above the market relative to what your position is likely paying and don't want to be screened out for being overqualified.

In either case, gently inform candidates that you need to know their current (or most recent) salary package details so that you have an understanding of where they stand relative to the market. Explain that you've seen people who were reluctant to state their salary details for fear of being over- or underpaid relative to the job at hand, but you've got to know where they've been so you have an idea whether they're in the ballpark or if you'll need to get additional information about flexing your current compensation package before they come in for an interview. That's only fair: You don't want to spend time interviewing a $200,000 candidate for an $85,000 position and vice versa.

Simply put: you've got to know where the salary anchor rests before inviting candidates into your office for in-person interviews.

Further, when you're evaluating candidates over the phone, jot down their base salaries and total cash compensation (TCC) in the left margin of their résumé next to each position they've held. Expect to generally see salary progression, or positive earning increases, over time. However, in today's competitive business environment and corporate America's constantly shifting priorities, it is not uncommon for workers to retool and learn new trades as former skills lose market value. Salary cuts typically go hand in hand with such skill shifts.

That being said, salary regression (meaning that the candidate has made less money each time over the past three or so job changes) could be a warning sign that the individual is incapable of assuming, or unwilling to assume, greater responsibilities. That's because salary and responsibility are inextricably linked. A candidate willing to accept less money often ends up accepting less responsibility, and that could definitely spell career burnout. Proceed with caution and keep questioning until you're comfortable with the individual's explanations for the negative earnings progression.

Section II, the Success Profile, and section III, the Self-Assessment of Candidate's Needs, of the matrix are fairly self-explanatory. Pay special attention to the Counteroffer Preparation question in section III. It addresses upfront the possibility that candidates will be enticed to stay with their current company once they return to give notice. If the candidates are currently employed, it's worth an initial query regarding the likelihood of their being propositioned to stay put. Likewise, you'll want to find out now if the candidates are deep into interview rounds with any other organizations. If so, the timing may not be on your side to bring them in at the present time. Again, it's better to ask now than be surprised later.

And there you have it: a one-page questionnaire with some of the most critical questions you'll want to have answered before someone walks in the door and takes up two hours of your time. The fifteen- or twenty-minute upfront investment that you make could save you hours of time on the back end because—let's face it—once someone is in your building, it's much tougher to cut the meeting short without embarrassing moments of discomfort. While these questions can be amended to fit the type of hire you're making—hourly versus professional, for example—this structure for conducting prescreening telephone interviews will go a long way in helping you work smarter by ratcheting up your efficiency and honing your candidate selection skills.

5   *Identifying Candidates Who Stand Out Among Their Peers: Criteria to Help You Define the Best and Brightest Talent*

Before we begin our discussions regarding high-yield interviewing questions that will help identify the best candidates, it's important that we define the key criteria that we're looking for in general when evaluating résumés and selecting finalists to come in to interview. Giving thought to the top three or four criteria you value in candidate selection in general is a critical step before journeying down the interviewing rabbit hole, so allow me to share the four key attributes that I look for:

1. Longevity
2. Progression through the ranks
3. Technical skills and education
4. Personality match/X-factor/personal chemistry

These are my recommendations; feel free to choose your own. But before you delve into isolating the core competencies for a particular position and generating behavior-based questions that highlight those competencies, you've got to develop your "philosophical four" values that drive your recruitment and selection efforts. Once you've done that, you've then got to determine which interview questions help you determine if a particular candidate meets those criteria.

The following subsections explain why the above four characteristics are so important to me in selecting new hires to join my team, and suggest a few interview questions that will help you determine if a particular candidate meets your criteria.

Longevity

Longevity represents the potential return on investment (ROI) that you can expect to get from a new hire relative to your involvement in that individual's onboarding and training. In many cases, candidates' résumés display a rhythm or cadence in terms of how long they remain with companies (barring exceptional circumstances that are outside a candidate's control, such as layoffs). When evaluating a résumé and interviewing candidates either over the phone or in person, therefore, focus on their reasons for leaving prior positions to gain a better understanding of what circumstances drive them to leave certain companies and join new ones. The reason for leaving serves as the link in career progression that defines an individual's values and career management strategies. And the most important reason for leaving is the current one: Why is the individual considering leaving his or her current company, and can your organization fill the need that the candidate is trying to achieve?

When evaluating reasons for leaving on an employment application or during an interview, distinguish between reasons for leaving that are within a candidate's control and those that are beyond a candidate's control. The aftermath of the Great Recession of 2008 has resulted in waves of layoffs that derailed many otherwise successful careers. Qualifying the layoff therefore is important to understand the nature of what occurred and how many people it impacted. In comparison, when candidates are orchestrating their own job changes, they often cite "No room for growth" as the number one reason why they left or are leaving a company to pursue greener pastures. Therefore, it's important that you're prepared to discuss both scenarios. Mapped out, your questioning strategy might look like this:

Layoff/Position Elimination due to Restructuring	Orchestrating Your Own Moves/Leaving a Company of Your Own Accord
"How many employees were laid off simultaneously?"	"What does 'growth' mean to you?"
"How many people survived the cut and why? What selection criteria did the company use in selecting positions and people for layoff?"	"What would your next logical move in career progression be at your current (past) company if you chose to stay there?"
"How many waves of layoffs did you survive before you were let go yourself?"	"How long would it take before your next promotion theoretically became possible?"

On the layoff side of the equation, always distinguish between group layoffs and individual layoffs. Group layoffs can impact hundreds or even thousands of people, so that's clearly a no-harm, no-foul type of reason for leaving a company. But if employees appear to be individually selected for layoff, that could be a red flag: companies may be opting to lay off specific individuals and offer a severance package as an alternative to pursuing progressive discipline and structuring a termination for cause. Likewise, if a candidate can explain objectively how the layoff selection criteria were applied without sounding bitter or resentful, those objective career introspection skills may demonstrate a high level of emotional intelligence. Finally, if someone survived multiple rounds of layoffs and was the last to leave and asked to "shut the lights off" on the last day, that could speak to a high level of trust and loyalty that the organization placed in him or her and weigh very favorably in that person's candidacy.

When candidates orchestrate their own moves and point to the most common response, "No room for growth," challenge their interpretation of what growth means to them. For some, it may mean promotion to higher levels of responsibility, and for others it may mean a lateral assumption of increased responsibilities (for example, an overseas rotation or exposure to other parts of the business). Still others view growth potential strictly in terms of salary increases and believe they're not paid their market worth. Candidates who expect your company (or any employer) to make up for their failure or inability to maintain market pay parity are making a mistake. It's not your organization's job to help restore candidates to their perceived level of market worth. So be wary of candidates expecting salary increases in excess of 20 percent.

The key question always when addressing "no room for growth" and career growth expectations is, "What would be your next logical move in progression if you remained with your current company, and how long would you expect it to take before your next promotion became available?" If the candidate responds, "Well, my company is in downsizing mode, and my current supervisor has been in her role for twenty years, so I don't see much upward progression opportunity," then pursuing a promotional opportunity with your company would make total sense. But beware of a candidate who responds, "I'd guess

I could expect to be promoted in the next six to twelve months." If that's the case, why are they here interviewing with you?

Such a red-flag response typically indicates that there's something else going on that candidates aren't mentioning; maybe they're fishing for a counteroffer at their current company and looking for a bona fide offer from a third party employer to use as leverage back at the office. Maybe while they technically could be promoted within six to twelve months, they're now on the outs with their boss and feeling politically isolated. Whatever the case, there's more to their reason for leaving than meets the eye, so explain your concerns and ask them what's really going on: "When candidates tell me they expect to be promoted in six months but they're interviewing here at our company, my antennae go up. There's clearly something else going on: otherwise, they'd be staying put, patiently awaiting their promotion at work. Can you give me a bit more insight into the story behind the story so I have a better understanding of what's primarily driving your decision to interview here or elsewhere?" Ah, nothing like injecting truth and honesty into an employment relationship—especially at the very beginning. Your transparency will go a long way in setting expectations and creating a healthy foundation for your potential working relationship.

Progression Through the Ranks

To identify and highlight candidates' penchant for promoting through the ranks, our second criterion, ask: "Walk me through your progression in your career, leading me up to how you landed in your current company and role." This question cuts right to the chase. It helps candidates frame their entire résumé, demonstrating where they began and how they got to their present company and level of responsibility.

The question could also be phrased this way: "Walk me through your progression in your current company, leading me up to what you do now in your current role." This wording provides candidates with an open invitation to explain where they began, how their roles have changed over time, and what led to specific promotional opportunities (e.g., did they apply internally or were they tapped by senior management to assume a certain position or level of responsibility). It's a great question for lending context to candidates' responses and gauging their ability to summarize large blocks of information succinctly and accurately.

What if a candidate began in his or her current role of controller eight years ago and is still in that role (i.e., there has been no vertical progression)? Of course, that's absolutely fine in terms of the candidate's credentials—who wouldn't want someone with eight years of dedicated service to a particular role within the same company? But this question itself may imply that there should be some sort of upward progression, and candidates may be embarrassed or feel bad about not being able to answer it within that context. To allow for an easy out, simply add a follow-on question like this: "It's great that you've been in your role for eight years. Let me ask you this: How has your role changed over the years, and how have you had to reinvent your job in light of your company's changing needs?" That follow-up question goes a long way in allowing the candidate to respond in a different way and explain the many challenges faced over that period of time and how the candidate adapted to them.

Technical Skills and Education

Technical skills and education provide a foundation that helps justify hiring one candidate over another. After all, if candidates have the right software or equipment skills, medical licensure, educational certification, and the like, they certainly qualify on paper as finalists for the position. But like all things in life, having the paper certificate or the background experience alone doesn't tell you much about how well they perform in a particular area or how they approach their work on a day to day basis. Therefore, engage candidates by asking questions such as this: "On a scale of 1 to 10, with 10 being a perfect match for this position based on your current understanding, how would you rate yourself from a technical standpoint?" Expect a typical response of 8; most candidates won't tell you they're a 10 because they don't want to come across as arrogant or as a know-it-all, but they probably won't grade themselves below a 7 for fear that you'll screen them out as underqualified.

Your follow-up question, then, would logically be, "Okay, tell me why you're an 8, and what would make you a 10?" Asking the question this way allows candidates to highlight their skills gap and explain why accepting this position would help them learn new things and be motivated by the role. Additional follow-up questions might then be: "Where do you think you'll need the most structure, direction, and feedback in your first ninety or 180 days?" and "Why would you consider accepting this position as a good move in progression from a career development standpoint?" Again, extend an offer to allow candidates to explain why they want to join your organization, what motivates them most, and why they see this opportunity as an excellent move overall within the context of their own career management planning. It's a healthy opening exercise for any interview, and candidates generally appreciate your interviewing style because you're helping them connect the dots in their own career development.

Personality Match/X-Factor/Personal Chemistry

My fourth criterion, personality match or personal chemistry, is often misleading. We all tend to hire in own image, but initial likability doesn't necessarily equate with compatibility on the job. Since many managers tend to hire people they initially like and hit it off with, be careful not to make this your first criterion; make it your last. Only use this issue as a swing factor once you've delved into the first three objective criteria in a diagnostic and dispassionate manner. I'll address "personality" and "personal style" further in Question 8. For now, though, understand that the glue that binds someone to a particular job or company is emotional in nature more than it is technical or cognitive, so this aspect of your interview questioning strategy will play a critical role toward the end of the in-person interview.

6 *A Twist on Traditional Interviewing Questions: The "Career Coaching" Approach to Getting Inside Candidates' Heads and Hearts*

Many employers jump into an interview prematurely: "Tell me about yourself, Paul . . ." followed immediately by: "Give me an example of a time when you've . . ." And before they know it, they're off and running into the formal question-and-answer paradigm that defines so many interviews in corporate America these days. Unfortunately, the relationship may not be quite ready for the formal Q&A structure right off the bat. There's actually a more practical and wiser way of approaching candidates at the outset of each interview, and it has to do with focusing on candidates' career needs and aspirations. Get them talking about themselves in light of their longer-term career planning goals, and you'll have a much more meaningful initial exchange of information—even with someone whom you're only meeting for an hour.

   "Piercing the veil" of the candidate façade is both an art and a science. We should simplify the interviewing process so that the interview itself becomes an exercise of value rather than a game of wits, strategies, and defenses, that is, an exercise that provides gateway access into your organization. You'll likely get much more from each interview meeting if you're willing to ask questions that help candidates learn from the process, think about their own priorities and longer term career goals, and articulate why the position you're offering may make sense for them in terms of building their careers.

   Reinventing your interview questioning strategy to focus on the individual's needs can be labeled as a "career coaching" approach to evaluating job applicants because it initially places their needs ahead of your own. As such, it serves as a roadmap for building immediate rapport and goodwill and for turning your current interviewing style, as sophisticated as it may be, into a more open and honest dialogue that focuses just as much on the candidate's needs as on the needs of your company. After all, you've determined that most candidates meet the technical requirements of a position by the time they come in for a face-to-face interview. But what will help you distinguish the most suitable individual for your organization or department will ultimately be based on a personality match, immediate rapport, and a compatible business style that complement your organization's corporate culture and unique personality.

   Pick up where you left off during the telephone screen to learn more about the reason for leaving the person's current organization. Repeat some of the questions you initially asked during the telephone screen, but dig deeper to refine your understanding of the individual's motivation to change jobs and companies. For example, ask again: "What's your primary reason for leaving your current company, and how would joining us satisfy that reason?" Likewise, you could ask, "What would joining our organization do for you in terms of building your résumé over the long term?" And then to really delve deeper, try this: "If you were to accept this position with us today, how would you explain that to a prospective employer five years from now? In other words, how would this job provide a link in your future career progression?"

For those employed candidates who may be considering a lateral move into your organization, be sure to ask, "What would have to change at your current organization for you to consider staying?" Similarly ask, "What would be your next move in career progression if you remained with your current company?" along with the follow-up question, "And how long would it take you to get there?" In essence, you'll be asking candidates to articulate what's driving the need to change companies, what's important at this point in their career, and why your organization makes sense in terms of building their career and résumé. It's very open and honest, and most candidates will appreciate your transparency—especially so early in the relationship.

Similarly, gain a deeper insight into some of the questions that you initially fleshed out during the telephone screen by picking up where you left off:

We touched on this during our telephone screening call, but tell me again about the three criteria that are most important to you in selecting your next company.

I know that industry, company, and the people you'd be working with are typically the three most important elements when selecting a new company where you'd like to work, but which of those three is the most significant to you at this point in time?

What are the top three companies (besides us) that you would pursue right now if you could, and what would the titles be for the positions you would plan on pursuing in those companies?

What jumped out at you when you researched us? What makes us stand out in your mind even at this early stage, and what do you picture the role you're applying for looking like in an organization like ours?

Yes, this may be a lot of information before you've formally begun discussing the individual's specific qualifications, but gaining candidates' trust and benefiting from their initial impressions will help you steer the interview in a particular direction. Assuming candidates have similar work experience, their responses will probably be pretty close to reality. More importantly, though, you'll be asking them to frame their responses within the context of the relationship you're creating by asking them to share more about themselves before you launch into your own technical questions.

You'll find that candidates may be a little thrown off by your self-assessment questions because they may never have been asked to articulate those considerations to a prospective employer in such detail before, but it will open the door to the bonding relationship you're looking to develop. That's because candidates will walk away thinking, "Wow, I've never interviewed with a company that took such a strong interest in me and my own career needs like that. They really forced me to think this move through, and if they put candidates' needs first, they probably do that for their employees as well." In short, forcing career introspection builds goodwill and trust early on.

Be prepared as well to offer candid career advice for the candidate's benefit. Be willing to think out loud and share your opinions upfront, especially if you think the role might not ultimately be a good fit for the individual. Your comments might sound something like this:

> Sam, I really like you, and I think you've got the perfect skill combination for this job, which has been so hard to find, believe me. You've been in a senior financial analyst role with your current company for the past five years, and you've got three years of senior staff accountant experience right behind it. Yes, you could certainly do this job. But it looks to me like your next step in progression should be to a manager level: your skills are in demand, you've got longevity, and it would make more sense to see a manager title on your résumé at this point. If I had a manager opening, you'd be my finalist candidate, no doubt. But you might have a hard time explaining to a future employer three to five years from now why you left XYZ Company for another senior analyst role at our firm. Do you see my concern for you?

I know that it would be tempting to hire Sam and let him worry about his own career progression. Truth be told, though, you want all the pieces to fit together both for the company and the candidate. If your position offers a learning curve, new skill sets, broader responsibilities, and more money, then everyone will be happy, and the hire will stick. If it only makes sense for your company, though, and you could see that the position may be to the longer-term detriment of the candidate, become the mentor and coach that you were meant to be and steer the candidate in the right direction.

You'll not only have helped a junior member of the workforce gain new insights into how he should be looking at his own career; you'll also have strengthened your reputation as a skillful and self-less leader and developer of people. In essence, you'll have shifted the "employee development" paradigm to the preemployment stage. And maybe candidates deserve those few extra minutes of your time to benefit from your expertise. You may just find that a little short-term sacrifice and career coaching on your part will lead to greater stability in your staff and a lot of goodwill in your own career as you build strong teams from this selfless leadership orientation.

7 Achievement-Anchored and Holistic Questions: Cutting to the Chase

Once your warm-up questions have drawn the individual into your selfless interviewing and leadership style, it becomes time to launch into more structured types of queries. Many employers prefer asking questions in a behavioral format that aims to extract real-life examples of past performance in order to predict future behavior. That's an excellent strategy, but I'd caution you not to use *only* behavior-based questions throughout your interview. A few well-placed questions that relate to the core competencies of the role you're looking to fill make sense, but too many examples end up wearing the candidate down, and the tendency to make up answers may result.

Let's say that one of the core competencies of the position you're attempting to fill focuses on strong communication skills. A typical behavioral interview-questioning paradigm might sound like this:

> Give me an example, Sam, of your communication skills. How do you typically communicate best, how do you confront problems head on, and how would your supervisor and subordinates rank your communication skills overall?

Okay, that's three questions in one, but it certainly gives the candidate plenty to ponder. You can also observe how he approaches multifaceted questions like this and compartmentalizes the information to feed back to you.

The beauty of this questioning strategy allows you to go off script. Depending on the candidate's initial response, you can then go deeper into the topic by picking up where Sam left off and asking for additional information about the individual's response:

> So you're not afraid of confrontation and believe it makes more sense to address minor issues before they become major impediments. I'd agree with that. So tell me how you'd typically approach an employee who appears to be falling behind on his work. What about someone who appears to display a bad attitude when asked to take on additional responsibilities: how would you go about addressing that?

Likewise you can ask,

> What is it about you that makes you more comfortable on stage leading an all-hands meeting rather than addressing someone one-on-one behind closed doors?

Clearly, the further you can get away from the structured Q&A response and personalize the conversation, the more you'll get to know the real person. You'll probably also pick up some gems via this interviewing strategy that you could later vet during a reference check with the candidate's prior boss at another company.

It's likewise important that you have a short list of key questions that focuses on the individual's strengths, achievements, and areas for development. You can launch into a behavior-based format with these questions if the opportunity arises, but try the following questions to help differentiate stronger players who are more self-aware of their accomplishments and career goals from those who go about their careers less consciously or purposely than may be ideal for your tastes:

> Overall, what would you say makes you stand out among your peers? I don't mean to make you feel like you have to brag to answer this, but share with me what makes you unique or a rarity relative to your peers.
>
> What have you done in either your current position or a former one that you consider a key accomplishment? Were you able to link your achievement to increased revenues, decreased expenses, or saved time?
>
> Tell me about your last few annual performance reviews. What types of scores did you receive, and do you feel they were an accurate reflection of your performance at the time?
>
> What would your most respected critic say about your areas for development? No one's perfect and there's no such thing as a perfect match for any particular job, but what are some of the real challenges you're focusing on in your career right now where we'll need to give you additional structure and support in order for you to excel in this role?
>
> What are the broad responsibilities of a [job title]? Where do you tend to focus most in your role, and what aspects of your job do you consider less crucial?

These questions tend to cut to the chase in terms of identifying an individual's level of self-confidence, job knowledge, and career focus. Does the candidate sit up and consider these questions to be challenging and an opportunity to be engaging in a healthy sense, or does the candidate sit back and shy away from engaging in these types of conversations? Not everyone you hire will need to be self-assured in his achievements and accomplishments or have a deep level of career introspection about his self-admitted shortcomings. But identifying candidates who demonstrate a heightened awareness of their strengths and weaknesses and who have given thought to quantifying their results will lead to stronger teams and higher performance.

Develop your own core achievement-anchored and holistic questions to help define who will excel on your team. Ask those questions consistently and be open to fine-tuning them over time. After all, interviewing is about a lot more than posing canned questions with little bearing on the candidate's career history. Questions like these tend to cut to the chase because they're meant to reflect your values about work. Using them effectively will help you differentiate candidates who excel from those who have a less accomplished track record of success and achievement.

8 *Hiring in Our Own Image: Likability Equals Compatibility*

Question 5 touched on the importance of hiring in our own image. We cautioned, however, that candidates' initial likability doesn't necessarily equate with compatibility on the job and that we have to be careful to make the likability factor the last, not the first, criterion in selecting candidates for final interview rounds. It's time to pick up with that topic because the personality match and personal chemistry issues belong toward the end of the interview—after we've gone through the "career coaching" portion of the meeting and the achievement-anchored questions described above, and the behavioral and other questions that you typically ask.

The beauty of the questions that follow is that they can be used in two separate arenas: first, they open the door of communication and transparency with the job candidate; second, they can then be asked of former supervisors during the reference checking process. In other words, these stylistic questions lend themselves to initial candidate responses and then vetting by a third party once all rounds of interviews have been completed. Here are questions that lend themselves to this dual usage format:

> What kind of structure and supervision would provide you with the most support from day one? Do you prefer a structured environment with clear guidelines and immediate feedback or more of an autonomous, independent, "hands off" type of working relationship with your boss?
>
> In hiring [job title], we look for a solid balance between quality and quantity in candidates' work. Still, most people lean more in one direction than another. Where do you typically fall on the quality–volume spectrum?
>
> Tell me about your ability to accept constructive criticism. Can your feelings be hurt, and should I be cautious about delivering tougher news, or do you pride yourself on having a thicker skin?
>
> As far as your natural and preferred pace of work, do you function better in (a) a moderate, controllable, and predictable environment; (b) a faster-paced atmosphere with deadline pressures and time constraints; or (c) a "hyperspace,"

chaotic, "management by crisis" culture like the floor of the New York Stock Exchange?

How would you describe your day-to-day approach to working with others? I don't like to use the word "attitude" because it's open to so many different interpretations, but how would people describe your overall demeanor in the workplace? Will people know when you're not having a good day and, if so, how can they tell?

How many hours a week do you find it necessary to work in order to get the job done? There's no right or wrong answer here: I'm just looking for what your historical time commitment has been and what you'd like to see it look like going forward.

Has anyone ever critiqued your reliability or dependability? I'm not asking about absenteeism or tardiness so much, but rather I'm looking more to see how you'd grade yourself in terms of your overall reliability to be present and to accomplish your work projects on time and under budget. What are your thoughts?

What motivates you? Is there anything that typically "unwinds" you or bothers you that you'd like me to know about?

Of course these questions can be adopted for the type of role you're hiring for. You'll ask different types of questions for salespeople versus Ph.D. research scientists. For example, here are some alternative questions that you might want to ask of potential senior leader candidates:

Would you describe your management style as more autocratic and paternalistic or geared toward a more participative and consensus-building approach?

How do you approach taking action without getting prior approval? Is it your natural inclination to report to someone else for sign-off, or do you prefer to operate more with independent responsibility and authority? Can anyone ever accuse you of asking for forgiveness after the fact rather than asking for permission up front?

Looking back at your past performance over the last few years, how effective have you been at orchestrating a corporate ensemble of functional areas? What area or department got most focus, and which one suffered a bit from benign neglect?

How would you describe your ability to cope with the significant pressures associated with senior management?

Have you ever delayed the inevitable in terms of disciplining or dismissing employees? Would people describe your communication style as more aggressive or passive overall?

What's important is that you give thought to what your questions and a candidate's prospective responses might look like. Remember that most new-hire failures are not a result of a technical mismatch; early turnover typically results from a difference in core values about leadership, communication, and expectations regarding teamwork. In short, it's the lack of compatible business styles that doom new hires. Find a way to inject those issues into your early discussions during the interview process, and then vet them during references. The chances of making a high-probability hire can skyrocket when you take such an honest and transparent approach to candidate evaluation and selection.

9 The Critical Importance of Reference Checks (and Scripts to Help You Maximize Each Call)

We all want to make "high-probability hires," but with human beings, there are no guarantees. You can hire someone who comes from a direct competitor, knows your systems inside and out, has great references and top-notch test scores, and that individual could fall apart in his first ninety days with your organization despite your best efforts. Likewise, you could pull a stranger off the street with little experience in your field who could end up being your employee of the year. That's what makes hiring and leadership so challenging and rewarding yet at times so frustrating.

Fear not: while you can't guarantee absolute success each and every time, you can ensure a high level of relative consistency in making high-probability hires. Simply put, that means that hiring someone with similar experience, skill sets, and communication and personal styles will typically yield better results than pulling a stranger off the street and hoping for the best. But the key to this process doesn't lie so much in interviewing and testing but rather in running your initial impressions by former supervisors at prior companies who can speak openly with you about the individual's potential based on his historic track record.

Companies often overlook the importance of reference checking, especially with candidates who had earlier careers in other fields. Yet there's nothing unlawful about checking references and, contrary to popular belief, former supervisors will speak with you if you set up the call in the right way. Just remember that hiring someone without checking references is like having a loose cannon on the deck of your ship: you're basing your entire decision on how well the individual interviewed, but as we all know, too many new hires can go "Dr. Jekyll–Mr. Hide" soon after starting in a new job. Further, there are such things as professional plaintiffs and union salts whose sole motivation is to take unfair advantage of a company and cause total disruption by organizing from within. Consider references your safeguard for ensuring that past behavior is a significant indicator of future performance and overall success.

Still, many employers shy away from checking references from candidates' prior employers under the mistaken belief that past employers won't speak with them, or that it's a waste of time because candidates only provide the names of people who will give favorable references, or that it's illegal to check references.

Nothing could be further from the truth! Until you've vetted your impressions with prior supervisors who have managed the individual on a day-to-day basis, you won't know what you're getting or what the real person behind the "interviewing facade" is all about until you're well into the relationship. And checking references is not illegal! People pick up the phone all the time and check with associates who work at a candidate's former place of employment to find out if the individual is a good performer. They look for shared connections on LinkedIn and other social media to see if they have any connections in common who could shed some light on what it's like working with the person.

To be on the safe side, have applicants sign a waiver that allows your company to investigate all information submitted on a job application, including the ability to conduct reference checks. Remember as well that it's true that a candidate's providing references could result in a lawsuit for invasion of privacy or defamation if the candidate believes he was denied employment because of false or misleading allegations.

Such claims are fairly rare, however, and are countered by a legal concept known as "negligent hiring." Under the negligent hiring theory, an employer may be found to have acted negligently in selecting an applicant for employment if the hiring company, among other things, neglects to contact the applicant's former employers to determine suitability. While negligent hiring claims typically result from acts of workplace violence, courts have generally held that companies may be liable for negligent hiring for certain acts of their employees that the employer should have known might occur. Further, even if the applicant's former employer refuses to give you information, documenting that you attempted to check the applicant's prior work history might fulfill your obligation to avoid or at least mitigate a negligent hiring claim.

The pro-and-con debates about references checks will undoubtedly continue and go well beyond the scope of this book. Remember, however, to keep notes demonstrating your attempts to pull information from prior companies regarding a job candidate's performance and behavior on that job. Keep the reference checking notes in a separate folder from the candidate's personnel file (should he ultimately be hired). Employees generally have access to their personnel files and shouldn't ever see documented comments from past employers under any circumstances. Instead, your reference checking notes should be placed in and remain part of the job requisition folder that was used to hire the individual.

The critical part of effective reference checking lies in how you structure your call and set expectations, both with the candidate and the prior supervisors. It's a lot easier than you think and yields outstanding results if you'll follow these three simple steps:

1. Tell the candidate that you're in the process of checking references on *several finalists* for the position in question. This builds a sense of competition into the process and will typically motivate

candidates to work harder to set up the referencing checking phone calls with their prior bosses. Also, since candidates will believe that they are one of several finalists under consideration, they won't be shocked if they don't get your job offer after the reference check step has been completed.

What you don't want to do is explain it this way: "Good news. You've completed all interviews and tested well, and now the only thing left to do is call your references." Clearly, this could be a problem if you then don't hire the candidate, as he'll assume it's because he got a bad reference from one of his prior supervisors. That could create unnecessary drama and potential legal exposure for both the referent and your organization in the form of a libel or slander accusation or a wrongful-failure-to-hire claim. That's easily avoided by saying that reference checks are the final step in the process for *all* finalist candidates, this individual included.

2. Have the candidate do all the legwork in terms of "reference bridging" and setting up the calls. Prior employers likely won't engage in a reference conversation with you if you're making a cold call. After all, their company has probably told them that giving a reference violates company policy. Further, if they haven't heard from the candidate in a few years and had no idea this call would be coming, then the standard response will typically be: "Sorry, all reference calls need to be referred to our HR department."

However, you can say to the candidate,

> Peter, our next step in the hiring process is to check references on our short-list of finalists. References are actually very important to us in the selection process, and I'd like to ask for your help. You listed four prior supervisors on your employment application, and I'd like to discuss them with you. I'd like to also ask you to reach out to them and ask them to vouch for you, so if you could call them and let them know that you're a finalist with us and tell them how excited you are, then they'll probably feel more comfortable speaking with us. In fact, your former bosses could either call me directly, or we could arrange a time for me to call them.

This approach shifts to the candidate the responsibility for tracking down the supervisors and setting up the calls, which is where it belongs. And if a candidate is excited about the new job possibility and asks a prior boss to speak with you, the chances are high that you'll have a very insightful conversation. In addition, it's generally safe to assume that former supervisors may be willing to speak with a prospective employer—even if it potentially could violate their company policy—if they like the person and want to help him land a job that he's excited about.

3. When opening a conversation with a past supervisor, spread honey on the situation and say, rather than ask, how you'd like the individual's help:

> Laura, Sam said some excellent things about your leadership abilities in terms of providing him with clear structure and direction in his job, and I was hoping that you could share some insights into his ability to excel in our company.
>
> [Sure.]
>
> Our challenge here at XYZ Company is to find someone whose personality best matches the temperament of this role. The position that Sam's applying for is very fast paced, it requires someone who enjoys working with the public and who can sometimes tame cranky customers, and it also requires an analytical eye because there's so much detail in the follow-up compliance reports. Did he tell you anything about the job or express interest in it at the time he asked you to speak with me?
>
> [Yes, he said he was very excited.]
>
> Great! Then how does that sound as an overall fit in terms of his personality, his ability to work with the public, and his attention to detail?
>
> [That sounds like a great match. It's very similar to what he did here with us.]
>
> I'm glad to hear that. Then allow me to ask you some specific questions about Sam and his ability to excel in this particular role.

Once you've set up the terms or context of your call this way, you can then begin asking specific questions about the candidate's ability to excel in your environment—communicate effectively, accept constructive criticism, balance quality and quantity, for example, as well as areas for professional development, eligibility for rehire, and the like. With the proper setup and a handy list of insightful questions that match what you discussed during the interview, you'll be well on your way to engaging prior supervisors in the preemployment selection process and developing an accurate understanding of what it's like working with this individual side-by-side every day. In short, you'll gain the advantage of developing a realistic glimpse of the real *person* whom you're hiring—not just the *candidate* behind all the interviewing hype.

What if the prior supervisor won't speak with you because of company policy? It depends. If one person won't speak with you but two or three others will provide accurate and detailed feedback, then the one referent withholding information shouldn't necessarily knock out the candidate as a finalist. In cases like that, ask the candidate to provide you with a copy of one or two performance evaluations from that company so that you could vet his strengths and weaknesses. That should suffice in terms of doing your good-faith due diligence and looking for similarities with the feedback you receive from the other references. If no performance reviews were given at that company or are otherwise attainable (for example, because the company is no longer in business), simply ask to speak with someone else in a leadership capacity from that company—a different supervisor from another team who's aware of the candidate's strengths and weaknesses or, depending on the level of the position, internal clients or subordinates who might be able to share insights into the candidate's working style.

But if none of the references from the various companies where the candidate worked will speak with you, be very cautious about bringing this person on board! At best he's a poor relationship builder and not someone that prior bosses would be willing to risk speaking about. At worst, the candidate could be a serial poor performer or a professional plaintiff. While you'll not likely get that level of specific feedback from a referent, the lack of information from any of the former supervisors may be a sign that this person was a troubled and problematic performer or had significant conduct issues across multiple companies.

References don't have to be an absolute knockout factor; that's a value judgment that you'll have to make for yourself. But making high-probability hires relies on in-person interviews, testing, background and credit checks, and, yes, reference checks to see if all the pieces of the puzzle fit together. They're a clear indicator of character and relationship building abilities, which are critical for any new hire. After years of working as both a headhunter and a corporate recruiter, I came to learn that poor references or no available references were typically a highly reliable sign of some significant problem or flaw either in performance or conduct. Proceed with caution when no one is willing to speak with you.

10 *Making the Offer and Closing the Deal: Don't Flinch at the Finish Line*

Hiring managers typically focus their interviews on questions that help them better understand the candidate: behavior-based questions, strength/weakness queries, discussions of long-term goals and desires, and the like. Although adding critical mass to the actual questioning process is essential, the most important part of the employment offer often gets overlooked: the finish-line negotiations. Questions are critically important there too!

Too many managers mistakenly assume that candidates will accept offers once they're extended. Hiring managers consequently extend offers without qualifying whether candidates are in "acceptance mode" or have otherwise had all their questions answered and needs met. It's important to remember, therefore, that the timing must go both ways: you'll want to ensure the likelihood that a candidate will say yes within the same timeframe that you're ready to extend an offer. To do otherwise would be to assume that the fish will simply jump into your boat once you're tired of all the reeling that goes into landing a big catch. What any good fisherman will tell you, though, is that the most important part of the whole process is hours after the initial connection—when the trophy fish is just a few feet under your boat and within reaching distance. One false move and the line snaps, and all your hard work floats quietly away.

Once you extend an offer to a candidate, the balance of power is shifted. Up until that moment, you're in control: you're the employer and you've got the job to give (no matter how tight a market or how qualified a candidate). However, once you say, "Janet, we'd love to have you join our team. You've got the job—congratulations! So let's talk salary and your availability to begin," you'll be on the candidate's terms. Beware!

You'll know you'll have fallen victim to a troubled negotiation when you've extended an open invitation to join the company and then candidates share new information at the finish line: "I'm so happy to hear that. I've got some updates that I wanted to share with you. First, I recently learned I was in line for a promotion if I stay with my current company. I believe that probably should have some bearing on my starting salary. Also, if I accept your position, I'd really like to give my current employer six to eight weeks' notice since it's such a busy time of the year for the company, and the team will need my help in reorganizing my department before I leave. And did I mention to you that I had a three-week trip to Aruba planned for two months from now?" Because candidates can throw you similar last-minute curve balls, you should be wary of extending offers and giving away your negotiation power prematurely—that is, until you have all the answers to your questions regarding the candidate's readiness to move ahead.

So how do you keep control of the negotiation and minimize the bumps along the way that are inherent in the salary negotiation process? Simple: Just ensure that no offers get extended until after you've taken the candidate through the "offer drill" delineated in the following subsections.

Question 1: "Has anything changed since the last time we spoke?"

Most of the time candidates will respond that nothing has changed, and so you're free to move to the next step of the negotiation process. But if something has changed, such as a sudden increase in responsibilities at the candidate's current company, a significant raise, or a job offer from another organization, then you've got to put the offer on hold and discuss these new developments. Don't assume that time has frozen since your last discussion. By inviting the candidate to make the first move in the negotiation, you'll save yourself time and also demonstrate respect for the individual.

Question 2: "Interest-wise, where do you stand right now in terms of the possibility of joining our organization? On a scale of 1 to 10, 10 being the highest, how motivated are you join us if we were to extend an offer?"

Now's the time to find out where things really stand. By implying that you may be in a position to extend an offer, you'll certainly get the candidate's attention. If she has any reservations at this point, now's the time to find out. What you don't want to do is learn about these new changes in plan *after* you've extended your offer. That would not only be uncomfortable for the candidate, it could be embarrassing for you as you appear to be chasing someone who may or may not want to join your organization.

Question 3: "If we were to make you an offer today, when would you be in a position to either accept or reject it?"

The ideal answer is, Right away! Beware candidates who suddenly request long time frames to come to a decision or tell you that they can't commit until next Friday. Ideally, candidates will have had enough opportunity during the multiple rounds of interviews to research your organization, speak with the key players, and determine the career benefits of joining your organization. Candidates who ask for more than a day to consider your offer may be delaying their commitment to you because they're more excited about another company's offer. Putting you off is the only way to buy time to see whether they can generate the offer they really want.

If you suspect that this is the case, then communicate your concerns openly:

> Janet, I want to start our relationship on the right foot, and I'd appreciate a candid response. I've found that people who suddenly need more time at the finish line usually have another offer on the table that they're more excited about. If that's the case, I understand. Still, I'd like to know where we stand relative to your other offer.

At that point, if your perceptions are correct, the candidate will admire your intuition and openness and respond to your legitimate concerns. You'll learn what your chances are of landing this individual, and you can prepare to either wait out her decision or line up additional candidates.

What you don't want to do is attempt to convince the candidate at the finish line that your offer is superior. Her focus is definitely on the other offer; otherwise, you would have heard an "I accept!" already. So persuading her that you're better than her other suitor puts you at a disadvantage in the negotiation process. It will appear that you're placing your company's interests above hers as you attempt to resell the benefits of joining your organization. In reality, by the time of offer negotiations, you'll have done all the selling you have to. Make a firm commitment to your own plan of action, and respect the individual's right to plan her own destiny.

Question 4: "If we were to make you an offer, tell me when you'd be able to start. How much notice would you need to give your present employer?"

Most candidates will need to give their current employers' two weeks' notice, and senior-level managers may need to give more than that because of their broad responsibilities. In analyzing a candidate's response, follow two general rules: First, watch out for candidates who don't feel obligated to give their current employers appropriate notice. An individual's failure to follow proper corporate etiquette may in itself play a role in your decision to extend an offer!

Second, remember that high performers are sophisticated consumers regarding the employment marketplace, and they realize that their current employers will be providing references for them for the next ten years. Therefore, don't pressure candidates to start earlier than would be appropriate. You could create a lot of resentment if you force individuals to walk away from their current companies without appropriate notice—not only for reason of loyalty but also for fear of a negative reference. In short, if you need someone immediately, hire a temp. In fact, encourage new hires to take an additional week off between jobs so they have time to catch up on things at home and in their personal lives. That selfless recommendation on your part will be very much appreciated and will set a very positive tone for the onboarding experience to come.

Question 5: "At what salary point would you accept our job offer, and at what salary point would you reject it?"

This is the million-dollar question, and that's why it's saved for last. Of course, you'll probably have already discussed initial salary expectations during the telephone screen and possibly during the interview process itself, so the answer shouldn't come as too much of a surprise. But depending on how motivated the candidate is at this point to join your company, the "interest–demand barometer" kicks in: If her interest is high, her demands will be low and vice versa. This is also typically part of the discussion where other factors come into play: requests to take additional time off, to work from home one day a week, to fly business class, and the like will typically weave themselves quite naturally into the conversation at this point.

Candidates typically expect to *hear* salary offers rather than volunteer numbers themselves. Still, it's best to open this critical piece of the negotiation this way:

> Janet, you've researched our financials, you've seen the job description, you have a general understanding of our benefit plans, and you've met the key players who you'd be working with every day. In short, you should have all the information necessary to come to an informed career decision. I'm asking you this question for two reasons: First, I'd like to gauge your perception of reality against ours in terms of what you believe the market worth of someone in this position should be. Second, I'd like you to discuss the minimum versus ideal salary for this job to again help me gauge your level of interest. Share with me what that walkaway point is for you.

Ideally, candidates will accept lateral offers to their current base salaries. It's more commonly the case that candidates peg an increase in their base pay to a percentage hike of 5 to 20 percent, depending on their desire for the job and their perception of their market worth. If any of those assumptions are within your salary range, you'll be safe to make the offer at this point.

Of course, by the time you get to this stage, you'll have already looked at internal equity considerations and determined a fair rate of pay. Still, you should find out if candidates' perceptions of reality make sense. Someone demanding a 25 percent increase in base salary

or looking to earn a contractor's rate for a staff position may lack business maturity. Simply stated, they may have an overinflated sense of
their own value or they may be looking for you to make up for lost
opportunities in the past. In such cases, delaying an offer may make
sense while you investigate the individual's concerns further.

Most importantly, you'll have retained control of the negotiation
until you've had all your critical questions answered. As an employer,
you wouldn't expect a candidate to accept an offer without all the
information necessary to come to an informed career decision. Expect
no less for yourself, because a candidate's behavior during the actual
"offer drill" may in itself strengthen your commitment to bring that
individual aboard or cast doubt on her ultimate suitability.

11 *Effective Onboarding to Maximize the Chances of Initial Success and Create True Believers*

When it comes to effective onboarding practices, many companies fail
by a wide margin. They spend significant amounts of time sourcing
and attracting candidates, interviewing and reference checking, and
background checking and drug screening, but when the candidates
show up for the first day of work, companies often underwhelm them.
Few organizations dedicate appropriate resources to the overall onboarding experience, which, unlike the new employee orientation
(NEO) that takes place on the first day, should occur over the first one
to three months, with a one-year follow-up for good measure.

Many companies do little more than NEO on a new hire's first
day. Some dedicate a full day to NEO, while others try to limit it to a
half day or even to one hour. That's a critical oversight on their part.
Transitioning new hires into your company has multiple cascading
events that take place over time—for the leader, the new hire, and the
organization. Much more than merely enrolling people in benefits and
setting up their payroll, it's your first chance to make a good impression and truly integrate the individual into your culture. Let's discuss
various aspects of onboarding to ensure that your investment in your
new hires is well spent and appropriately planned.

While NEO typically introduces new hires to company policies, codes of conduct, safety requirements, organization charts, and key leaders within the organization, the onboarding process provides you with an opportunity to orient new hires to ensure maximum engagement and productivity right from the start. On a very broad level, onboarding provides you with an opportunity to do the following:

1. Explain what your organization emphasizes and values. These issues need to be clearly demonstrated over time because they define your company at its core and clarify what differentiates your organization from your competition.
2. Create "true believers" and sell your company's story while highlighting its history and achievements. Not everyone needs to understand your company's financial statements and SWOT (strengths, weaknesses, opportunities, and threats) analysis, but all new hires should understand what your company does, how it does it, and what it wants for its employees. This is a very special opportunity to sell your organization's uniqueness, and trying to unload everything in one day will surely miss the mark in helping your new employee appreciate and value your culture and heritage.
3. Set expectations regarding the customer service experience. What is it that you expect from your new hires in terms of servicing both internal and external customers and clients? What are your rules of engagement so that everyone knows what you value and what you model? Figure 1.2 is an example of a handout that can be given to new employees explaining the company's expectations.
4. Set appropriate standards for how you want new hires to value their work and see their connection to the bigger picture. As the Walt Disney Company aptly puts it, do you teach your employees to lay bricks or build cathedrals? Do your employees understand their connection to the broader picture? Do they know why the founders created the organization and how? Do they recognize the value your organization brings to its customer base and the community overall?

5. Explain that a new hire's performance is reviewed at ninety days, six months, and one year, and that merit increases are based on annual reviews. New hires can use these review opportunities to better understand where they are now, where they want to be, and how to get there. Explain how performance review templates, goal-setting worksheets, and self-review forms are used, as well as individual development plan templates to help employees set their sights on longer-term achievements and goals right from the start.

In short, how you handle the employee's first hour, first day, first week, and first three months on the job provides you with multiple opportunities for contact, feedback, suggestions, and clarifications. Compared to the "sink or swim" onboarding method used by many companies during NEO, this strategic approach to new-hire onboarding will drastically increase your chances of success and long-term retention.

Assign a mentor to the new employee. Weekly one-on-one meetings with a mentor on the same team can provide a terrific return-on-investment for both the mentor and the new hire. New employees appreciate having someone to guide them through the ins and outs of the organization and the hidden "land mines" that could otherwise derail an early career, and to be a resource to help them get to know the players and their personalities and penchants that much better. Such relationships build trust and camaraderie, but more than that, they help new hires integrate into your company with more confidence because of the safety net they provide. And what a great stretch assignment for more senior or tenured team members! Placing people into leadership roles on an intermittent basis increases their sense of self-worth. It provides them the opportunity to grow and develop new team members—a great strength to add to someone's personal brand and reputation. And it provides a healthy sense of competition where the more senior member has skin in the game to ensure that the new hire is successful. These are all important elements of a healthy working environment that focuses on employee growth and development while capitalizing on the organization's investment in the new hire.

Figure 1.2. Leadership expectations handout. CEOs, general managers, and department heads should select eight or ten key principles to discuss with new hires regarding culture, communication, behavior, and the like. The examples listed here will help you draft the items that meet your department's unique needs.

Leadership Expectations

This is *your* company. *You* create and sustain the culture, your team's work experience, and our productivity and performance!

Principles	*Communication*
Mutual Respect	Say "Hi" and "Thank you"
Pride in What We Do	Create a culture of openness and
Passion for Who We Serve	information-sharing
Strong Work Ethic	Praise in public; censure in private
Exceed Customer Expectations	It's okay to say "I don't know"
Welcome Change as an Opportunity to Learn	Proactively feed information up and out
and Grow	Provide consistent feedback in a
Give Credit, Don't Take Credit	constructive manner
Drive Creativity and Innovation	Keep others informed and leave no one
Safety First	flying blind
	Listen openly and look for common ground

Leadership	*Teamwork*
Lead by example	Always assume good intentions
Practice MBWA (Management by Walking	Create a positive and inclusive work
Around) and raise visibility	environment
Make others feel welcome and included	Err on the side of compassion
Celebrate successes and learn from mistakes	Practice the adage "What you want for
Create a work environment where team	yourself, give to another"
members can motivate themselves	Place others' needs ahead of your own
Create a continuous learning environment	and expect them to respond in kind
Teach what you choose to learn	Always look to bring out the best in others
Respect others' points of view and value their	Share best practices
opinions	Resolve team conflict without drama or
Focus on bringing out the best in others	angst
Demonstrate the highest level of ethics and	Foster a sense of shared accountability
values at all times	and group responsibility

What should you focus on in your follow-up meetings with your new hires? Your primary focus should be on developing their understanding of the business, its key players, and its current initiatives. What are the high-level goals that your company is focusing on, and how does each person's role contribute to those goals? What opportunities exist where new hires can make a difference? Further, these segmented and extended onboarding programs provide you with opportunities for one-on-one feedback with a member of management outside of the new hire's immediate team or department. For example, the recruiter, HR representative, or a department head may want to spend one-on-one time with new hires at various intervals, conducting a "pulse check" to see how their onboarding experience is progressing. Further, according to the editors at Business Management Daily (www.businessmanagementdaily.com), some questions that you might want to ask include:

- 30-Day One-on-One Follow-Up Questions

  Why do you think we selected you as an employee?

  What do you like about the job and the organization so far?

  What's been going well? What are the highlights of your experiences so far? Why?

  Tell me what you don't understand about your job and about our organization now that you've had a month to roll up your sleeves and get your hands dirty.

  Have you faced any unforeseen surprises since joining us that you weren't expecting?

- 60-Day One-on-One Follow-Up Questions

  Do you have enough, too much, or too little time to do your work? Do you have access to the appropriate tools and resources? Do you feel you have been sufficiently trained in all aspects of your job to perform at a high level?

  How do you see your job relating to the organization's mission and vision?

What do you need to learn to improve? What can the organization do to help you become more successful in your role?

Compare the organization to what we explained it would be like when you initially interviewed with us. Have you experienced any surprises, disappointments, or other "ah-ha" moments that you're comfortable sharing?

How does it go when your supervisor offers constructive criticism or corrects your work?

• 90-Day One-on-One Follow-Up Questions

Which coworkers have been helpful since you arrived? (Goal: Pinpoint which employees can be influential in retaining new hires.)

Who do you talk to when you have questions about your work? Do you feel comfortable asking?

Have you had any uncomfortable situations or conflicts with supervisors, coworkers, or customers?

Does your supervisor clearly explain what the organization expects of you? How would you rate leadership communication overall on a scale from 1 to 10 (with 10 being highest)?

Do you believe your ideas and suggestions are valued? Give me some examples.

In retrospect, what could we have done differently in terms of setting your expectations appropriately for working in our company overall and for your job specifically?

The end result: better performance, improved engagement, and stronger retention. After all, it only stands to reason that employees who are engaged in these types of activities from the first day will feel a stronger connection to your organization over time. They'll feel acknowledged, included, and more excited about their prospects for long-term success and commitment so they'll likely demonstrate greater loyalty and productivity. What's interesting is that it won't even take that much time. While traditional NEO may still last one full day, follow-up meetings on days 30, 60, and 90 may be scheduled for four hours, two hours, and one hour, respectively. All in all, your total hour commitment may be little more than 16 hours, but because the meetings are spread wisely over the new hire's 90-day introductory period, the constant follow-up and ongoing contact help cement a relationship that will stand the test of time. And of course, you can extend this initial contact period to six months and then to the one-year anniversary if you agree that the feedback you're getting is worthwhile.

Is there an "opportunity cost" (i.e., a downside or disadvantage) to removing the individual from the field at these various intervals? Of course there is, but think of all you'll be gaining. You'll have a chance to identify your top performers, provide special assignments to those looking for more, spot individuals who may be challenged and need to course-correct, and flag others who may not have been cast in the right role during the hiring process. Your extra attention will help new hires incorporate new concepts and skills into their natural learning process when the timing is right for them, and your extra set of eyes will identify opportunities that your organization may not have otherwise been aware of.

An extended onboarding program is a rare opportunity to help your organization maximize its investment in new hires and increase the chances for success. Employ this strategy for the next six months and measure your new-hire retention results as a before and after. Don't be surprised to see a superior return on this particular investment in your new hires' futures because of the time you'll save, the opportunities you'll identify, and the ongoing commitment that will benefit your organization over the long haul.

2 Effective Leadership and Outstanding Communication

GREAT LEADERS are great communicators. When you look at success-ful work teams and fully effective departments, you'll typically find a leader at the top of the org chart who seems to understand intuitively how to talk to people and engage them to create rapport. Successful leaders simply get it—they know how to communicate effectively, practice MBWA (management by walking around), recognize and praise often, and know their employees personally. In comparison, it's rare to find an effective leader who doesn't follow certain Golden Rules of communication. The two concepts—successful leader and excellent communicator—seem to go hand in hand in many if not most cases of effective leadership.

But how do you get there? Communication skills are relative, meaning they're viewed differently by different people and can al-ways be improved. And even the strongest natural communicators among us could arguably strengthen their talents and skills in this critical leadership area at any given time. More than knowing what to say, effective leaders know how to say it—not because they're poli-ticians but because they care, and not because they're trying to manip-ulate but because they want to motivate. Simply stated, their values shine through in terms of what and how they communicate. So com-munication doesn't stem so much from what you do as from who you are. Yet there are ways and opportunities to communicate that allow you to motivate others and create an engaged work team and also address problematic situations openly, while setting and maintaining high expectations. It's in these common workplace challenges that you can hone your communication skills and demonstrate your true value as a leader and caring human being.

12   *The Nature of Positive, Constructive Communication*

What are the top three attributes associated with strong leaders? If you responded great communication, the ability to build strong teams, and consistency in turning talent into performance, then you're well on the way to appreciating the importance of excellent leadership and communication. What most studies will show, and what many organizational feedback tools such as employee opinion surveys and exit interviews will tell you, is that communication typically ranks number one when it comes to how employees grade their leaders and what employees want more of.

It's particularly challenging to provide constant and immediate communication in an environment that operates at the speed of the Internet. Thanks to smart phones and tablets of all sorts, we're all used to real-time updates, constant stimulation, and immediate gratification when we need to know something. Clearly human beings can't respond quite that quickly, no matter how well intentioned or how tech savvy. Corporate America is undergoing a tremendous shift in information sharing and change management; we're experiencing evolutionary change at revolutionary speed. So what's realistic in terms of expectations for leader communication? What makes certain leaders great communicators while others fall behind significantly in this mission-critical area?

First, no one is expecting leaders to provide constant, real-time information as on the Internet. No one can be "in the know" to that degree on a constant and ongoing basis, especially while companies continue to merge and conglomerate at such a stunning pace. However, it's critical to understand that your communication style reveals who you are and what you value—especially how much you value your team members. Do you treat them like adults? Do you hold them accountable and maintain high expectations? Do you share information appropriately so that team members understand the reasons for your decisions? Do you put their needs ahead of your own and practice servant leadership so they respect and appreciate your selflessness and dedication? Do you lead by example? Do you work late the Friday before a long holiday weekend so that your people can go home early, or do you insist that they work late so that you can leave early instead?

All these issues speak to your character and your values—the DNA that makes you who you are. People respect competence, they respect passion for what their leaders believe in, and they honor leaders who get to know them personally, demonstrate sincerity, and look to make their relationships personal and meaningful. And all of these values and belief systems reveal themselves in leaders' communication style—the respect they demonstrate toward others; their willingness to teach, coach, and develop people; and their readiness to make themselves vulnerable so that people can relate to them in the sincerest way possible.

What are some of the key tenets that mark exceptional communication styles? First, great communicators are willing to engage in tough conversations and hold others accountable—the *sine qua non* of exceptional leadership. They don't delay sharing immediate praise and offering constructive feedback, but they likewise address minor impediments before they become massive roadblocks, thus lessening the drama inherent in most business environments.

Second, great communicators demonstrate care and sincerity in all they do. That means they listen well and are empathetic, typically putting the employee's needs above their own. They listen attentively and make people feel heard so that no one feels isolated or apart from the inner sanctum. Likewise, they recognize the psychic income that comes from group interaction and the benefits of working together closely to achieve a common goal. They look to have fun, build camaraderie, and keep work in perspective. It's that type of wisdom that creates charisma and draws people to them.

Third, they understand that communication is a two-way street. There are two sides to every story, and they strive to always see both sides. They are aware that if they see everything in black and white, ignoring the gray areas, they may be missing some critical components of the story. This give-and-take aspect of communication creates and fosters a sense of empathic leadership where no one rushes to judgment, and all accept that there may be more to a particular story or scenario than initially meets the eye. As such, their message is gentle, no matter how stringent the content: not "You're fired" à la Donald Trump on *The Apprentice* television show, but "I'm afraid this job may not be a good fit for your talents, and I'm afraid we'll have to part ways. Thank you for all you've done for us in trying to help us move our organization forward, and we wish you continued success in your career and in all you'll continue to do." The end result may be the same: the individual is terminated. But Trump's exit line strips the individual of his dignity and humiliates him when he's most vulnerable, while the longer message allows him to exit the company gracefully and with his dignity intact, realizing it's nothing personal and simply may not have been a good match of individual talent to organizational need.

And while all these characteristics may appear to be almost impossible to reach and incorporate into your overall communication style, remember that we're not talking about your becoming the next President Kennedy or President Reagan. Great workplace communicators, at their core, are not necessarily superior orators or motivational speakers. Their actions speak louder than words, and they come from a simple, quiet wisdom that others can emulate and strive to repeat. Their communication shows itself in what they do, how they do it, and their concern for others along the way.

So now that we know what great communicators and great leaders have in common, the question becomes, How do we get there ourselves? What is it that we need to do to display role-model behavior that pierces people's hearts and helps them feel connected to us and cared for? How do we want our communication style to be described and, in a broader sense, how do we want to be defined as leaders?

While many books and articles have focused on communication and leadership, keeping it simple is probably the best overall approach. With specific principles in place, we can measure ourselves throughout our careers as change dictates.

To start, let's borrow some of the communication phrases outlined in my book *2600 Phrases for Setting Effective Performance Goals* (AMACOM Books, 2012). That's a great place to start because they help put communication talents and skills into particular buckets that can be broken down, analyzed, and strengthened with a helping of focus and effort.

The Golden Rules of Effective Communication

According to *2600 Phrases for Setting Effective Performance Goals*, always remember to:

1. Recognize achievements and accomplishments often.
2. Celebrate success.
3. Deliver bad news quickly, constructively, and in a spirit of professional development.
4. Praise in public, censure in private.
5. Assume responsibility for problems when things go wrong, and provide immediate praise and recognition to others when things go right.
6. Create a work environment based on inclusiveness, welcoming others' suggestions and points of view.
7. Listen actively, making sure that your people feel heard and understood and have a voice in terms of offering positive suggestions in the office or on the shop floor.
8. Share information openly (to the extent possible) so that staff members understand the *Why* behind your reasoning and can ask appropriate questions as they continue along in their own path of career development and learning.
9. Remember that thankfulness and appreciation are the two most important values you can share with your employees and teach them to live by: make them the core foundation of your culture.
10. Put others' needs ahead of your own and expect them to respond in kind (a.k.a. "selfless leadership," otherwise known as "servant leadership").
11. When dealing with others' shortcomings, always err on the side of compassion.

12. Solicit ongoing feedback and suggestions from your team in terms of how you could do things differently, thereby stimulating creativity and innovation.

Most importantly, build trust through regular, open, and honest communication. After all, your reputation is the coin of the realm when it comes to building strong teams of satisfied workers who laud your ability to lead and communicate effectively and help them grow and develop in their own careers. Great communicators and great leaders enjoy high productivity, high employee engagement and satisfaction, and low turnover. And it all stems from you—your values, your ability to relate and communicate, and your willingness to help others grow and excel in their careers through the work that you do together. Trust is the foundation of true leadership and communication, but it's typically hard-earned and often tested.

13 *The Art of Successful Communication: Guidelines to Help Your Message Soar*

We've discussed what strong communication looks like, and we recognize that certain natural barriers make it difficult for people leaders to master the fine art of effective communication. Let's focus now on some practical ways to communicate more effectively in the workplace.

"Please" and "thank you" still work!

As trite as this may sound, be sure and say "please" and "thank you" to your teams. You'd be surprised how often exiting employees make comments along the lines of, "You work so hard around here and you never hear a word of thanks. But make one mistake and you'll be hearing from your boss like there's no tomorrow." Along the same lines, follow the mantra of "What you want for yourself, give to another." That's not just spiritual guru talk—it's practical advice that injects greater humanity into the workplace, which in turn fosters a culture based on respect and more open communication.

Get to know your employees on a more personal level.

Marcus Buckingham and Curt Coffman's bestselling book *First, Break All the Rules: What the World's Greatest Managers Do Differently* captured the Gallup organization's findings after studying 80,000 managers and over one million employees, and the results were clear: People join companies but leave managers. In other words, they join a company because they're excited about its reputation, accomplishments, mission, and the like, but then leave a few years later because of ongoing challenges they have with their immediate boss. Gallup found that of all key retention factors—for example, company brand, benefits, and learning and development opportunities—nothing trumped employees' relationships with their immediate supervisors as the glue that bound them to the organization. The relationship should be personal—at least to some degree—so that team members know you care about their own personal interests and lives beyond work.

How do you accomplish this? Meet one-on-one with your direct reports and (occasionally) with your extended reports to find out how they're feeling about things. You might want to ask:

How are you doing, and how do you think we're doing overall as a department and team?

What could we be doing differently around here that would make a change in the results we're getting? If you could snap your fingers and change one thing about the way we do things, what would it be?

On a scale of 1 to 10, with 10 being the highest, how engaged and motivated would you say you're feeling these days, and how would you grade the rest of the team?

Tell me about my communication style. And be honest—I really want to know. Do you get enough information to do your job well and keep yourself and your customers informed about upcoming changes? Likewise, do you feel that you have a voice and can make a difference in terms of how you do your job and how we get our work done?

What would you add or subtract to the way we communicate with one another as a team? Is there enough respect? Would you say we're good at teamwork? Do you trust that we have each other's backs and provide the right amount of internal support so that all team members can perform their work every day with minimal drama and full peace of mind?

The questions, of course, are endless, and you could customize these to address your own personal values or some of the challenges you may be facing as a team at any given point in time. What matters most, though, is that you ask. Being a leader who cares doesn't mean that you have to know details about what's going on in your employees' personal lives (although some understanding of that is arguably very natural and healthy). It means that you're taking the time to ask them about what matters most to them in the workplace and in their careers. Listen actively, seek their advice, and appreciate that the best suggestions will often come from those in the trenches who are closest to your customers' needs.

When delivering bad news, don't come from anger.

If you show that you're angry at your employees, their natural self-defense mechanisms will kick in, and the entire conversation will be off to a failed start. That's why yelling and shouting never works: at best, employees will comply out of fear or compliance, but fear and compliance will rarely get you to 100 percent in terms of effort and dedication. Instead, people will perform only to the minimum necessary to get the job done because they'll act either out of spite or out of resentment. What you're looking for is 110 percent on the effort scale—employees going above and beyond for the sake of their company, coworkers, or boss. It's that marginal difference that distinguishes strong, high-performing teams from those that struggle to satisfy minimum expectations.

Along the same lines, avoid using the word *why;* "Why did you do that?" will typically trigger a self-defense response that focuses on deflecting criticism and avoiding blame. Instead, open the conversation with: "Share with me how that came about and what you were considering at the time." By stating your question as an open invitation to provide subjective input, you'll typically get a much more candid and objective response that allows others to explain their side of the story (even if what they ultimately did was a mistake).

Turn "Yes . . . but" into "Yes . . . and" statements.

"Yes . . . but" responses often shut down a conversation right from the get-go. For example, instead of: "Yes, I know we spoke about that, but you should have known . . .," you can turn your statement into: "Yes, I know we spoke about that, and I'm wondering what other choices were available to you at the time that you could have opted for . . ." So don't become a "Yes . . . but" communicator—an individual who's a naysayer, who always seems to focus on the negative, and who tends to crush initiative and spontaneity. It's okay for you to spot weaknesses—that's a critical part of your role as leader. How you bring those weaknesses to others' attention or help them realize the shortcomings in their reasoning, however, will help you foster and nurture talent rather than shut it down.

Speak from guilt more than from anger.

We're not talking about old-fashioned guilt that stems from putting people down or otherwise shaming them into doing something. Instead, we're looking at guilt as a natural human emotion that helps people look inward for solutions and come from a more selfless orientation where it's safe to feel vulnerable and assume partial responsibility for an issue gone wrong.

When it comes to expressing dissatisfaction with an employee's performance or conduct, coming more from guilt than from anger typically garners much more favorable results. First, anger is an external emotion: If people feel angry, they're pointing their energy outward at someone or something else. They feel defensive and instinctively look to justify their actions by proving the other person wrong and themselves right. On the other hand, guilt, as a human emotion, helps people look inward for answers and, as such, helps people make themselves partially responsible for a problem so they could help resolve it in a more cooperative spirit.

For example, if you believe a subordinate was inappropriate or somewhat disrespectful during a staff meeting, you could raise the stakes by going toe to toe either during the meeting or in private afterward: "I can't believe you used that tone of voice with me in front of the rest of the team. You report to me, and the stripes on my shoulder are a bit higher than yours!" While that may make you feel better for a moment as you let off steam, clearly it does little to help you understand what was really going on that led to the inappropriate comment or remark.

Instead, if you handle the matter quietly and in private, you'll arguably get a much more desirable response by stating something like this: "Mary, I'm not quite sure what happened in that meeting. We've always had a mutually respectful relationship, but it seemed to me like you needed to work out a lot of pent-up anger in there, and the fact that you did that in front of the rest of the team really *disappointed* me. I respect you too much to call you out like that in front of others, and I wouldn't have expected you to act that way toward me, especially in front of the rest of the team. Can you understand why I might feel *let down* by your actions in there?"

Said quietly and softly with a serious tone of voice, no drama was needed—no escalation, no threats, and no pulling rank—and your message will likely have a much stronger impact than had you escalated emotions by yelling. The typical employee response might be, "I'm sorry, I didn't intend to embarrass you in any way, especially in front of the rest of the team. I apologize for my actions in there and promise that'll never happen again." Enough said.

Speak of "perception" and holding your employees accountable for their own "perception management."

Finally, when delivering bad news, add the words "perception" or "perception management" to your vocabulary. Feelings aren't right or wrong—they just are what they are. The same goes for perception: you're entitled to your own perception, and sharing what things look like from your vantage point isn't right or wrong—it just is what it is. For example, telling a member of your staff that he has a *bad attitude* will likely trigger all sorts of drama. Adults tend to get all weird when they're told they have an attitude problem, so let's approach it a different way:

> Michele, I think it's time that we sit down and address some concerns that have been on my mind for quite some time. Working with you can be challenging, and I'm guessing this isn't the first time you're hearing this. Let me share with you what things look like from my vantage point as your supervisor. From a perception standpoint, you come across as angry much of the time. I'm not sure what triggers hostility on your part or what I may be doing in terms of pushing some sort of hot button when I'm working with you, but

your responses with me tend to be aggressive and confrontational. Truth be told, I tend to avoid you at times because I'm not sure what kind of response I'm going to get.

Likewise, your mood fluctuates often, and I've heard from others that you never know what kind of response you're going to get from Michele because it depends which way the wind is blowing. That's been my experience as well on a number of occasions.

I'll make a commitment to you now that I won't walk on eggshells around you anymore or avoid working with you. I shouldn't have to, and neither should anyone else. Regardless of your reality or however you've been justifying your behavior in your mind up to now, I'll simply not accept irrational or moody behavior from this point forward. You've got a significant *perception problem* on your hands, and from now on, I'm holding you fully accountable for your own *perception management*. If you're not successful managing how you come across to others or in any way make it difficult for people to work with you, then my response will be in writing in the form of formal progressive discipline. And depending on the nature of the complaint and who informs me of it, I'll arguably be starting the corrective action at either the written or the final written warning stage.

If you feel you can't or won't reinvent yourself in terms of how you're coming across to others and to me, then you may want to rethink remaining with this organization. You've been here for eighteen years, which I respect, but in my last three months since joining the firm, you've shown me what feels like resistance at every turn. You come across to me as if I'm interrupting you or bothering you. I feel that you don't have my back, are leaving me flying blind, and are otherwise not supportive of my success.

If you're willing to turn a new leaf and reinvent your relationship with me and with others, then I'm fully on board and will support you in any way I can. But if you're not willing to make that commitment to me, to the organization, and to yourself, then I'd ask you to please not put me in a situation where I need to reach out to HR to initiate corrective action that could ultimately lead to your termination. You deserve better as a long-term employee, but I deserve better as your supervisor as well. What are your thoughts?

Yes, that's a tough conversation, but you'll have created a clear verbal record of your impressions and your expectations, and that's a very healthy place to start. It's now up to the employee to measure herself by how others view and describe her and to remain open to reestablishing her relationship with her boss, coworkers, and clients.

14   *Human Nature: The Path of Least Resistance Is Avoidance*

No one wants to confront others at work if they can possibly avoid it. (In fact, if they do want to, they've probably got other, more serious problems on their hands!) But we have to focus on human nature to understand why communication can be so difficult and challenging. People tend to shy away from discussing uncomfortable issues and prefer to take a "let's wait and see if it fixes itself" approach whenever possible. And sometimes things do end up straightening themselves out without any form of external intervention, but most of us would agree that's more the exception than the rule.

In reality, this natural trend toward avoidance shows itself in many untoward ways in the workplace: an unwillingness to address minor impediments verbally before they become large-scale road-blocks, a reluctance to issue formal corrective action for fear of upsetting or demotivating an employee, and most commonly in the form of grade inflation on the annual performance review. These very common land mines may plague us throughout our career if we don't acknowledge them and determine a strategy for communicating effectively through them, and the time to hone that skill is right now. And here's a hint: this isn't as hard as it seems! Remember, it's not what you say but how you say it that holds as an evergreen rule of human interaction. Let's focus on building the *How* in the equation so that it actually becomes easier to deliver challenging news and hold people to higher expectations. (By the way, the approaches we'll discuss work with spouses and kids just as well as they do with coworkers and team members.)

First, though, we have to spend a few minutes understanding how we're naturally wired. Whether it's via our quirky individual personalities or millennia of practice, adults have certain hang-ups about communication. Understanding where we come from is therefore important because it can shed light on where we're going. More specifically, knowing that any and all of these quagmires face us as managers at different times and to differing degrees, it's important that we explore and understand that certain adult behaviors are actually built into us from childhood and have to be overcome to attain recognition as a great communicator.

The easiest way for us to view communication challenges in the workplace in a more common context can be seen in its parallelism to parenting. For the sake of this argument, let's assume that Dad is taking care of the kids at home while Mom is out working. If little Nina and Sam are driving Dad crazy because they just won't get along with one another, how does Dad stop the annoying behavior, raise behavioral expectations, and stop the roller-coaster ride so that the problem doesn't keep popping up?

Let's look at three models of parenting that reveal the choices at hand very clearly. In each scenario, let's assume that the kids are at it again and Dad is about to go ballistic and is at the end of his rope. See which model sounds most familiar to you in terms of your own upbringing:

> Model 1: Dad shouts, "Kids, you're driving me crazy! Go out and play and when you come back, I don't expect to hear any more bickering!"

Okay, not an uncommon response; the core logic is that the problem will fix itself once the kids are otherwise distracted. But if this approach does work, it's usually not for very long, as the frustrated father realizes once the kids are back in the house and the bickering picks up where it left off.

> Model 2: Dad shouts, "Kids, you're diving me crazy! If you don't knock it off, you're both going to be in so much trouble when your mother gets home."

Again, a fairly common approach, although Dad just totally minimized his role and gave total power over to Mom, who isn't even home and doesn't know there's a problem. The kids typically figure out pretty quickly that Dad's threats are pretty hollow, he'll forget all about it by the time Mom gets home, and they're at liberty to pick up the fight anytime and anywhere they want because they know that Dad isn't going to do anything about it other than make some hollow threats about Mom's wrath (which never materializes).

Model 3: Dad shouts, "Kids, you're driving me crazy! Come in here right now and close the door behind you. We're going to talk about what's going on because I expect more of both of you."

Ah, a very interesting twist. Once the kids sit down, Dad calmly opens the discussion by saying, "Nina, I want you to say something nice about your brother." (Nina rolls her eyeballs and begrudgingly says, "You've got pretty eyes, Sam.") Dad then turns to Sam and says, "Sammy, something nice about your sister Nina." (Sam harrumphs and says, "I really like the painting you made me this morning.")

Okay, now we're getting somewhere: we set the tone of the "intervention" to be positive and constructive. Now that the kids have settled down a bit and gained some perspective (although reluctantly) on the situation, they're prepared to discuss why the other is bugging them. At the conclusion of their explanations, Dad then has the opportunity to reset expectations in a calm voice and reassure them that in this household, a certain level of behavior is expected of the children and it's his job to ensure that they don't forget that. The kids can then give each other a hug, smile, and move on to other things.

Notice the paradigm shift in model 3: There's no avoiding (model 1) and no deflecting (model 2). The wisdom that the father shows in model 3 is that he's in total control, he's there to remind the kids of the expectations that he has of them, and he's there to support them both through an uncomfortable set of circumstances.

However, there's a critical difference between this scenario with Dad and the kids and what you'll typically find in the workplace: siblings can sit down cold in the midst of an argument and settle their dispute amicably. Not so with adults—they can't be brought into your office cold and asked to sit down and fix a problem right on the spot. Adults aren't made that way: sibling kids can do it because they've grown up together and know each other intrinsically, while adults in the workplace don't have enough trust to solve the "what" of the problem as well as the "how" of the solution all in one sitting.

Instead, adult coworkers typically need to participate in separate meetings (preferably with a night of sleep between both meetings) to first determine the "what" (i.e., the facts and allegations) and then—after a good night's sleep—to work on the "how" (i.e., the solution and their commitment to avoiding such behaviors again in the future). So if you bring two warring parties cold into your office to end an ongoing dispute and order them to "knock it off," expect a whole lot drama and tension. Adults are too afraid of being attacked (again, the "what" of the issue and the ensuing allegations) and typically will not listen openly. Instead, they'll be prepared to jump on the other person as soon as something "wrong" is said, leading to rolling eyeballs, glares, sarcastic laughter, and the like. (Remember the best defense is a preemptive offense!)

So don't expect warring parties to fix the "what" and "how" in one sitting: They're simply too socialized and not trusting enough at this point in their social development to simply assume good intentions and make themselves vulnerable. But there is a way for you, as their leader, to make it relatively safe to address their concerns openly and even assume partial responsibility for the problem at hand. As in most things in life, it's all in the setup. So let's explore how to make this happen successfully and consistently in your workplace in our next question.

15 Mediating Employee Disputes and Communication Breakdowns: The Strategy Behind Constructive Confrontation

Brokering employee disputes and communication breakdowns isn't easy. People possess differing levels of self-awareness, business maturity, and spiritual evolution. Some are quick to assume responsibility, forgive, and move on, while others will harp on every point, act on principle, and leave no man standing in order to prove a point. How you customize your approach, therefore, will depend highly on the players involved. That being said, there's a construct or formula that will allow you to maximize such meetings time after time, and it's very much based on how adults process information and admit shortcomings. Only you can guess how participants will react under a particular set of circumstances, but if you set up the foundation as if you're on each participant's side, then you're more likely to gain buy-in, even among the toughest, most stubborn personalities.

When mediating employee disputes or otherwise brokering disagreement in the workplace, follow this three-step formula to maximize the likelihood of success:

Step 1: Meet with each individual separately to learn the "what" of the issue.

When two of your staff members are "at war," meet with each one individually. There are two sides to every story, and it's important that you inject yourself into each person's vantage point. First, it helps you assess the situation more objectively. Second, it helps you cement your relationship with each person so that both feel you're on their side. Third, it positions you with all the information necessary to serve as a wise and objective arbiter of the dispute.

Privately find out Fred's side of the story before meeting individually with Jennifer. But tell Fred right upfront that whatever he shares with you now, you're going to share with Jennifer in your one-on-one meeting with her that follows. Total transparency, no drama: Fred needs to understand that you're a conduit to their communication and are not taking sides.

Further, in your meeting with Fred, ask him why Jennifer may be feeling the way she does. Ask him what he'd like to see happen ideally in terms of his working relationship with Jennifer, and then ask him what he'd be willing to change about his own behavior to elicit a different response from Jennifer in the future. At the conclusion of the meeting, inform Fred that you'll be meeting with Jennifer next and will share his sentiments. Likewise, once you've completed your meeting with Jennifer, you'll get back to Fred and let him know her specific feedback.

Setting up a meeting with those ground rules automatically de-escalates feelings of angst or distrust in the participants. It also gives you the chance to take a gentle approach to interpersonal issues that, like scars, sometimes run long and deep.

Step 2: Prepare to meet the next day as a group to work out the "how" of the issue.

Let both participants know that you want to meet with them together in your office the next morning to open the lines of communication. But give them a night to sleep on the matter and process the "what" of all that they have learned during your feedback session from the one-on-one meetings you held. Unlike young siblings who can address the "what" and the "how" all in one sitting, adults typically respond a lot better when they learn the "what" in one meeting and then have time to compose themselves and prepare for the "how" session that's to follow the next day. (Don't delay the second meeting by more than one day: it's not fair to keep people holding on when they feel a need to talk and resolve their issues and still have to work together in the interim.) When you open the meeting with your two subordinates, share these three rules at the onset of the meeting:

> Let me share some critical rules and guidelines for our meeting right now. First, you shouldn't hold anything back. You both know the "what" of the problem—what's bothering the other person about your performance and/or conduct and why. You've also both had a night to sleep on this and give thought to your approach to this group meeting this morning in terms of addressing the "how" of it all.

> This is your chance to get it all out in the open, and if you withhold anything, then you'll have missed a golden opportunity to share your side of the story. You're not going to get another chance to readdress these issues in the future—this is a once-in-a-career benefit, and I'm not going to permit a "roller-coaster" effect develop out of this where we need to address it more than once. After our meeting today, I'm re-welcoming you both to the company as if it were your first day of employment. I'm also holding you fully accountable for reinventing your working relationship from this point forward.

> Second, everything you share has to be said with the other person's best interests in mind and in a spirit of constructive feedback. There is no attacking and no need for defending anyone's actions; this is really more a sensitivity session where you both get to walk a mile in each other's shoes and hear first-hand how the other is feeling.

> Third, once the meeting is about to conclude, I'm going to ask you to give thought to and potentially share what you're willing to do on your end to

elicit a different response from the other person. In other words, Fred, you can't control Jennifer, and Jennifer, you can't control Fred. However, you both could make commitments to amending your approach, your communication style, and whatever else in order to elicit a different response from the other person in the future. That's only fair after an intervention like this, and I'm looking forward to hearing your comments once we get to the end of this meeting.

For right now, I'm going to ask you, Jennifer, to give us a broader overview of the issues that have been concerning you about Fred's interactions with you since you brought the issue to me first. Let's approach this like mature and supportive adults, and since we already know the broader issues from our discussions yesterday, we can simply recap here. Jennifer, the floor is yours: What's your two-minute overview of what's been bothering you in your communications with Fred, and what are some of the highlights from our conversation that you'd like to share with him now?

And you're off to the races, engaging in a healthy dialogue in a safe environment. The issues are already known: this is simply an opportunity for the warring parties to share their concerns and perceptions in an open and honest manner with little surprise involved, while hearing the other person's concerns directly as well.

Step 3: Conclude the meeting.

Conclude the meeting this way:

Jennifer and Fred, you've both heard the other side of the story now. I'm not asking you to hold hands and sing "Kumbaya," and I don't expect you to go bowling together after work tonight. But I do expect you to openly communicate so that the work in our department isn't negatively impacted and nothing falls through the cracks because of a lack of communication between you both.

The final questions I have to ask each of you are, Now that you've heard the other person's perceptions of what's going on, what are you willing to change in terms of your own behavior that will elicit a different response in the other person? My other question is, How should I, as your manager, react if this situation were to rear its ugly head again?

And voila—you'll have given each employee his or her day in court, so to speak, where each vents and shares perceptions of the problem. You'll end the meeting on a constructive note where both parties agree to change their behavior. And you'll also create a "healthy sense of paranoia" where both realize that if the problem surfaces again, there will be a more formal management response, most likely in the form of disciplinary action. Congratulations—you've treated your warring parties as adults and held them accountable for fixing the ongoing problem that exists between them.

Allowing adults to hash out their differences in a controlled, safe environment removes a critical roadblock that could otherwise hinder someone's success. No matter how much you care, you can't manage their differences. Only they can do that. Still, you can provide a mechanism for solving employee disputes that brings out the best in people. Establishing a culture of openness means confronting "people problems" in an environment that maintains the individual's dignity and trust. It enhances your position as a leader and establishes your reputation as a fair arbiter of disputes—truly a leadership trait that will set you apart from your peers.

Much like the Dad in the scenario in Question 14, who allows the kids to share their concerns but then resets expectations going forward, this approach to warring adults will likely yield similar positive outcomes. Are you expecting them to become best friends again overnight? Of course not. But you have every right to ensure that communication doesn't fall through the cracks because of either individual's willful stubbornness to work with the other person. Should that happen and output and productivity suffer, you'll unfortunately have to hold a separate meeting with them both, the results of which could be far less benign and caring than the intervention outlined above.

Additional Note

Encourage your two staff members to use the phrases "This is how I feel" and "Can you understand why I would feel that way?" Feelings aren't right or wrong—they just are. Since perception is reality until proven otherwise, it's each individual's responsibility to sensitize the other regarding the existence of the perceptions that have developed over time.

16 *Bearing Bad News: The Creative Art of Give and Take*

Hollywood lore echoes a true story of the fear of bearing bad news: In 1939, the subordinates of Adolph Zukor, Paramount Pictures' founder and studio boss, were terrified of telling him of the box office success of rival MGM's *Gone with the Wind* for fear of his suffering a heart attack. Maybe that seems a bit exaggerated and overly dramatic, but it makes an important point nonetheless: We all walk the delicate line of balancing the delivery of bad news with the fear of being blamed for holding it back.

Giving and receiving bad news is a common part of business. However, focusing on how to deliver bad news to senior management or others as well as ensuring that your subordinates are keeping you abreast of unpleasant changes in circumstances are critical in our information-driven work environment. A simple rule to share with your employees is this: "I don't mind that bad news occasionally hits the fan; I simply want to know which way to duck when it does. You're responsible for communicating any problems to me before I learn about them from anyone else. There can be no exceptions while I'm at the helm."

Okay, simple enough. But what about delivering bad news to CEOs and other senior executives who have a tendency to shoot the messenger? Unfortunately, too many managers avoid unpleasant confrontations with senior managers, even if this is to the detriment of the company. Only you can assess how welcome your comments and suggestions will be to your senior leadership team. And the purpose of this chapter is certainly not to damage your career by suggesting that you boldly volunteer bad news when others are reluctant to do so. That being said, though, as a leader within your organization, you are indeed responsible for the well-being of the enterprise and the fulfillment of its mission. If you choose to deliver bad news to the CEO or other member of senior management, here are some tips on communicating your message:

Step 1: Confirm your commitment to keep the enlightened CEO informed.

Simply stated, every CEO relies on her immediate core of senior managers to remain abreast of changes in company circumstances and employee attitudes. When a member of senior management finds out about a critical problem that was not communicated in advance, the tongue lashing typically sounds something like this:

> Why am I finding out about this now for the first time? I can't be everywhere all the time, and I rely on you to keep me abreast of changes in the organization that impact our business. I shouldn't have to reprimand you for failing to fulfill an essential function of your job. What am I paying you for anyway?

Okay, point well taken. The CEO never seems to acknowledge at the point of castigation, however, that the last time a manager brought bad news to her attention, that manager was pummeled and bloodied and became the hot topic of water cooler banter for a month. A strategic opener to this dialogue with your senior manager consequently might sound like this:

> I've got to share some unpleasant information with you, and I'm not looking forward to this conversation, but it's important that you know. This won't make you particularly happy, but we've got a few options that I'd like to discuss with you to help us through this. Here goes: The employment marketplace is coming back, and we're seeing an increase in the number of resignations among our key employees. If we don't address the hiring freeze and the hold that's been placed on equity adjustments and promotions over the past year, I'm afraid that other "keeper" employees may jump ship at the first offer that comes their way.
>
> The bad news is, this will cost money. The good news is, if we institute a management training program for all directors and above and also reward a small number of key players with promotions and equity adjustments, then I think we'll have a greater chance of stemming the tide of turnover that's upon us right now and keeping within a reasonable budget.

Step 2: Overcome the CEO's initial objections preemptively.

After your opener, make a business case that preempts the boss's objections. For example:

> I know what you're thinking: We've not faced this problem in several years, so why change the practice now? Our turnover has been exceptionally low over the past three years. We've been averaging 12% annual turnover, so why pay attention to some of the key resignations of late? The reasons why turnover has been artificially low is most likely because there were few outside jobs

available for our people to turn to. We responded logically to the market down-turn by not back-filling open jobs and by freezing promotions and equity adjustments. Obviously that environment wouldn't last forever, and it's time to gear up for change in the recruitment marketplace.

We have a lean staff that is very talented and committed, and changes to the lineup at a point when we have little bench strength could be very costly. The level of job dissatisfaction is high right now among most companies, though, and people are tired. Many of them feel their careers are stalled, and they're looking to make up for lost time in terms of their earnings potential. If we don't put a formal retention program in place and communicate and publi-cize it adequately, we'll remain vulnerable to losing additional key players in our operation. In short, our lack of proactive change at this point could make us penny smart and pound-foolish.

Step 3: Do the math when focusing on the "how."

A proposal like this needs to be tied to the bottom line: cost contain-ment and budget variances. Any "lofty" proposals that haven't been logically thought through or financially justified will seem naïve at best and could result in your loss of credibility. Here are some consid-erations you might include in your closing:

We could hire an outside training firm to put on a series of management sem-inars over the next three months for $35,000. We've looked at promoting six key employees and giving equity adjustments to 12 others, for a total payroll cost of $125,000. We believe we could show a permanent savings offset of $40,000 by cutting certain underused employee programs that don't give us much return on investment, but we'd still end up $120,000 over budget. Still, it's a strategic investment for our key players, and we've looked at external market surveys as well as internal equity, so we believe the fundamentals are in place and the timing is right. I also think we could cover $80,000 of that bud-get shortfall by outsourcing our temp desk, although it would take 18 months to show those savings. What are your initial thoughts?

Regardless of the senior manager's ultimate decision, you'll have created a compelling presentation with a logical business conclusion. More importantly, you'll have couched the bad news in a contextual framework that forces your boss to consider your proposal on its objective merits. Likewise, you'll have fulfilled your responsibility of providing organizational insights that the senior manager may not have focused on—a well-done opener that, it is hoped, will lead to further questions and investigation.

In comparison, when it comes to working with your own subordinates, creating a culture of trust is an amalgam of formal guidelines that you establish as well as informal, unspoken cues that you give. Of course, there are tools available to help you do this. For example, inviting your employees to evaluate themselves before you critique them during the annual performance review process allows them to involve themselves in their own career development, while placing you in the role of career mentor and coach rather than unilateral judge and decision maker.

Similarly, adding a question to a one-on-one meeting with a subordinate like, "What could I do differently to provide you with more structure, direction, and feedback or otherwise help you prepare for your next move in career progression?" would likewise help establish trust in your relationship. Simply stated, if your subordinates feel that it's safe to stick their necks out of the foxhole and share bad news with you, there's a greater chance that you'll hear about problems proactively while you could still fix them.

But what do you do if a subordinate stubbornly refuses to provide you with negative feedback? If a feeling of "flying blind" plagues your relationship with a particular staff member, a more formal response may be an appropriate measure. Some organizations call this coaching and counseling, while others describe these types of actions as "verbal warnings." However you categorize them, the verbal message needs to be clear and incontestable in its intent. For example:

Kelly, your failure to meet the deadline for our Estimate 3 financial projections resulted in my having to work till midnight last night to ensure that your information was properly integrated into the divisional report. More significantly, your failure to notify me in advance of your inability to meet your project deadline precluded my assigning additional staff or resources to help you. As such, your failure to communicate is a separate infraction that demonstrates an inability to meet the fundamental demands of your job. If I were documenting this in some form of progressive discipline, the language would read something along the lines of: "Failure to demonstrate immediate and sustained improvement may result in further disciplinary action up to and including dismissal." We're not at that stage, but I'm disappointed that you left me feeling like I was flying blind. I didn't see this coming, and that's a major misstep. I'd like your commitment right now that we won't have to have a conversation like this again.

Just in case this issue recurs, be sure to document in your notes that you discussed your expectations regarding open communication, especially surrounding potentially negative news. It's critical that each member of your team understands that communication remains the subordinate's ultimate priority in all business dealings. Oh, and here's the good news about Mr. Zukor at Paramount Pictures: his staffers had nothing to fear. He not only survived the bad news about *Gone with the Wind*'s box office success, but he also shaped Paramount Pictures into one of the greatest movie studios in the world, serving as honorary chairman until his death in 1976 at the age of 103.

17 *Staff Meeting Tune-Ups: Upgrade Your Group Communication to Strengthen Team Performance*

Opening the lines of communication with your staff starts with healthy group dialogue, and a regular, ongoing, and predictable forum to voice new ideas and safely suggest alternative ways of doing things will always be your best place to start. No matter how strong your relationships with particular individuals on your team or how long you've all been working together, the group dynamic takes on a life of its own during the weekly staff meeting. It, more than just about anything, gives you an opportunity to open the lines of communication with your team, demonstrate recognition for a job well done, and place individual contributors into rotational leadership roles.

There are three basic steps to a successful staff meeting. First, invite all of your subordinates to discuss what's going on in their worlds. Brief updates and overviews of achievements, roadblocks, and opportunities to reinvent the workflow are hallmarks of healthy group get-togethers. It's not only important for individuals to talk about themselves, however; it's also critical that all members of the staff hear what their peers are doing. Too many times employees dig foxholes for themselves and develop an entitlement mentality where they believe they're doing all the work. Once they hear what everyone else is working on, they tend to develop a greater appreciation for their peers' contributions. Their sense of entitlement will typically diminish as a result.

Second, focus on what you, as a group, could have done differently in the past week to make the company a better place. After all, that's what work is all about. We're hired to increase revenues, decrease expenses, and save time. Any lost opportunities to impact the company's bottom line in one of those three ways should be discussed, studied, and revisited in this postmortem exercise. "What could we have done differently?" is a natural counterpoint to our opening question because it mirrors what's going on in your group at any given time. It also allows for a healthy dose of self-critical insight and makes it safe to learn from past mistakes.

Third, introduce constructive criticism into the decision-making process. Specifically ask, "What do we need to be doing differently to reinvent the workflow in our area?" The best ideas will always come from the people on the front line. The frustration that many employees share with HR during employee opinion surveys is that they didn't feel that their ideas mattered or that management was listening. They went through the motions day in and day out but had no real impact or influence over their working environment. This simple invitation satisfies the basic need to be heard and to make a positive difference.

Where do these weekly staff meetings lead? First and foremost, you'll strengthen the overall culture of the work unit when communication, recognition, and trust are encouraged. Second, by giving your people more "face time" with you, the boss, and with each other, a spirit of camaraderie will develop. Finally, these meetings optimally will expand from the micro view of work assignments and project updates to the more macro level of organizational impact. All in all, your investment in a group meeting like this will likely end up being the most important hour of the week in terms of enhancing productivity and teamwork.

In fact, one of the surest signs of a dysfunctional group is that it doesn't hold regular staff meetings. The "informal feedback" response tends to be a copout in all but the most trusted situations where team members have been working together for a long time and work independently. Instead, when you hear that staff meetings "aren't really necessary because we all know what everyone is working on," your antennae should go up. If staffers aren't talking collectively on a regular group basis, it's more often the sign that people are working in silos and that cliques exist that create a more exclusive working environment.

If this is the case in your group or in a team that you're now responsible for overseeing, it could be very simple to inject a staff meeting structure into the workweek—no matter how busy everyone's schedule is or how little time they have to take the focus off their work. You can instruct your team as follows and, depending on what your team is responsible for, focus your team efforts on the critical issues at hand. You might try something like this:

> Everyone, I called this meeting to let you know that I want to begin holding formal weekly meetings. I think there's a lot of value in that sort of group interaction because I want you all to have an opportunity to share with your peers what priorities you're working on, what challenges and roadblocks you may be facing, and how the rest of us could help you in terms of additional support or resources. I also think it'll give us a chance to share and celebrate successes, which is something we don't do enough of.

> Here are my recommendations: First, be prepared to give an overview of the top three projects or assignments you're working on in terms of progress, deliverables, and timelines. If you suspect that you may have any challenges meeting deadlines, this is the place for us to find out so we can all make ourselves part of the solution. Second, I'd like you to address the biggest programs or projects you're working on—David, in your case that would be metrics development; Jennifer, in your case that would be employee communications in light of the recent employee opinion survey; Travis, I'd ask you to share your insights into the mentoring relationship you have with the two recent new hires and how that's helped them assimilate into our culture more successfully.

> Finally, I'll ask you all to discuss what we could be doing differently as a team and how I could support you further by removing roadblocks and facilitating progress toward the goals you're working on. Let's try this, assume good intentions, and give it our all. I think this could be a game-changer in terms of our team's productivity, and more important, I think this could be a lot of fun. I'm

looking forward to your contributions, so let's tee the first meeting up for this Thursday at 8:30.

Resist the temptation to back-burner weekly staff meetings, no matter how much pushback you get from your staffers. This is one of those situations where they might not know what's good for them, but formalizing the lines of communication and giving yourself multiple opportunities to reset expectations and hear about feedback in real time is an advantage and an opportunity that you won't want to do without.

18   *Leadership SOS: Effective and Successful Turnaround Strategies for Failing Teams*

What do you do when you inherit a department that is functioning poorly? Likewise, what happens if you've been ignoring or avoiding ongoing friction on your team, and people are starting to act up, using terminology like "hostile work environment," or even grumbling about organizing a union? Well, you may not have a "Save our Ship" button on your desk, but there are ways to turn around even the most dire situations where it looks like a team may be about to implode. In fact, more often than not, if you peel back the layers, you'll often find that there are root causes driving particular issues and key players that keep driving a wedge into the team's relationships.

"Strawberries. It was all about a silly gift of strawberries. That's when everything changed." So reported a nurse at a hospital who was in tears in the HR officer's office. Perplexed, the HR person asked to learn more about what a gift of strawberries could possibly have to do with the ongoing interpersonal problems plaguing this team of experienced and long-tenured nurses. Five nurses showed up in HR unannounced that day complaining about one particular nurse, Debbie, who harped on them, threatened to sue them, and created voodoo dolls of each of them.

That last element was significant in the case: These particular nurses were from an island nation where voodoo was a credible force, and they were legitimately frightened. Further, HR learned that Debbie also carried around a little black book, which she told them was where she kept notes on each of her peers for her lawyer so that she could sue them personally for harassment, bullying, and retaliation should they challenge her in any way.

These six nurses had worked together for years. A breach occurred in the group friendship about three years earlier when, according to the five complainants, Debbie started acting differently. She no longer wanted to go to lunch with them, get together after work, or participate in group events. One day, one of the nurses brought in four small baskets of strawberries. She only had four baskets at home that morning when she picked the strawberries from her garden. She knew that Debbie wouldn't be in that day, so she brought strawberry baskets for the other four nurses.

As fate would have it, Debbie came to work that day even though she wasn't scheduled. And when she found out that everyone got strawberries except her, she apparently went ballistic. She cursed and threatened her peers, she told them she'd create voodoo dolls of them all, and she said any form of friendship or personal association was over. And that's how this real-life story turned into a crisis where five nurses almost walked off the job in anger, frustration, and fear. HR also learned that Debbie wouldn't cover for them while they were on break or answer their patients' call lights when they weren't available, so there was a true concern about compromised patient safety.

The wise HR person reasoned that there were two sides to every story and invited Debbie in to learn more about her experiences with the team. Debbie wasn't hesitant to launch an attack on her peers for harassing her, discriminating against and bullying her, and creating a "hostile work environment." (Caution: When employees start using legal words like "hostile work environment," your antennae should go up because they're often contemplating suing.) HR went on to ask her for examples about the harassment and bullying, and Debbie stated that the nurses were doing things subtly to exclude her and taunt her.

HR reasoned fairly quickly that something was very odd about the whole setup: How could five employees be so intimidated by one person, and how could that one person appear to yield so much power over them? The answer, of course, lay in the voodoo dolls and that little black lawyer's book. After speaking with the nursing management team, it was decided that the six nurses needed to remain in that particular wing of the hospital because of their specialties, and transferring Debbie to a different unit wouldn't make sense. So it was time for HR to partner with the nursing leader and reset expectations for the entire team.

First, the HR person and the nursing director of that unit met with Debbie. The conversation went like this:

> Debbie, after doing our investigation, we found out that you've threatened your peers with voodoo dolls and that you've shown them the dolls, which are in their likeness. You admitted to carrying a little black book that you told them you use to document anything that you feel is inappropriate so you could sue them. Is that correct?
>
> [Yes.]
>
> Okay, both of those practices must stop immediately. Threatening people with voodoo could potentially create a hostile work environment, and threatening to sue people and writing their names in your legal book can do the same. Based on your actions, we're placing you on a final written warning that states that if you ever again engage in conduct like that, it could be considered hostile or offensive toward your peers, and you'll immediately be dismissed for cause.
>
> Further, you claim that you're the victim of harassment and bullying from your peers, but aside from a few indirect examples that you provided, you've offered no proof of inappropriate behavior on their part other than a "gut feeling" and a "suspicion" you have about their talking behind your back. As a result, I see little merit in your allegations against your peers but will assume that they may be acting inappropriately at times. What you need to understand, however, is that we are holding you fully accountable for your own perception management. That means that you are responsible for fostering a healthy and inclusive work environment where your coworkers don't need to fear you or avoid working with you. Is that clear?
>
> [Yes.]
>
> Finally, we're holding a group meeting tomorrow with all six of you to reestablish our expectations and clarify the rules of respect and inclusion in the workplace. All six of you will be asked to sign a letter of confirmation recognizing these rules of engagement and respect, and if anyone violates the rules, then further disciplinary action, up to and including dismissal, may result.

In short, Debbie, we're putting an end to this highly inappropriate conduct in our hospital. The fact that you're receiving a final written warning for your particular conduct will not be shared with other members of your team. Only you can break that confidentiality if you choose to disclose it. Note, however, that after tomorrow's meeting, we're going to re-welcome everyone back to the hospital as if it's their first day of employment. We don't expect people to forgive and forget right away because we realize that if it took three years for your relationships to deteriorate to this level, it may take at least that long to simply get back to the baseline. Still, we wanted to meet with you individually and in private to explain our findings and reset expectations. We'll draft the final written warning and issue it to you in the next few days. Do you have any questions about how we're handling this and why?

[No.]

Okay, thank you for meeting with us, and we'll schedule our follow-up group meeting for first thing tomorrow morning.

HR and the nursing director then met with the other five nurses later that afternoon and explained that the investigation was completed, that their complaints were taken very seriously, and that the voodoo dolls and little black books should no longer be a problem. HR and the nursing director instructed the team to notify management and HR immediately if those items ever popped up in the workplace again or otherwise were made mention of. All agreed, but they seemed nervous and apprehensive about the next day's meeting.

The group meeting the following morning went like this:

Everyone, as you know, we conducted an investigation into what's been plaguing your team and learned about voodoo dolls and little black books that seemed to threaten a number of you, which is understandable. The good news is now that we've found out about them, we have an agreement from Debbie that this will no longer be an issue. Debbie, is that correct?

[Yes.]

Good. Thank you. Further, I want to share on a personal note how sad I feel to see six people who have worked together for so long, who used to be close friends, and who save people's lives on a regular basis, creating so much drama and making accusations against one another, constantly assuming bad intentions about the other side's motivations.

We're placing you all on notice that this type of behavior—whether direct or veiled, overt or in undertones—must stop immediately. First, we respect you too much as long-term employees to allow any of you to work in an unfriendly environment or feel excluded in any way. Second, you could potentially all be creating a "hostile work environment," as some of you have called it, and we're clearly not going to allow that to happen for legal reasons. And third, it's time to reset expectations: we exist for patient care. Our mission is to cure and mend people with serious healthcare issues—not to get lost in our own dramas about strawberries and what not. We expect more of you as a team and as individuals. We expect you to appreciate this hospital for what it does, we expect you to respect each other and create a friendly work environment where people feel comfortable to express ideas and work with peace of mind, and we expect you to be thankful for the opportunities this hospital has given you to build your careers and care for your families. Anything shy of an appreciation for this hospital, your jobs, and your awareness of the opportunities available to you as a result of working here, will lead to failure.

I don't expect you all to become best friends after this meeting, but I do expect communication among you all to remain open and clear. If someone doesn't respond to a patient's call in the primary nurse's absence, I will consider that a terminable offense and the ultimate in patient disregard. If problems arise because of a lack of communication among you, we'll have another group meeting, but it may result in far more serious consequences, and I would ask you please never to put us in that situation.

Finally, we've drafted a letter of confirmation outlining these points that we've just discussed. We'll ask you all to sign the letter to acknowledge that we've held this meeting, reset expectations, and clarified the consequences of repeating these types of behaviors. This is not a disciplinary document and won't be placed in your personnel file. However, if you ultimately violate the commitment that you're about to sign about maintaining and fostering a respectful and inclusive work environment and following hospital standards of performance and conduct, then the document you sign today as a clarification letter could be attached to formal corrective action notice in the future or be used as justification to move to immediate dismissal. Is this clear to all of you?

[Yes.]

Then thank you for bringing this problem to our attention, and we'll consider the matter concluded for now.

This scenario may sound very fact-specific, and it is. But that's by design: when departments or teams seem like they're about to crash or otherwise implode, in most cases it's because there's an antagonist who's probably behaving oddly. It may be a supervisor who undermines her boss, a peer who engages in gossip and rumor mongering, or an individual who continually stirs the pot by pitting one person against another. In almost all cases, look for the ringleader. Find out who's driving the ill will, angst, and drama, and address that individual privately. Then bring the entire team together to heal the wound and reset expectations. Verbal interventions like these may have written consequences (like a final written warning) for certain key players, but no one else needs to know that. Your job is to solve the problem. In this case, you called the players out, addressed the overt and veiled behaviors causing the ongoing angst, and concluded the matter cleanly, professionally, and respectfully. Job well done and crisis avoided.

19 Addressing Uncomfortable Workplace Situations and Personal Style Issues

Leadership and communication go hand in hand when it comes to motivating staff, recognizing employees' achievements and accomplishments, and explaining your reasoning so that employees understand why they're doing what they're doing and how to best get there. But as we know, communication tends to break down when it comes to sharing more challenging news, and addressing uncomfortable workplace situations clearly falls under this category. No, the employee isn't typically doing anything wrong per se, but certain personal issues tend to make their way into the workplace and impact coworkers in awkward and uncomfortable ways. When that's the case, it's time for you to step in and gently move things in a new direction.

Many all-too-common workplace issues get short shrift in the press because they're simply too uncomfortable to deal with: employees' inappropriate dress and body odor are two issues that managers are reluctant to address. Unfortunately, the workplace isn't usually that forgiving: if you don't handle it yourself, the problem will likely continue. But how do you approach it without embarrassing the employee, and what do you do if the employee challenges you and claims that she has every right to dress as she wishes?

My book *101 Tough Conversations to Have with Employees: A Manager's Guide to Addressing Performance, Conduct, and Discipline Challenges*

(AMACOM, 2009) discusses many of the most common but also most challenging conversations you may have to have as a manager; the examples below represent a sample. So let's address your responsibilities to your immediate subordinates and to the rest of your staff when it comes to uncomfortable workplace situations.

You've probably seen one of these variations on a theme before: Several of your staff members come to see you because a long-time coworker has developed a body odor or halitosis problem. Or perhaps an individual arrives at work with her hair in a mess looking like she just got out of bed. Maybe a subordinate's face has a new, prominent piercing, or maybe a visible tattoo is being shown off to make a statement. How nice it would be to pull out a policy that dictates workplace behavior in instances like these. More likely than not, however, you'll need to verbalize an ad hoc solution to the particular circumstances that you're facing.

Bad Hair Days

Publicly shaming or ridiculing an individual will only develop resentment and anger. The goal of any management response in situations like these is to ensure that the individual is treated with dignity and respect. So here's how we might address our first scenario, bad hair days, by making light of the situation and using a little humor:

> Victor, I have to share something with you, and I don't want to hurt your feelings or embarrass you in any way. This is private just between the two of us. Victor, your hair . . . Something's either happening too much to it or not happening enough. You're making a bit of a statement because it's looking rather "severe," if you don't mind me saying so. I thought it would be a good idea to address it with you quietly before anyone else seems to notice. Where are you with that [pointing to the coif]?

Typically you'll find some nervous shuffling along with an apology: "Oh, Paul, I woke up and went to the gym and didn't have time to comb it out the way I normally do. I'll run to the restroom right now and fix it and make sure that I come to work dressed for work from now on—including my hair! I'm sorry about that. Did anyone else say anything? I'm so embarrassed!"

Body Piercing

Okay, that first one was easy enough: a very common scenario with a predictable outcome. If only all employee relations interventions were that easy! Now on to a larger challenge: Assume that your customer service manager walks in one day with a new ring in his eyebrow and a metal post in his tongue. After you gasp and think, "He can't service customers looking like that!" you devise a way to position your message so that he arrives at that same conclusion himself:

Michael, I need to talk with you privately about your fashion decision. First, let me say that I don't mean to embarrass you in any way. I respect you as a person, and I don't mean at all to dictate what you do in your personal life. But I've got to ask you: Are you sure that you've given sufficient thought to your eyebrow ring and tongue post in terms of how they might impact the customers that you service in our bank? I guess what I'm getting at is, Knowing that that kind of look might alienate some of our customers, would you be willing to remove them while you're at work? Or would you consider removing them whenever you have to deal with the public? What are your thoughts?

The value to this approach lies in its subtlety and reasonableness. Few companies have policies restricting facial hair on men or insisting that women wear dresses in the office. And even the large accounting firms' consultants now arrive at their consulting assignments in more of a "casual dress" mode than in the blue suit and red tie combinations of the past. Still, body piercing tends to result from revelations and epiphanies of what's cool, what's important in life, and what rights people believe they have over their own lives. In short, it's not something to brush over lightly.

If your conversation leads to some kind of compromise where the employee agrees to leave the hardware at home or to take it off whenever dealing with customers, then you'll have accomplished your goal. Employees who feel they've been treated respectfully and not simply been told "what to do" will almost always agree to some kind of modification, which will please the company and allow them to maintain their individuality.

Tattoos

Eyebrow rings and tongue posts are removable. Tattoos aren't. (At least not for the sake of this conversation.) How would you address the ankle bracelet tattoo or back-of-the-neck black widow spider tattoo that seems about ready to climb into the employee's hair? The phraseology may be different, but the strategy is the same: Discuss your concerns openly, listen to the individual's side of the story, and then look for some resolution or compromise that you can both live with:

> Eileen, a few of the staff members brought to my attention that you'd gotten some new tattoos over the weekend. I respect the fact that you have the right to do body art, but as the nursing supervisor in the ICU, I'm a little concerned about how some of our patients might respond. In essence, you know that we're a little bit more of a conservative hospital, but that doesn't mean that we want people to act like robots and repress their individuality. I wanted to talk with you and see if there could be a way where your desire to express yourself has a minimal impact on the patients and their families who come to us for care. What are your initial thoughts about that?

Once again, most people will offer alternatives that minimize the problem in the workplace: "Maybe I'll wear pants rather than a dress to cover the ankle tattoo, and I'll wear blouses with collars so that patients won't be able to see the spider tattoo on my neck." A reasonable approach begets a reasonable response.

Body Odor

Suppose your subordinates meet with you *en masse* to complain that a coworker's odor is making the workplace intolerable. Odors come from bad breath, garlicky diets, insufficient personal hygiene, unclean clothing, and sometimes from chronic medical conditions like obesity, Crone's disease, or colostomy bags. These conversations are a little trickier because they're not necessarily something your employee can physically control. In addition, the Americans with Disabilities Act (ADA) may govern these matters, so it may be more than workplace sensitivity: it may be a matter of law.

First, a caveat about the ADA: As a civil rights and antidiscrimination law intended to bring disabled workers into the workplace and to keep disabled employees in the workplace, its remedies can include punitive damages, so be careful! In addition to defining a "disability" as a physical or mental impairment (or record of such an impairment) that substantially limits one or more major life activities, the ADA also covers individuals who are "regarded as having" an impairment. In other words, even if no "disability" technically exists, a plaintiff's lawyer could argue that you, the employer, "regarded" the employee as having a disability and that your company was therefore governed by the Act (and subject to its penalties).

Finally, in preparing for any workplace discussions with your employees regarding physical or mental conditions that may be governed by the ADA, remember that the law does not merely prohibit discrimination against the disabled; it imposes additional affirmative obligations upon employers to accommodate the needs of people with disabilities and to facilitate their economic independence.

Now that I've gotten your attention, proceed this way:

> Joan, I need to make you aware of a situation that's come to my attention, and I'll need your help to solve it. A few of your coworkers came to me out of concern for you, but also out of concern for themselves. Apparently there is an odor coming from your office that makes it difficult for them to approach you. The odor is described as being a combination of sweat and urine, and apparently this is the third time that they've noticed it. It's happening about the same time every month, and they've asked me to address it with you. You don't need to share any specifics with me regarding the cause. I'd rather you address some possible solutions with me, assuming that you agree that this could be a problem. Is this something you're aware of, and did you realize that your coworkers might have noticed anything?

Expect the employee to identify some underlying cause for the medical problem, but stop her before she gets too far. Under the ADA, you're not obligated to accommodate a disability that you're unaware of, so the fewer details you have, the less you have to formally "accommodate." Likewise, for privacy reasons, you probably don't want to know anything more than you have to. So after she shares that her monthly cycle aggravates her problem, ask her how she might want to resolve the matter. "Well, I'll make a doctor's appointment for to-morrow and see how this can be solved."

Medical intervention is the only real direction in which an employer can lead an employee under these circumstances. Just be sure and close your conversation this way: "Joan, you just take care of yourself. If you need time off, if your doctor recommends any special considerations that we can help you with, just let us know. We're all concerned about you and want to make sure you're okay."

Practically speaking, you'll have demonstrated care and compassion to an employee in need of your help. That's what effective leadership is all about. Legally speaking, you'll have begun the process of fulfilling your obligation under the law to engage in an "interactive process" with the employee to determine an appropriate accommodation, if one is applicable. More importantly, you'll have risen to the occasion and addressed a workplace issue appropriately. That's what turns managers into leaders who stand out among their peers.

Dealing with Outright Refusals

Most employees will respond reasonably to your request if your presentation is respectful and reasonable as well as appreciative of people's differences. However, there can be an occasional instance where a subordinate chooses to make a stand over a hairdo, eyebrow ring, or tattoo. If the employee refuses to discuss it with you, and if you feel you have a legitimate business reason for disallowing a nose ring or tattoo, then you may be within your rights to terminate the individual since body piercings and tattoos are generally not protected under the law.

Termination may be a bit extreme, of course, but depending on your industry and culture, it may be the only plausible outcome. Most states recognize the at-will employment relationship, and "at-will" means that companies can let go of employees for any reason or for no reason at all with or without cause or notice. The only catch is that you can't let go of an employee for an *unlawful* reason. Body piercing and tattoos are generally not protected categories under the law, so it likely wouldn't be unlawful to dismiss an employee who, for example, might intimidate your customers. In extreme cases like that, be

sure to discuss such terminations with qualified legal counsel before
proceeding. Consider the legal costs a cheap insurance policy to ensure
that you're not missing anything, you're asking the right questions to
qualify the individual's reason for refusing to make an adjustment,
and you're coached appropriately on what to say (and what not to
say) during the separation meeting.

20   *Situational Coaching: How Do You "Coach Someone to Normal"?*

How do you effectively deal with supervisors and other frontline
leaders who report to you but just don't seem to get it? Whether they
continually make off-color or political remarks, refer to female staffers
as "sweetie" and "honey," or simply enjoy good old-fashioned public
shaming sessions where they censure others openly and inject ongoing embarrassment and resentment into their working relationships,
these leaders apparently don't want to play nicely or otherwise get
along with others. In fact, some are "spoken to" and even disciplined
for past behaviors, yet their inappropriate conduct continues to roller
coaster up and down every few months. At some point, frustrated
and angry employees challenge why such behavior is allowed to continue, and company leaders often don't take the situation seriously
until people threaten to quit, file a lawsuit, or organize a union.

How do you stop these roller-coaster patterns from recurring in
the workplace? How do you tell leaders that they've got a significant
perception problem? And how do you stop these types of toxic behaviors and encourage errant leaders to behave appropriately? The key,
like most things in business, lies not in what you say but how you say
it and how you structure your expectations going forward. You must
gain the leader's commitment to fix the problem.

Such meetings often require a combined front. Let's assume you're
a director and have a manager reporting to you and a supervisor reporting to him. The individual in question is the supervisor. You've
heard banter about this supervisor's conduct, but your manager hasn't
been able to correct it. In such cases, it might be time for you to step in
and join forces with your manager to ensure that the errant supervisor

hears two levels of consistency in terms of the organization's expectations. In fact, if your company has an HR department, then it might make sense to invite the HR director to the meeting so that all three of you can provide a clear and consistent message about the ongoing problem and future expectations.

Next, determine upfront whether your organization can risk losing this individual, either via termination or resignation. If the answer is yes, then the suggested scripts that follow can be strengthened in terms of the consequences that you are prepared to apply; but if the individual is too valuable to your organization to risk losing, then you might want to change the language that follows in our example.

What's critical, however, is that you not come across as judgmental. "Why do you keep making inappropriate and disrespectful remarks in public about people on your team?" won't accomplish anything. The individual will simply become defensive and place blame elsewhere. Instead, come from observation—the "what's so" rather than the "so what"—to explain the challenges as you see them:

John, you've had discussions about this before with your manager, and you've committed to undoing some of the damage that occurred when you admitted to engaging in public shaming sessions with some of your staff members in the past by censuring them at group meetings in front of their peers. You agreed at the time to follow our guidelines that you praise in public and censure in private. Yet yesterday two members of your team came to me as the department director to complain of that very same behavior repeating itself at your staff meeting. From what I was told, you reverted to using the F-word and questioned why people "aren't thinking" and "are acting like f-ing idiots." Is that an accurate assessment of what occurred yesterday?

[Yes.]

Based on our prior discussions and reflecting on your handling of yesterday's meeting, can you look back and see some sort of justification for your behavior?

[No, not really: I just lost my head.]

Would you be surprised then if I told you that both employees are now considering quitting because of how they were treated in front of the rest of the team?

[No, I guess that could be a reasonable reaction on their part.]

Then based on that, John, you've got a real perception problem on your hands. They say that perception is reality until proven otherwise, and people are simply assuming bad intentions when dealing with you. In fact, your actions yesterday are very much now part of everyone's reality—perception issues aside. We're holding you fully accountable for your own perception management from this point forward. In other words, regardless of your intentions or how you think others may be receiving your message, you've got to raise your awareness level about how you're coming across. You can no longer engage in public diatribes about your entire team or individuals on your team, especially using that kind of language. Is that a fair request on our part?

[Yes.]

Now would be an optimal time to remind leaders about personal liability surrounding what are known as "managerial bad acts" as follows:

John, you've also got to remember that you may be putting yourself at risk from a liability and financial standpoint. When a leader engages in what could be construed as harassing behavior or in potentially creating a hostile work environment, a lawsuit from a disgruntled ex-employee will typically name you separately from the company. We don't pay you enough money to warrant risking your savings and your home in a personal lawsuit for what's deemed to be "managerial bad acts" or "acting outside the course and scope of your employment."

But the threshold for individual liability is fairly low, and I've read that one out of four managers in corporate America will become personally involved in some sort of work-related lawsuit during their career. What executives don't realize is that, in some states, they can be sued for up to $50,000 of their own money; in California, there's no cap on how much they can be sued for. As a frontline leader in our company, you may be seen as a juicy target who's worth pursuing separately and apart from the company, and you can't risk your personal savings because you keep losing your temper or otherwise striking fear in your staffers. They could all serve as witnesses to your behavior in a court of law.

Remember, you've been to training sessions on respect in the workplace, which included modules on bullying behavior and hostility. Just so you're aware, we have proof that you attended multiple training workshops. In essence, the company uses that documentation to demonstrate that it was a good corporate citizen and trained its employees appropriately. However, this particular supervisor, John Smith, decided to engage in egregious behavior nevertheless and, as such, was acting outside the course and scope of his employment. Therefore, the company will logically argue, "Please don't sue us—sue him. We did everything right, yet he continued on in this behavior nevertheless."

The next question from the judge or arbitrator will clearly be, "Well, why didn't you fire him then?" And you need to fast-forward to where we are right now: If this type of behavior shows itself again, we will indeed have to separate you for cause. This is your last chance, John, and if you fail to abide by our guidance here in terms of controlling your temper, you'll be firing yourself. Is that clear?

[Yes.]

Okay, so you're confirming that if we ever have to have another conversation like this, it will be your final day of employment with us, check in hand. Agreed?

[Yes.]

Fair enough, then. We'll be codifying this conversation and our expectations in the form of a final written warning. Note as well that it won't have an expiration or "stay clean" period. The document will specifically state that if you *ever again* engage in behavior that could appear to intimidate or threaten your team members or otherwise strip them of their dignity or humiliate them in public, you'll be immediately discharged for cause. Do I have your commitment at this point that we're all clear on our company's expectations and the results if you ever go down this road again?

[Yes.]

Then thank you for coming in, and we'll prepare the final written warning for your signature shortly.

You may, of course, soften the message, depending on the circumstances, and provide alternative courses of action:

John, we want you to be successful here. We're having this meeting to confirm for you that you're a valued and key member of our company's leadership team, but that this sort of conduct has to stop. We want you to think about options and resources that may be helpful, including an executive coach. If you feel you would benefit from having one-on-one guidance from an external expert who could help you navigate through these types of situations, especially when you're feeling frustrated, let us know. If there are other resources—education, additional staff, or otherwise—that you feel are necessary at this point to relieve some of your stress and pressure, we'd like to hear about them. Likewise, remember that you can contact our Employee Assistance Program confidentially if you want to discuss your reactions and emotions with a professional. You tell us what will help, and we'll do our best to accommodate.

But I'd like a commitment from you now that we'll never have to have a meeting like this again. This is totally within your control, and as much as we value you and want to support your success, we don't want to risk unnecessary turnover or the potential of lawsuits because you can't or won't control your temper. In short, the roller coaster needs to stop as of today. This type of meeting is uncomfortable for us, and we know it's uncomfortable for you, but once you give us your commitment, I expect that this will become water under the bridge and ancient history. We're re-welcoming you to the company today—a fresh start—but it's up to you to accept our olive branch and make this commitment. Are you willing to commit to us now that you'll hold yourself fully accountable for your behavior and actions and ensure that we never have to have a meeting like this with you again?

[Yes.]

Great. Then I'll consider the matter taken care of at this point. That being said, if you have any additional suggestions or concerns that you want to share with me separately, my door is always open. Thanks for joining us today.

Said quietly and without a lot of drama, a respectful discussion scenario like this, led by the individual's immediate supervisor, next-level supervisor, and HR, will more than likely quell the drama. After all, you've placed John in control, listened to him openly, and offered additional resources and options to support him. Even if it doesn't work and you're forced to pursue this issue again, you'll have created an outstanding record of having accorded the supervisor with "workplace due process" in the legal sense. Any further actions on the company's part—whether in the form of progressive discipline or ultimately termination—will be strengthened by this healthy and fair verbal intervention.

21   *The Danger of "Off-the-Record" Conversations and Over-Promising Confidentiality*

Regarding communication, we've addressed issues of transparency, recognition, delivering difficult news, and even incorporating the concept of "perception" into our analysis: all make for critically important concepts in becoming an effective communicator. But listening is equally as important, if not more so. Being a good listener means acknowledging what others are saying, hearing their side of the story with an open mind and objective mindset, and allowing them to finish their thoughts before interrupting them or otherwise talking over them.

Another crucial aspect of effective communication lies in knowing what not to say. Too many leaders have inadvertently stepped on land mines without realizing it because they either said too much or otherwise made promises or guarantees that they simply couldn't keep. Knowing what *not* to say, therefore, is an important part of effective communication. One common area where such land mines exist has to do with over-promising confidentiality.

If an employee asks to speak with you off the record, train yourself right now to respond like this:

> Maybe. It all depends on what you have to say. If it has to do with one of three things, Laura, then I can't promise confidentiality because I'll have an affirmative obligation to disclose it to senior leadership: The three things are harassment or discrimination, potential violence in the workplace, or an inherent conflict of interest with the company's business practices. If it doesn't have to do with any of those three things, I'd be happy to speak with you. But if it does, then understand that you may not want to tell me because I'll be obligated to bring the matter to the attention of senior management or HR.

Wait! Is it reasonable for leaders to instruct their subordinates *not* to tell them something that's on their minds or that's otherwise bothering them? I would argue yes. If employees want to talk off the record and not have the information escalate, then they shouldn't tell their bosses if one of the three categorical areas above is in question. Likewise, leaders need to know not to provide blanket authorization to talk about anything and everything on the employee's mind because they may have to disclose the matter, breaching their agreement of confidentiality with the employee and that individual's trust.

Here are some common examples where you shouldn't promise absolute confidentiality when an employee asks to speak off the record:

> I'm afraid that Susan is feeling threatened and harassed by Ken's constant requests for a date. She told me not to say anything to anyone, but I don't know what to do and want to help her.

> Jack, an IT programmer, pulled a bullet out of his shirt pocket and banged it on his desk three times this morning, shouting: "No one better bother me

today." I think we all got pretty freaked out because we know he keeps rifles in the trunk of his car so that he could visit the rifle range after work every night. Wasn't that weird?

I know you're not my supervisor, but I always enjoy spending time with you. I've got an opportunity to moonlight with XYZ Corporation. I know they're a direct competitor of ours, but they're willing to pay me $60/hour for 20 hours of work every week over the next three months to help them meet a project deadline. It sure would be helpful to make that extra money, but I wouldn't want anyone to know. I'm really excited!

In situations like these, you have an affirmative obligation to disclose your findings. Why? Because in the eyes of the law, once an employee places a company leader (i.e., supervisor, manager, director, VP, and the like) on notice, then the *entire company* is deemed to have been placed on notice. Here's how it works in reality: An ex-employee of your company decides to meet with an attorney to discuss what she believes was a wrongful termination from the company. During questioning, the employee volunteers to her attorney that she's felt threatened by her supervisor on occasion because of his aggressiveness and disparaging comments about her weight. The lawyer questions further and learns that other indirect comments were made about her age and her choice of clothing (along with occasional references about her "sexy legs" and, on one occasion, large breasts).

Bingo! The wrongful termination claim just added harassment and discrimination to the charges—both potentially entailing the awarding of punitive damages. The next question is key. The lawyer asks, "Did you ever inform anyone in management about how you were feeling?" The employee hesitates and responds, "Well, yes and no. I told Jim, who's a supervisor, but he's not my supervisor. He's in favor of the plaintiff's attorney. And I made him promise me to keep it confidential, which he did and which I appreciate. Besides, I'd never want him to get into any kind of trouble."

Too late! The case for discrimination and harassment has now swung decidedly in the plaintiff attorney's favor, and Jim, your friend and confidant, is going to be the main reason why. He'll be taken through a series of interrogatories, depositions, and may ultimately be asked to take the stand to establish why he, as a leader of the company, failed to affirmatively disclose the harassment and discrimination complaint that was made to him. His sheepish and apologetic response will sound something along the lines of, "Well, Doris asked me to keep it confidential, and I wanted to respect her request."

Boom! The land mine just exploded. The entire crux of the case will be shifted to Jim's failure to disclose the harassment he learned of. The plaintiff's lawyer will skillfully argue that in the eyes of the law, once Jim was placed on notice, the entire company was deemed to have been placed on notice, and the company did absolutely nothing to stop the egregious misconduct that subjected Doris to harassing and discriminatory behavior. So much for being a nice guy! Jim, as a supervisor, fell for the biggest sucker punch in the book: he failed to disclose something that he had an obligation to escalate to senior management or HR. He'll unfortunately feel the full brunt of his decision because the entire lawsuit will rest on his ultimate failure to do his job.

Plaintiffs' lawyers aren't in the business of protecting old friendships. Their job is to expose a company's shortcomings, and "company," in this instance, refers to the individual leaders who didn't have a clear of understanding of their responsibilities under the law. Therefore, it's critical that you avoid over-promising confidentiality. This particular error or oversight on leaders' parts has gotten them into tremendous amounts of trouble and has cost people their jobs. Remember, if anyone asks you to speak off the record, respond "Maybe," not "Yes"! Then follow the script above to clarify your expectations before the employee lets loose with her innermost secrets. Employees may not know how much trouble they're getting you into, but now you know how to protect yourself from this particular land mine, which has derailed many a successful career for way too many leaders in corporate America.

22 *Special Circumstances: From Coaching and Mentoring to Verbal Warnings—Communicating with Skillful Aplomb*

Communication is such a broad and all-encompassing topic that no one chapter or even book can come close to addressing its variations in the workplace or elsewhere. Still, our goal in this chapter is to address common workplace opportunities where leaders can become

more effective communicators, especially when it comes to employment offense (motivation, engagement, and positive recognition) and
employment defense (tough conversations, resetting expectations,
and addressing consequences when desired performance or conduct
outcomes aren't achieved). It's appropriate for us to complete the
chapter, then, with special circumstances that may be a bit more common that you'd think.

Coaching and mentoring employees is a critical aspect of effective
leadership, and it all hinges on appropriate communication. On the
other end of the spectrum, however, we need to discuss how to incorporate crucial conversations into the progressive disciplinary process
to create a thorough record of according employees due process—the
legal concept that employees know about problems before they're terminated for cause. Let's look first at coaching and mentoring—your
opportunity to train and develop those employees who are following
in your footsteps or otherwise growing and developing in their own
respective careers.

When people feel valued, acknowledged, and appreciated, they
will typically respond with increased commitment and enthusiasm,
which naturally translates into higher productivity. Even though performance reviews typically occur only once a year, most experts in the
field of leadership and management (including me) will argue that the
optimal amount of time devoted to formal performance feedback is
four hours per year or one hour per quarter. This is a fourfold increase
over what most companies do and what most workers experience, but
the strongest leaders provide formal feedback four times per year to
catch up on progress, redefine goals in light of new information, and
provide timely information and guidance to their team members.

So how do you coach and develop your employees throughout the
year in way that will lead to a highly fueled, self-aware, and engaged
team? Follow this general outline to structure your conversations:

1. Specific: Use real examples. Detailed feedback that is recent and
   "real" becomes actionable and much more meaningful to the
   recipient.
2. Balanced: People need to hear both what they are doing well
   and where they need to improve. The age-old advice still holds:

You'll garner much greater results as a leader if you spend your time and energy on building people's strengths rather than managing their weaknesses. It's likewise true that as a leader, you'll be better off focusing on people's natural talents and encouraging them to become more of who they already are rather than on trying to fix their weaknesses or making them perfect. That's what teams are all about—diverse groups of individuals with varying strengths and talents that complement one another so that the whole is greater than the sum of its parts. Still, hearing both positive and encouraging information in addition to areas of development and opportunity provides a balanced approach to coaching and mentoring because employees generally want more input to focus on their self-development and heighten their self-awareness.

3. Timely: Waiting months to deliver feedback dilutes its impact and sends the message that the matter wasn't very important. Providing actual, real-time feedback between formal performance reviews should become a matter of practice and expectation. The ongoing feedback loop will garner you high points as a caring leader who's focused on employee development. Also, don't be afraid to shift the responsibility for timely feedback back to your employees: Simply instruct them to call intermittent update meetings to discuss their progress and keep you informed of any surprises along the way—pleasant or otherwise.

4. Continual: In the same way we need to keep our cars fueled with gas, we need to keep our people fueled with feedback. That's the psychological oxygen that keeps them engaged and refreshed, and it removes any awkwardness when it comes to addressing minor issues before they escalate. After all, if feedback is ongoing and continual, then it simply becomes a cultural imperative under your leadership.

Likewise, when meeting with an employee whom you're mentoring or coaching, ask questions such as the following:

Do you have a clear understanding of what's expected of you at work?

Could you articulate what would garner a "meets expectations" score on your annual review versus an "exceeds expectations" or "superior" rating for your particular role?

Do you have the materials, equipment, and training that you need to be successful?

What's your biggest concern currently?

Do you feel that your opinion counts and that you have a voice on our team?

If you could change one thing right now that would make things better for us as a team or how we get our work done, what would it be?

Do you feel you have adequate opportunities to learn and grow in your role? Are there any types of rotational or stretch assignments that you feel could help you progress in your career more effectively?

These questions are easily customized, of course, but the examples above should help you launch into a conversation fairly seamlessly. More important than the particular questions you ask, however, is your sincere interest in the individual's growth and development.

Finally, on the other end of the verbal communication spectrum, companies often issue corrective action verbally before proceeding to more formal, documented stages. The typical corrective action paradigm in corporate America is a three-step process that looks like this:

Step 1: Verbal warning (which may be documented for the sake of clarity and confirmation)

Step 2: Written warning

Step 3: Final written warning

Regarding step 1, you might be wondering why it is documented if it's a *verbal* warning. A very logical question, of course, but there's also a very logical answer: By documenting a "first warning"— something many companies label a "verbal warning"—companies establish a record that the meeting occurred and the content of the discussion is codified. This avoids claims that the meeting never happened or that the meeting was more of a "coaching session" and not part of the company's formal progressive discipline process.

However, let's assume your company doesn't document first warnings (i.e., that your verbal warnings are truly "verbal"). In such circumstances, it's critical that you use the words *verbal warning* during the meeting—especially if you work in a union environment. Any lack of clarity or wiggle room in terms of whether the meeting was part of your organization's formal corrective action process or simply a "coaching" or "mentoring" meeting could be used against you if challenged by a union or in a court of law. Simply state:

> Donna, we're considering this a formal verbal warning, which, as you know, is the first step in our company's corrective action process. I want to make sure this is clear to you, and I'm happy to discuss this further if you'd like. But the next step in the process would be a formal written warning if the situation doesn't improve itself, and I just want to make sure that you're clear on how the corrective action system works and, more importantly, that it isn't something to take lightly because it could ultimately result in your being separated from the company. Tell me what questions you have about that at this point because we want to make sure that this first, verbal meeting addresses the issue so we don't have to hold any further discussions about it. Do you agree that's a fair approach to how we're handling this?
>
> [Yes.]
>
> Okay then, thanks for your commitment, I'm glad we're on the same page in terms of future expectations, and I appreciate your taking this in such a professional and cooperative spirit. I'm here to help you any time you want to talk and will always make myself available if you need me. Thank you.

Whether you're delivering coaching and recognition for a job well done or directly addressing problematic performance and conduct issues that may arise in the workplace from time to time, remember that being a great communicator doesn't only mean delivering good news. It also means delivering challenging news in a positive and constructive manner. Great leaders are great communicators, and there are few areas that you could invest in that will yield greater results than becoming a stellar and transparent communicator and leader.

3 The Importance of the Written Record

EVERY EFFECTIVE LEADER in corporate America must be a master of the written record. While documenting someone's achievements and accomplishments is an important part of visionary leadership, the importance of documentation is typically found on the defensive side of the leadership equation; simply put, you have to know how to document problematic performance and conduct to protect your company and yourself from unwanted liability. So the discussion in this chapter focuses on how to document critical issues that hinder performance or give rise to lawsuits. Presumably, you already know how to motivate, recognize, and reward your employees by documenting their achievements, so there's not much need to discuss offensive HR practices in the documentation arena. This chapter's importance in terms of insulating your organization from legal challenges can't be overemphasized, so pick up your highlighter and follow along closely!

23 "Document, Document, Document:" Heightening Awareness of the Record You're Creating

If you've ever heard your organization's leaders, HR director, or attorneys pontificating on the importance of documenting employee performance—both good and bad—you're not alone. This one piece of management advice is typically shouted from the rooftops, but it's actually only half the equation. The documentation itself isn't really the key to changing behaviors, improving performance, or creating a written record of the challenges that a particular employee may be facing; instead, it's discussing your documentation with the employee in a timely fashion that's the most critical part of this exercise. After all, documents in and of themselves mean very little unless they are acted upon and communicated while they are still fresh and relevant.

For example, too many managers have found themselves frustrated with a subpar work product, such as a document, from a team member. The manager corrects the document and returns it to the employee for finalization. The employee returns it, however, with uncorrected edits and new errors! The manager then rolls the document into a ball in frustration, hurls it into the wastebasket, and works late that night fixing the employee's errors for the next day's deadline.

Big mistake! The supervisor just threw out an important piece of evidence that exemplifies the nature of the problem: careless work and lack of attention to detail. Rather than throwing that particular work product into the wastebasket, it should be retained and discussed with the employee, for a number of reasons. First, it can be used as a teaching tool so that the employee understands how his carelessness led to additional work and late night hours for the supervisor. Second, if the employee needs to be written up (i.e., issued corrective action documenting the problem), this piece of evidence should be attached to the written warning demonstrating the nature of the ongoing problem. Third, the employee will take the matter much more seriously if a poor work product requiring multiple rounds of rework is brought to his immediate attention when it happens.

Next, understand how your documentation will be viewed in the eyes of the law or in front of a jury. Plaintiffs' attorneys will typically argue that their client (your ex-employee) was denied workplace due process and subsequently terminated without cause if you terminate without prior corrective action on file. (An exception would be for egregious misconduct issues like theft or embezzlement, for example, which typically warrant termination for a first offense.) The wrongful termination claim, once established, can then support punitive damage claims such as discrimination, harassment, and retaliation, which is where plaintiffs' attorneys make their most money. Therefore, you'll want to cut off the avenue for a wrongful termination claim in the first place, and to do so you need to understand how the record will look to a dispassionate, objective third-party observer.

What's wrong with the following picture?

1. April 2016	First written warning: substandard job performance/productivity
2. June 2016	Second written warning: substandard job performance/poor customer service
3. August 2016	Final written warning: substandard job performance/productivity
4. September 2016	Annual performance review score: "*meets expectations*"
5. November 2016	Request to terminate for violating terms of final written warning: substandard job performance/productivity

Does the major roadblock in this written record jump out at you on paper? Steps 1 through 3 are very clear and logical: the progressive discipline steps for first and second written warnings in addition to the final written warning outlining ongoing performance problems that the employee continues to experience. All clear up to that point.

But then in step 4 in September, the supervisor throws a monkey wrench into the record by codifying that the individual "met expectations" for the entire year. Ouch! That supervisor just validated the entire year's performance despite the final written warning issued just one month before. As a result, the organization is clearly not in a position to terminate for cause: the record is now confusing and inconsistent, and the employee's attorney will likely argue that the company sent mixed messages about the individual's job being in jeopardy. If you throw a log in the way of your path, you'll get tripped up or significantly slowed down, either in your ability to terminate now or the negative consequences stemming from your decision later during trial.

Think of it this way: annual performance reviews are like massive battleships. They displace tons of water and cover an entire year's performance. Written warnings, in comparison, are like tiny PT boats that serve to break the chain of positive reviews on file. In fact, a written warning could result from just one bad day in the office. So expect plaintiffs' attorneys to place a lot more weight on annual performance reviews than on written warnings. That being said, the written warnings did their job in steps 1 to 3 to demonstrate that the individual's work was substandard and the consequences were becoming more serious; it's just that the inflated performance review score damaged the record the employer was trying to create in informing the individual, with notice, that his work wasn't acceptable (i.e., workplace due process).

The end result? In this case, the employer opted not to terminate the employee at step 5 in November. Instead, the employer issued yet another formal notice informing the employee that the performance review score of "meets expectations" was issued in error and that the final written warning issued at step 3 in August was still active and valid. In addition, the employer added "last chance" language to ensure that the employee understood that his position was now in immediate jeopardy of being lost:

> Further, please understand that this is your last chance. Your position is now in serious jeopardy, and failure to demonstrate immediate and sustained improvement will result in immediate dismissal.

The moral of the story: Performance reviews make for very different records than written warnings. Don't put battleships in your way when creating a written record of according workplace due process. Make sure that your corrective action and annual performance review's "overall score" are in sync (i.e., demonstrating that the individual is not meeting expectations for the entire review year because of the number and types of correction action notices on record during the review period). And don't fall prey to the mistaken assumption that saying employees "meet expectations" when they're really failing will somehow motivate them. It will only make your job that much harder if and when the time comes to recommend termination for violating the terms of a final written warning. It's true that confrontation is difficult and it's easier to just assign a passing score, but proceed at your own risk if you opt for that course of action; you'll severely limit your ability to terminate if the record doesn't show a consistent theme and story.

24 *Performance Reviews: The 800-Pound Gorilla in the Room*

With a better understanding of the consistency you need in your written records of employee communications before recommending a termination and the importance of being able to demonstrate "good cause" through the use of carefully crafted corrective action documentation, it's important to focus on the employee's annual performance review—that massive battleship we referred to above. It captures an entire year's worth of effort, production, productivity, and overall contribution to your department and your company. However, proceed cautiously: most managers misunderstand the key strategies behind using performance reviews as motivational tools for employee self-development, and, worse, they sometimes step on land mines by carelessly completing reviews without giving much thought to the record being created.

Understand that the annual review is meant to be a culmination of prior activities and communications that have occurred throughout the review year. The performance management cycle has three stages:

1. Goal setting and planning
2. Ongoing coaching and feedback
3. Appraisal and reward (i.e., the annual performance review)

Exceptional leaders get to know their staff members' goals and needs throughout stage 2: Is the individual looking for an upward trajectory within the organization, looking to assume broader responsibilities and higher levels of accountability, a more stable work–life balance, or the acquisition of new skills or educational credentials? As a manager, are you meeting with your staff members formally on a quarterly basis to spend one-on-one time with them and getting to know how they learn best, whether they prefer public or private praise and recognition, or whether they want more formal or more relaxed communication from you? Furthermore, what amendments need to be made to their goals established in stage 1, and what ideas and recommendations can each member of your team share to reinvent the workload in light of the organization's changing needs?

Simply put, if you don't know how to answer questions to this level and degree, you're shooting in the dark in terms of assessing your staff members' performance and future goals. The result? You're left filling in the blanks on a performance review form at stage 3 of the cycle using stereotypes, generalizations, and misguided notions in terms of each individual's true strengths, areas for development, and inclinations to recommend innovative and creative solutions to better the organization. You probably know managers who muddle through the annual performance review as a rote exercise and paper chase because they have very little information or personal insights to draw from. When the review process becomes a mandatory exercise and headache that simply justifies giving someone a merit increase, you'll know you're upside down in this process—a process that is meant to be a rewarding and satisfying experience for the employee.

Instead, encourage your employees to draft their own self-evaluations, including their goals, at stage 1. As I pointed out in my book *2600 Phrases for Effective Performance Reviews* (AMACOM, 2005), ask them to answer the following three groups of questions with as much or as little detail as they prefer to contribute:

1. Address you overall performance track record for this review period. Specifically highlight your achievements that have resulted in increased revenues, decreased expenses, or saved time. Why is XYZ Corporation a better place for your having worked here this past year? How have you had to reinvent your job in light of our department's changing needs? How would you grade yourself in terms of work quality, reliability, production, teamwork, and technical skills?
2. In what areas do you need additional support, structure, and direction? Specifically, where can I, as your supervisor, provide you with additional support in terms of acquiring new skills, strengthening your overall performance, or preparing you for your next move in career progression?

3. What are your performance goals for the next year? What are the measurable outcomes so that we'll know that you'll have reached those goals?

With these three groups of questions, you'll have invited your team members to involve themselves in their own career development, make you their coach, and motivate themselves to build "achievement bullets" on their résumés, as well as contemplate next year's self-evaluation exercise.

Not all employees will participate, of course, and some may only provide cursory information. That's okay: the real target audience for this exercise is your top performers—the top 5 to 20 percent of your team who look for ways to build their careers and acquire new skills in tandem with you, their supervisor. Don't be surprised when those superachievers present you with spreadsheets that contain all the bells and whistles: career goals, specific skill acquisition, achievement milestones, and the like. Remember, as a leader you're not responsible for motivating your team members; motivation is internal, and you can't motivate them any more than they can motivate you. However, as a leader in your organization, you *are* responsible for creating an environment in which people can motivate themselves. This self-evaluation exercise achieves that very goal; it gives all your employees, but especially your top performers, a chance to involve themselves in their own career development and point out areas where you can help them.

Next, be sure and review the employee's prior year's performance review before attempting to draft this year's appraisal. Remember that when creating a written record, the consistency and the common themes within the documentation are exceptionally important. There shouldn't be weaknesses from two years ago that became strengths last year but are now weaknesses again. If that were to be the case, the conflicting record could cause confusion in the employee's eye, and the inconsistency could be used against your company if the individual were to later claim wrongful termination. Generally speaking, there should be a clear progression or decline in these documents, and they should be able to stand on their own and tell their own story without your having to explain anything. It stands to reason, though, that if the cause of the inconsistency in the individual's record is due to the employee's erratic and unsustainable performance, then be sure to document the issue appropriately. Specifically, document the ups and downs and erratic performance inconsistencies that have created a "roller coaster" effect and that are forcing you, the supervisor, to re-address issues that should have been cleared up months, quarters, or even years ago.

As far as assigning scores, don't give everyone a score of 3 ("meets expectations") across the board. There's not enough discernment there, and you should generally have a healthy distribution of superstars (5's), those who excel on a regular and consistent basis (4's), and those either partially failing (2's) or totally failing (1's) in their roles. That being said, it's okay to give a 5 ("exceptional"). Don't be like those college professors who never give A's. That, in effect, simply reduces your five-point scale down to a four-point scale, and that obviates that need for the flexibility and discretion that the five-point scale allows and encourages.

Next, be wary of following the idea of "forced ranking" too closely. Forced ranking basically posits that there should only be so many 5's, 4's, 3's, and the like in any particular group. The system was made famous by Jack Welch at General Electric when he created the fabled "rank and yank" system, in which 20 percent of the organization should be superstars, 70 percent should be performing at a high level but striving to get into that 20 percent box, and 10 percent need to be fired every year. No matter how well that bottom tenth percentile performed, it was all relative: 10 percent of the organization needed to be let go every round when performance reviews were completed.

Does a system like that make you uncomfortable? Does it make you feel that everyone was in it for themselves and had to get into that first-tier 20 percent box at all costs? Possibly so, and you're not alone. While no one can argue with GE's success under Jack Welch, as it became a virtual factory of CEO talent that ultimately manned the largest corporations in the world, it was likely due to factors other than stack ranking. And many companies today have rejected the "rank and yank" concept because of its destructive nature. Still, performance management and performance appraisal were critically important to one's career success at GE, whether you agree with its Darwinian interpretation under Jack Welch or not.

That being said, codifying people into absolute categories is probably a mistake in most organizations and departments for one simple reason: they're too small to justify such differentiation. For example, a typical bell-curve distribution of performance review scores might look like this:

	Typical Bell Curve Distribution Across Large Populations
≤5 percent	Distinguished performance (score of 5)
30 percent	Superior performance (score of 4)
50 percent	Fully successful performance/meets expectations (score of 3)
10 percent	Partially successful performance/partially meets expectations (score of 2)
≤5 percent	Unsuccessful performance/fails to meet expectations (score of 1)

The catch to interpreting these types of scores, however, lies in finding such patterns and trends over large populations—in this case, containing thousands or even tens of thousands of data points. A typical department with only ten or one hundred team members is too small to try to fit into this neat box. Therefore, generally speaking, while this score distribution template could be helpful as a guideline, don't force all your people into a box that requires, for example, that less than 5 percent of the people on your team will qualify as "distinguished." You may have more people than that this year, so don't let the forced ranking concept limit your ability to award scores based on individual merit.

But beware of the biggest trap awaiting many unsuspecting managers: grade inflation. The difference between scores of 1 ("does not meet expectations"), 2 ("partially meets expectations"), and 3 ("meets expectations") is monumental. Award a score of 3 or higher (assuming a five-point scale with 5 as the highest), and you'll make it exceptionally difficult to terminate a worker in the near future. That's because your anchor document—the annual performance review—validates an entire year's work, despite prior warnings and final written warnings. While the path of least resistance may be avoidance, and placating the employee with a higher score than deserved may somehow "motivate" them, don't be naïve: you'll have placed a major impediment in your way by inflating a score that clearly wasn't warranted. As a general rule, if you expect to terminate someone in the upcoming review year, your score in this year's annual performance review will need to show that the individual failed to meet (or at least partially failed to meet) expectations. Speak with your HR representative or company attorney about how to structure the content of the annual review to minimize legal risk.

25 *Performance Reviews: Dealing Effectively with Incorrectly Assigned Individual Grades*

Remember that the annual performance review is a *process*, not a form. When done correctly, the annual performance review is one step in a continuing cycle of ongoing performance measurement, progress against goals, and shifting priorities. Those twelve months of historical performance culminate in the annual performance review document—much like a balance sheet reflecting a snapshot of an organization's financial and operational performance at a given point in time.

But what if you mistakenly assigned the grade of 3 ("meets expectations"), communicated it verbally and in writing to the employee, and the individual already received a merit increase in a recent paycheck? Undoing your error is always a sticky wicket, but you've basically got three choices:

1. Say nothing, because it's too late to make any changes and may unnecessarily upset the worker.
2. Reissue the review with a failing score and recoup the additional merit payments already made.
3. Allow the employee to keep the money, but write an amendment letter for the record that documents that the review's overall score was issued in error.

Under normal circumstances, either the second or third option typically makes the most sense. After all, doing nothing about the problem and not even addressing the matter is short sighted, especially if you're planning on terminating the employee in the near future. But option 3 may have better results than option 2 because it appears to be fairer and less punitive. After all, trying to recoup the money under option 2 may arguably smack of retaliatory action against the employee and could be considered to be in bad taste from a perception or corporate image standpoint. (It *was* the company's error, after all!) But clarifying the record on paper under option 3—while allowing the employee to benefit financially from the company's mistake—shows the company to be wise, transparent, and constructive, which is always your goal when creating and correcting formal employee records.

If you opt to pursue this third option, then here's a draft of what your written communication to the employee might look like:

Dear [employee]:

We have determined that your recent annual performance review showing an overall score of "meets performance expectations" was issued in error. The purpose of this letter is to establish a clear understanding of your path forward with our organization.

- **2016 Annual Performance Review:** The review you signed on 12/16/15 was completed erroneously by your immediate supervisor and delivered to you in error. Your performance rating for 2015 was entered at the "meets expectations" level, and you received a 2 percent merit increase. However, as indicated by the numerous corrective actions that you received throughout the review year, and particularly in the last six months of 2015, the correct performance rating should have been at the "needs improvement" level. As such, we wanted to take this opportunity to clarify the record.

- **Corrective Action Notices:** You received three documented warnings in various forms for failure to follow equipment processing guidelines, which occurred in July, August, and November 2015. This notice serves as a reminder that these corrective action items are still active in your employment record. Furthermore, any future incidents of failing to follow equipment maintenance rules or instructions may result in further disciplinary action, up to and including dismissal. You are currently on a Final Written Warning, which remains active for six months from the date of issue on November 1, 2015. This is your final opportunity to improve your performance and policy adherence, or your position may be in immediate jeopardy of being lost.

- **2016 Merit Increase Status:** Your 2 percent increase will not be reversed or retracted. However, the purpose of this memo is to clarify that your overall score for the 2015 review year was issued in error and that had it been issued correctly, you would not have been eligible for a merit increase this year.

In addition, as discussed with you during today's meeting, I will remain available to help you and to discuss areas where you require additional support. Please let me know what I can do to help you succeed in your role from this point forward.

Sincerely,

[supervising manager's name]

Grade inflation occurs often, and companies have to find smart ways of clarifying the record and ensuring that employees have clear expectations going forward when such errors are identified after the fact. By correcting the record with a memorandum of understanding like the sample drafted above, you'll not only have clarified the record in terms of the failing score; you'll also have reset expectations regarding the final written warning remaining active, the individual's job remaining in jeopardy, and the manager's willingness and availability to help. That approach will clearly place the company in the best light possible should you later need to terminate the individual's employment despite the inflated annual review score.

26   *Performance Reviews: Correcting for Grade Inflation Across Your Department, Division, or Company*

Unfortunately, there are no set criteria to distinguish a performance review score of a 5 from a 4, or a 3 from a 2. What's important, however, is that leaders within each division or department and across divisions and departments should discuss what those scores might look like in a performance "calibration" meeting. That's where they can discuss key employees and decide where they should fall on the performance-rating continuum. To do so, however, they'll need a tool to help them talk through these very subjective types of considerations.

Imagine this: The president of your company tells you that on a scale of 1 to 5 (5 being outstanding, 3 meeting expectations, and 1 being a failure), he expects all of the managers who directly report to him to be 5's. "If they're not 5's, they should all be fired" is the president's logic. But the head of finance tells you that she believes that the vast majority of her team is meeting expectations and performing well and that she intends to award "overall scores" of 3 to the majority of her staffers, reflecting that they're meeting expectations and performing well. (Good answer!) Then she hesitates and says, "Then again, the managers in sales and operations will probably award more 5 scores than anything else, so maybe I'll need to award 5's as well; otherwise, my group will receive lower merit increases relative to the other departments."

Is it okay if a manager expects everyone on the team to be a 5 ("outstanding")? Does it bother you that the head of finance doesn't feel comfortable awarding what she feels is the right score for the majority of her team, which is 3 ("meets expectations"), because the managers in other departments will inflate scores for their own teams? How do you get everyone on the same page in terms of distinguishing appropriately between scores and assigning grades that truly reflect the level of performance in that group?

The simple answer lies in communication—discussing perceptions of what the scores actually mean and which scores should be assigned to which employees. The rater definition consistency tool (Figure 3.1) can be used as a point of reference for all involved. It helps open the lines of communication and get all leaders "speaking the same language" about what success looks like relative to individual contributions and performance levels over the past year. The definitions aren't exaggerated, but they're spelled out to paint a clearer picture of just what makes someone exceptional.

The percentages next to each scoring category reflect what you'd normally expect to see if your company's scoring results fell under a typical bell-curve configuration. Also, notice that the 3 category—

Figure 3.1. Rater definition consistency tool.

Rater Definition Consistency Tool

5: Distinguished Performance (≤ 5 percent)

Role model status. Potential successor to immediate supervisor/highly promotable now.
Performed above and beyond under exceptional circumstances during the review period.
Generally recognized #1 (top 5 percent) ranking among peer group.

4: Superior Performance (30 percent)

Overall excellent performer and easy to work with—smart, dedicated, ambitious, and cooperative, but may not yet be ready to promote because there's still a lot to learn in the current role.
May not have been exposed to exceptional circumstances or opportunities that would warrant
a higher designation. However, definitely an exceptional contributor who exceeds people's
expectations in many ways and is a long-term "keeper"—just needs more time in current role
to grow and develop and gain additional exposure.

3: Fully Successful Performance (50 percent)

3(a)	3(b)
Consistently performs well and is reliable, courteous, and dedicated. Always tries hard and looks for ways of acquiring new skills but doesn't necessarily perform with distinction. Works to live rather than lives to work. May not stand out as a rarity among peers but consistently contributes to the department's efforts and is a valuable member of the team.	Meets expectations overall but may be challenged in particular performance areas. May perform well because of tenure in role and familiarity with workload but does not appear ambitious about learning new things or expanding beyond comfort zone. While performance may be acceptable, conduct may at times be problematic.

2: Partially Successful Performance (10 percent)

Fails to meet minimum performance or conduct expectations in specific areas of responsibility.
Is not able to demonstrate consistent improvement. May appear to be burned out or lack
motivation, and fails to go the extra mile for others. Lacks requisite technical skills or knowledge
relating to particular aspects of role. May perform well, but conduct is so problematic that the

(continued)

Figure 3.1. (cont.)

---

entire year's performance review score may be invalidated. A partial merit increase or bonus
may be awarded.

1: Unsuccessful Performance (≤ 5 percent)
Fails to meet minimum performance or conduct expectations for the role in general. The individual's position is in immediate jeopardy of being lost. The performance review may be accompanied
by corrective action documentation stating that failure to demonstrate immediate and sustained
improvement will result in dismissal. No merit increase or bonus should be awarded.

Source: The Performance Appraisal Tool Kit: Redesigning Your Performance Review Template to Drive Individual
and Organizational Change (AMACOM, 2013)

meets expectations/fully successful performance—has two subsets:
"a" for those who really try hard but don't necessary perform with
distinction, and "b" for those who perform satisfactorily but don't
necessarily give their best effort. Distinguishing between a 3(a) and a
3(b) can be particularly helpful when engaging in discussions regarding individual contribution levels.

How these general parameters fit your organization and what
they might look like at any given time should indeed differ from year
to year. What makes the most sense is to present Figure 3.1 in Power-
Point or a similar medium and openly discuss it with the management team to determine which employees clearly fall in the various
categories. Start with the highest generally recognized performers first
and see if you can gain agreement as to why the 5's are 5's. Your discussion can then proceed to 4's and 3's, although you may not want to
address 2's and 1's in an open forum like that. The point is to get the
conversation going. From senior leaders to frontline supervisors, conversations like these need to happen to raise awareness of your organization's expectations and to provide leaders with benchmarks and
guideposts to align their assessments.

What's the difference between a 4 and a 5? Is it simply a matter
of someone who's able to be promoted into the boss's role now as
opposed to two years from now? Is the difference attributable to outstanding circumstances that allowed employees to assume responsibilities well beyond their job description? Likewise, what's the difference

between a 3(b) and a 2? Is it acceptable to have employees on the team who are technically capable due to long tenure in their role but who demonstrate little ambition or interest in anything outside of their immediate area? What about occasional inappropriate conduct? How "occasional" does it have to be to fail someone for the entire review year? Should we award partial merit increases to anyone who receives an overall score of 2, or should we take that money and return it to the pool to reward the higher performers?

As you know, there aren't necessarily right or wrong answers to these questions, and much of this is subject to debate. But it's healthy debate, and it's wise to have at least one discussion like this before all the managers start writing the performance reviews. Otherwise, without any guidelines or structure, you'll end up with all the managers using different criteria for what the organization wants to see in terms of proposed overall performance review scores. These group meetings set the tone for the upcoming performance review discussions and documentation strategies.

In fact, as the general level of performance increases across your company, raising the bar and setting higher expectations should become the norm and should change the interpretation of these definitions over time. For example, what looked like superior performance last year may only appear as fully successful performance this year. And if that's the case, it means you're using this tool and your organization's performance management system correctly to leverage productivity across the enterprise.

So kick off a conversation that's long overdue, and remember that total agreement isn't necessary. Discussing performance interpretations openly, however, is. And that's how successful organizational calibration sessions fine-tune performance over time in a performance-driven company.

27 Workplace Investigations: Understanding Your Role and Knowing Your Limits

Conducting workplace investigations is as much an art as it is a science, and this exercise should generally be left to HR or some other neutral third party, especially if the claim is against you, the manager.

But it's important that you understand the basics of workplace investigations in case you need to partner with HR, an external consultant, or an attorney who may be looking into allegations that potentially involve members of your team. It's critical that all members of management who are involved are clearly operating under the same assumptions and conducting their fact-finding missions consistently.

While no book on a topic this broad can replace sound legal advice based on fact-specific situations that may come your way on a case-by-case basis as an employer, it's critical to understand the basics of workplace investigations because so many companies trip themselves up by not following their own internal rules or basic guidelines for fairness and due process. Your goals in conducting workplace investigations should be threefold:

1. Ensure fairness and consistency on the one hand while protecting your company legally on the other.
2. Know when to recuse yourself from an investigation due to a potential conflict of interest or the possibility of garnering a retaliation claim by simply participating in the process.
3. Communicate appropriately both verbally and in writing when it comes to documenting your findings and reaching a timely and reasonable conclusion.

Regarding goal 1, understand that workplace investigations, by their very nature, create tremendous anxiety and angst among the affected team members. As a result, investigations should be completed as quickly as possible and shouldn't remain in limbo or be open ended. In other words, strip the bandage off all at once if at all possible.

In terms of your formal legal obligation as an employer, here is what courts expect of employers involved in such activities: *The employer is obligated to conduct a timely investigation and to reach a reasonable conclusion.*

That's it! You're not expected to have a magic wand or to look into the heart and soul of your employees. Courts realize that investigations are limited by their very nature and as a result have deemed that legal standards such as "guilty beyond a reasonable doubt" or "guilty by a preponderance of the evidence" are not thresholds that apply to workplace investigations. You simply have to act reasonably, responsibly, and in a timely manner to reach a reasonable conclusion. That being said, you have to use common sense: Listen to both sides of a story before taking action, investigate any witnesses or review documents that can substantiate someone's claim, and ensure that the written record in place that justifies a particular course of action (especially termination) is thorough, well documented, and well thought through. Also, take prompt and remedial action to put an end to a problem that you learn about as a result of a good-faith complaint.

Regarding goal 2, there will be times when you're not allowed to participate in an investigation in any way because of the nature of your role within the organization (for example, as an immediate supervisor, department head, or division head). If someone on your team could accuse you of potential retaliation for participating in an investigation, you have to respectfully decline to be involved. In fact, you might consider suggesting that you work from home on the day the investigation takes place so that no one can accuse you of somehow influencing the outcome of the investigation by being present on the company premises.

If you work in a publicly traded company, your organization very likely has a documented business conduct statement or code of ethics. (Even many privately held organizations publish a code of conduct for practical reasons, even if not required by the Sarbanes-Oxley Act of 2002, which is discussed in Question 39 in Chapter 4.) If so, you'll likely find language in the code of business conduct that reads something along the lines of, "Employees and supervisors may not conduct your own investigation." Heed those words carefully: Trying to unduly influence an investigation can have far more damaging results than the original underlying cause of the investigation itself! That's because any perception of attempting to influence or impact what should be an objective and dispassionate workplace investigation is a significant breach of workplace conduct that could result in immediate dismissal.

Companies can't mess around with bending ethical rules at the time of an investigation, and propriety may dictate that anyone trying to unduly influence the outcome of an investigation be terminated because of the ethical perception problem created. After all, when it comes to matters of ethics in the workplace, the issue drives the outcome: No matter how much tenure you have, how popular you are, or how successful you might be, a significant ethical breach may leave a company with no choice but to terminate—even for a first offense. In short, you may be messing with fire here, so be very cautious so as not to get burned.

Likewise, don't ever make statements to your staff members about "not going to HR" or "keeping everything that goes on within our department *within the family.*" Too many managers try to control their teams by throwing out veiled or even direct threats about employees escalating issues outside the group. This is a career land mine for one simple reason: You'll have created a public record that all employees on your team can attest to regarding the fact that you somehow threatened them—either directly or by employing some type of veiled threat—that they'd be disciplined, terminated, or otherwise retaliated against for escalating matters beyond your immediate control. Again, that fact alone could warrant significant corrective action or even termination against you—regardless of the severity of the issue at hand.

And remember that angry employees have long memories: If someone on your team suspects that you may be looking to discipline or terminate them six months or a year later, that employee—likely a very sophisticated consumer—may report to HR that they feel intimidated working for you and that you're creating a hostile work environment. How? "My boss threatened us last spring by telling us if anyone was thinking of going to HR to lodge a complaint, he'd find out who they were and find a way to terminate them." And HR of course can very easily determine that this threat was true: after all, the manager warned the entire team all at the same time! So fifteen employees are witnesses who can substantiate this aggrieved worker's complaint to HR. That muddies the waters when you may otherwise have legitimate performance reasons to discipline or terminate this individual.

Instead, encourage the employees on your team to escalate matters to your boss, to the department or division head, to HR, or even to the company's in-house counsel if they feel that's warranted. Explain that you would generally appreciate a heads-up of a complaint escalating beyond your department to some other member of the company's leadership team, but that's optional. What's more important is that all your team members understand and feel comfortable with the fact that they may escalate a matter outside of your group at any time if they feel it is warranted. That's the public record you want to have in place in terms of formally addressing your team regarding workplace complaints or other concerns. It's open, reasonable, and fair. Likewise, it builds trust and creates a healthy culture of transparency. But at its core, it creates a record—witnessed by others—attesting to your willingness to allow your staff members to escalate matters beyond your immediate group if they feel that's necessary. Simply put, establishing your expectations publicly this way will indeed protect you one day if a workplace investigation ever materializes where you're accused of some type of wrongdoing.

Regarding goal 3, remember that you're not in this alone. When a workplace investigation occurs—whether you're accused or you're involved in the fact-finding mission—remember that you cannot overcommunicate to HR, the investigator, or your in-house counsel. Play-by-play action is expected and is the norm: the timeliness of your investigation is one of the expectations that a court will have of you both as the supervisor and as the employer. So the rule is "communicate, communicate, communicate" in terms of your findings, new leads or additional witnesses, or potential changes in course that you learn of. I can't overemphasize how important timely communication is during an investigation. Besides, you're not a professional investigator—this is only one of a hundred things you're asked to do at any given time—so depend on the professionals and keep informed to protect both yourself and the company.

Finally, never rush to judgment at the finish line. If you need additional time to look into particular matters, simply place the accused employee on a paid, investigatory leave. This buys you additional time to confirm your facts, to research the documents, and to interview witnesses. Too many companies rush to the firing stage, only to learn in the litigation arena that they didn't do their homework, hadn't interviewed the witnesses or reviewed the documents recommended by the complainant (i.e., the accused ex-employee who's now bringing suit against your company for wrongful termination), or otherwise acted reasonably and responsibly in reaching a sound conclusion. Slow down at the finish line before you reach a final decision and make sure all involved parties (the Operations, Legal, and HR departments) are in agreement with the final decision. This way, if a lawsuit does eventually arise, there will be no surprises and everyone will be on the same page in terms of defending it.

28   *Workplace Investigations: Harassment, Discrimination, and a Cautionary Tale*

We can't complete our discussion of workplace investigations without addressing some of the "big guns" out there in the workplace: harassment, discrimination, and retaliation complaints that can be so damaging to company morale and so potentially costly to organizations from a liability standpoint. Here's what the scenario typically looks like: A supervisor fails to disclose to HR or organizational leadership that an employee reported that she was feeling harassed. The employee may have asked the supervisor to keep the matter confidential as a personal favor, but in matters regarding (1) harassment, (2) discrimination, (3) retaliation, or (4) potential violence in the workplace, supervisors have no discretion: they must affirmatively disclose to the employee that they will be escalating the complaint to HR (or some other party that typically handles employee complaints). In the eyes of the law, once the worker puts a supervisor on notice, then the *entire company* is deemed to have been placed on notice. A supervisor has what's known as an "affirmative obligation to disclose," and any failure to do so will leave the company seriously vulnerable.

There's another, less direct, scenario that's commonly seen where complaints regarding harassment, discrimination, retaliation, or hostile work environment claims go unchecked: A supervisor or member of management simply assumes that if no one makes a formal complaint, then the company has no obligation to act. The "reasonableness" standard holds that if you (i.e., the supervisor or the company) either *knew* or *should have known* (i.e., "actual" versus "constructive" knowledge) about a worker being harassed, retaliated against, or the like, you have an affirmative obligation to intercede. The icon of the monkey covering its eyes, ears, and mouth—that is, not wanting to know what was going around it—won't hold up in court and will do very little to sustain positive employee relations at work. In court, your organization is treated as a corporate citizen, and questions will be raised as to whether that "citizen" acted responsibly and appropriately by interceding on behalf of its most vulnerable and disadvantaged members.

Further, supervisors, managers, and officers of a company are required to affirmatively disclose any and all complaints regarding potential harassment, discrimination, retaliation, or workplace violence without exception, even if the complaining employee asks that no investigation be conducted. Managers cannot and should not promise confidentiality in matters relating to discrimination, harassment, or potential violence in the workplace.

Next, understand the broader, loosely defined terms that employees may throw your way when airing complaints. Many times, they're not quite aware of what these terms actually mean in the legal sense, but they drop them like bombs hoping to intimidate management by threatening a lawsuit. Here are the definitions of some terms that drive much employment litigation and that you should understand at a high level:

- **Discrimination:** Under federal law, employment discrimination is a form of discrimination by employers based on race, sex, religion, national origin, physical or mental disability, and age. In addition, states have their own discrimination protection laws and categories that typically exceed those under federal law. A "disparate treatment" claim arises when employees or applicants allege that they were treated differently in terms and conditions of employment based on their race, sex, color, religion, national origin, age, disability, sexual orientation, or any other factors that are not legitimate business reasons.

- **Harassment:** Harassment is a subset of employment discrimination and generally is defined as subjecting an employee to unfavorable working conditions without business justification. Workplace harassment complaints are divided into two areas:
  - **Hostile Work Environment:** A form of harassment that is so severe or pervasive that it negatively impacts the conditions of the employee/victim's work environment. Hostile work environment claims make up 80 to 90 percent of all harassment issues that are litigated. The harassment must be offensive to the recipient and to a reasonable person. A hostile work environment can entail sexual harassment and can also be based on race, religion, national origin, color, disability, sexual orientation, age, and other protected categories.
  - **Quid Pro Quo:** A Latin term meaning "this for that," quid pro quo harassment typically makes up about 10 to 20 percent of harassment claims and is often depicted by the "casting couch" scenario: For the starlet to get the part in the movie, she must sleep with the casting director. In quid pro quo harassment, a supervisor, or someone who has authority over the employee, conditions the terms of employment upon sexual behavior and where a tangible job detriment (e.g., poor performance review, demotion, or termination) occurs when the employee refuses to cooperate.
- **Retaliation:** Retaliation may occur when an employee's terms and conditions of employment are negatively impacted because he or she complained about someone within the company or served as a witness against the company regarding claims of discrimination, harassment, or other violations of law or public policy.

Discrimination, harassment, and retaliation are common problems in corporate America. Whether you're a passive investigator in a claim, based on your leadership role in your company, or you're the person being investigated, because the claims are aimed at you, simply remember this: Follow the lead investigator's instructions as closely as possible. The lead investigator may be your HR representative, the director of employee or labor relations, or an outside consultant or attorney. Whatever the case, such claims have the potential to result in significant liability for the company and could lead to a corporate leader's "summary discharge"—meaning an immediate termination without prior steps of progressive discipline or corrective action.

Let's look at an unfortunate but all-too-common example, which will serve as a cautionary tale about how summary discharges often result from cases of supervisors dating subordinates without disclosing the relationship to management: An administrative assistant reports to HR that she's been sleeping with her boss, the VP of Operations, for nine months. She knows it was wrong because her boss is married. However, she felt compelled to do so for fear of retaliation if she didn't submit to his advances. The HR person listens carefully to the administrative assistant's claims. He then wisely sends her home on an investigatory leave with pay so that HR can notify the appropriate parties (e.g., higher levels of HR, in-house legal, and the VP of Operations' immediate supervisor—the Chief Operations Officer [COO]) and prepare to launch an impartial investigation without the administrative assistant present on company premises.

Once HR has escalated this claim to the appropriate parties and developed an investigational game plan and strategy, HR and the COO call in the VP of Operations to explain the nature of the allegation and learn his side of the story. Lo and behold, he readily admits to the affair but claims it was consensual: "We fell in love with one another, my marriage is on the rocks, and I don't know why she's coming forward to disclose this to you because it's a private matter just between the two of us."

With this he-said, she-said scenario in place and the female subordinate likely reaching out to an attorney to claim quid pro quo harassment, the company swiftly decides to terminate the VP of Operations. First, the investigation isn't able to prove much beyond the administrative assistant stating that she felt compelled to engage in sex for fear of retaliation and the VP of Operations stating that their affair was consensual. Second, under most organizations' codes of conduct or employee handbooks, the supervisor is responsible for disclosing a romantic relationship with a subordinate. Failure to do so typically warrants "summary dismissal" in cases like this because of the tremendous liability that such nondisclosures entail (as this case study demonstrates). Third, the organization must immediately protect itself from further legal liability by showing that it acted as a responsible corporate citizen in terminating the VP of Operations as soon as it learned of the problem, so as to mitigate the damage. Fourth, the organization must uphold the integrity of its mission statement by providing a safe and healthy workplace for its workers at all times.

So the VP of Operations is fired pretty much on the spot, and the company is now on the hook for the administrative assistant's potential claims of harassment under the legal concepts of "strict liability" and "vicarious liability." Strict liability posits that a company may be automatically ("strictly") liable for the acts of its managers in cases of harassment simply by the nature of the role and responsibilities they hold as leaders and regardless of their intentions or any negligence or fault on their part. Similarly, vicarious liability makes the company responsible for the acts of its subordinates (in this case, the VP of Operations), even if the subordinate technically did nothing wrong.

It then gets worse for that VP of Operations: Under federal anti-discrimination law, an employer may be legally responsible for discrimination and harassment that occurs in the workplace or in connection with a person's employment unless it can be shown that "all reasonable steps" have been taken to reduce this liability. While "reasonable steps" are left to legal interpretation during litigation, the primary way of showing that a company acted responsibly and took the reasonable steps necessary to prevent such occurrences of quid pro quo harassment can be found in its training programs. If the executive attended harassment training and code of conduct training, and signed off on the employee handbook that likely addressed discrimination, harassment, and the obligation to disclose personal, romantic relationships that develop with subordinates, these steps all serve as proof that the company acted responsibly and demonstrated that the executive unilaterally acted "outside the course and scope of his employment."

As such, the company can then look to shift liability toward the defendant (the former VP of Operations) and away from the company, thereby mitigating the company's legal exposure. Unfortunately, that means that the former VP of Operations could be sued personally for such "managerial bad acts." In many states, individual managers can be sued for up to $50,000 of their own money for such transgressions; in other states, such as California, however, there is no monetary cap.

It's important that you, as an organizational leader, understand the role of training, your organization's code of conduct (in terms of disclosing romantic relationships that develop with subordinates), and your company's probable course of action should you ever fail to disclose such a romantic relationship. Be aware that an accusation of "consensual" versus "forced" sexual relations can very easily be made by a subordinate against a supervisor.

This "cautionary tale" is all too real for executives who risk such behaviors. Your organization doesn't pay you enough to warrant your risking your savings and your financial security for such indiscretions!

29 *Effectively Invoking Attorney–Client Privilege*

During the course of a workplace investigation, you may want to protect certain communications or recommendations from being legally discoverable in litigation. Attorney–client privilege, if utilized properly, should accomplish this task, as it may be invoked when a complaint involves serious concerns (including potential criminal claims) that may develop into a lawsuit or may have the potential to impact a large number of employees (e.g., class-action status), among other considerations. It is always best to contact your legal department in advance of launching an investigation when you suspect that the gravity of the situation may give rise to significant liability. So be sure to discuss upfront whether your in-house counsel or outside defense attorney wants any particular emails or document exchanges protected. Further, if you have any question about whether or not you should be invoking attorney–client privilege, always err on the side of caution and protect the documentation trail as much as possible.

Note that there are no guarantees when it comes to invoking attorney–client privilege. Just because you mark a document "Privileged and Confidential" doesn't mean that a plaintiff's attorney won't challenge the privilege and that a court won't overturn it. Therefore, let caution rule the day when it comes to exchanging emails, documents, or other electronic communications that you mark privileged. After all, it could come as quite a surprise if a judge allows the communication to be shared with the other party and made part of the public record, even though you thought you followed the rules properly. These rules, listed below, will help increase the chances that a particular communication or series of communications can withstand legal scrutiny and remain privileged. However, without a crystal ball, you can't guarantee that the privilege will be sustained because a court has the discretion to disallow the privilege.

That being said, you've got to know how to structure an attorney–client privileged communication to maximize the chances of it not being overturned by a court at some point in the future. To do so, follow these general rules and see the example in Figure 3.2:

1. Address communications to your attorney, such as the in-house counsel or an outside counsel, but for attorney–client privilege to become effective, it must be addressed to an attorney who is providing legal advice and counsel. The privilege does not protect communications between workers when no attorney is present. In other words, you can't send an email to your non-attorney boss and mark it "privileged and confidential" because without an attorney on the receiving end to provide legal analysis and advice, there's no mechanism to protect the communication from legal discovery.

2. End the communication by asking your attorney for a legal opinion and analysis. You may be challenged in sustaining the privilege if you simply copy your attorney on your various emails without asking for official legal advice. Instead, to sustain the privilege, a judge will generally want to see that you reached out to your attorney for a legal opinion and recommendation. If successful, your description of the facts and your attorney's recommended course of action will be protected from the plaintiff's attorney's eyes (and from a jury's considerations) should the case proceed to trial.

3. Label the top of the communication or the subject line of an email as follows: "Privileged and Confidential: Attorney–Client Privi-

leged Communication." This notice should be prominent and easily viewable as soon as someone receives the communication.

4. Copy only a limited number of people who have a legitimate business need to know the information. Do not copy or share the document with others, or the privilege may be lost. After all, if you copy fifteen people on the communication, a court will likely infer that it wasn't all that confidential or proprietary to begin with. So including too many people in the communication could jeopardize the privilege. As a rule, try to limit the audience to just the attorney or to the attorney and one other person (for example, your boss).

5. Do not communicate the information discussed with the attorney with others unless instructed to do so. The nature of attorney–client privileged communications is that they are highly confidential, limited in distribution, and created at a particular point in time on a strictly need-to-know basis. Failing to create the document under such criteria could result in the loss of the privilege and the subsequent sharing of the material as part of the plaintiff's attorney's case against your company.

Figure 3.2. Example of an attorney–client privileged document structure.

Subject Line of Email:

Privileged and Confidential: Attorney–Client Privileged Communication

Heading of Email Body:

Privileged and Confidential: Attorney–Client Privileged Communication

Email Content:

Dear [attorney's name]:

I'd like your advice and counsel on the following matter:

[Provide details]

Please provide your legal analysis and opinion at your earliest convenience.

Thanks very much.

Paul

Again, not all attorney–client communications will be deemed privileged once submitted in court, so always proceed with caution and continue to communicate in writing as if your document may be used as evidence in court and presented to a jury. You can't be too careful when it comes to the possibility of your own communication to your attorney being employed as evidence *against* your company. When in doubt, call your attorney for advice before hitting the send button.

30   *The "E" in Email Stands for "Evidence"*

When we talk about the importance of communication during the investigation process, both verbal and written communications can be subjected to intense legal scrutiny. But what's written down and documented typically outweighs what may have been communicated verbally because memories can change over the months and sometimes years that litigation consumes.

First, understand that the "E" in email stands for "evidence." Email has become to civil law what DNA has become to criminal law: a rich source of indisputable evidence that can change the outcome of court cases. Managers arguably write an average of one hundred emails per day, and as a result, email has become an almost casual means of quickly communicating thoughts and ideas. And it's just this casual informality that makes it so deadly: every email that you write as a manager has the potential of being presented to a jury as evidence of your state of mind at the time you wrote it—a state of mind that may reveal some form of animus that you harbored against a plaintiff or ex-employee based allegedly on that individual's age, race, disability, or other protected characteristic.

As a result, most defense lawyers will tell you not to commit anything to email that you wouldn't otherwise post on the front page of the *New York Times*. The same holds for instant messaging and text messaging: all forms of electronic messaging are fairly easily obtained from forensic IT consultants who are trained to scour systems for written communications about a particular plaintiff. And all it takes is one or several off-color remarks or exchanges about the individual's background, slowness relating to age, or other protected characteristic to sink your legal defense strategy. In addition, your comment can be taken totally out of context, but all's fair in the world of employment litigation.

Further, never attempt to destroy email evidence because electronic communications can almost always be traced back to its metadata source. To repeat: it's practically impossible to destroy electronic communication records. For example, if a manager were to delete an email, empty the recycling bin, and somehow reach into the bowels of the hard drive to attempt to delete the "deleted" recycling bin contents, she wouldn't be successful in eradicating the message from the system or from the discerning eyes of a forensic IT specialist. Worse, that manager may inadvertently create an electronic record of attempting to destroy evidence, which could arguably lead to claims of "obstruction of justice" or "spoliation of evidence." You don't want to inadvertently add criminal sanctions to a civil case, so do not attempt to destroy electronic evidence under any circumstances.

Furthermore, if another member of management sends you an email with inappropriate information, don't just delete it! Instead, respond back to the manager stating that you cannot give credibility to it contents or recommendations. Then forward the original email, along with your response, to your supervisor, HR, or in-house counsel. Your response, in essence, "nullifies" the problematic email by confirming that the company will not consider it. As a result, you'll be able to defend the company should that email later come back to haunt you in litigation. For example, you receive the following email:

> Paul, we're going to have to lay off one of our four staff accountants because of budget constraints, and John is the one who's got to go. He's the poorest performer with the worst attitude among the bunch, and his computer skills are from the Dinosaur Age, so please let us know what to do to prepare the appropriate notice that he's going to be let go. Thanks.
> Michelle

You respond to the operations manager as follows:

> Dear Michelle,
> I'm sorry to hear that you're going to need to layoff one of your four staff accountants. Just for the record, though, the company can't consider any of the

recommendations that you've outlined in this email. As you know, our company practices peer group analysis (PGA), which entails considering all four staff accountants based on their tenure, documented performance, education level, and the like. Once we've compared them, we'll then look to see who is the least qualified individual to assume the remaining job duties after the position elimination has taken place. If John ends up being the least qualified individual once all those objective criteria are established and examined, then he'll be the individual selected for layoff. If not, then someone else on the team may be selected instead.

In addition, Michelle, your comments about his computer skills coming from the "Dinosaur Age" are inappropriate. His level of technical competence will be considered along with everyone else's as part of the objective analysis that will be conducted, but please eliminate any reference to the "Dinosaur Age" as part of any future discussions or documentation. I'll work on developing a PGA now and get back to you with our initial recommendations along with projected severance costs. Please call me with any additional questions. Thanks.

Paul

You can forward the completed email to your supervisor and/or in-house counsel for future reference. In addition, before you send a response like this to Michelle, you might want to call her and explain the problem with the email she sent you. Give her a heads-up that you're going to write her back a fairly stringent email stating that you can't and won't consider any of her inappropriate remarks in the layoff selection process. This way, she'll learn the proper way to proceed in cases like this and won't be shocked by the tone of your response, which will probably sound to her like a reprimand.

31 *Progressive Discipline: Appropriate Documentation for Addressing Substandard Job Performance and Attendance Issues*

Progressive discipline is a series of increasingly severe steps taken when a worker fails to correct a problem after being given a reasonable opportunity to do so. Each step brings with it some added sense of urgency that the problem issue must be resolved or the worker's job will be placed in jeopardy and ultimately could be lost. The concept is a matter of fairness (see Question 37). Employees need to:

1. Know what the problem is
2. Know what they need to do to fix the problem
3. Be given a reasonable time period in which to fix the problem
4. Be made aware of the consequences if they fail to meet the standards outlined

In my book *101 Sample Write-Ups for Documenting Employee Performance Problems: A Guide to Progressive Discipline and Termination* (AMACOM, 2010), I categorized 101 common problems according to performance, conduct, and attendance—the three broadest categories of worker infractions. What's important to keep in mind is when dealing with performance and attendance issues, most corrective action measures of the same sort or in similar categories follow similar documentation patterns:

Part 1: Narrative

Part 2: Performance Improvement Plan (PIP) and expectations

Part 3: Outcomes and consequences

While the narrative will differ from case to case based on the specific facts, most types of infractions follow similar formats for parts 2 and 3. So, for example, while the details surrounding a typical write-up documenting substandard job performance or work quality will clearly change and need to be customized, parts 2 and 3—the PIP and Consequences—will generally remain the same for those types of problems as well as for tardiness, lack of customer service, failure to adhere to policies, and the like.

The key to documenting corrective action effectively, however, is creating a consistent record that outlines the company's attempts at proactively rehabilitating the employee while shifting responsibility for improvement away from the organization and back to the employee where it belongs. Following are certain rules and guidelines that will help you document corrective action that your employees will find fair and your company's defense lawyers will approve.

Rule 1: "Three strikes you're out."

Our current employment environment typically encourages companies to follow a three-step approach to accord employees with workplace due process in the form of progressive discipline as follows:

1. Verbal: first written warning
2. Written: second written warning
3. Final written warning

As a general rule, you, the employer, should follow this three-step approach to dealing with problematic employee performance, poor attendance, or tardiness, unless there are mitigating factors that justify an exception. For example, a new hire in a typical sixty- or ninety-day introductory period may not require any documented corrective action at all or possibly one piece of documentation (rather than three) because of the lack of tenure with your company. That depends on the nature of the issue, of course, but courts and plaintiffs' attorneys typically don't expect employers to accord much workplace due process to someone who recently joined a company.

Generally speaking, though, I recommend one documented warning of some sort, even for probationary employees. Why? Because "Did the company ever formally discipline you?" remains one of the first questions that a plaintiff's attorney will ask when deciding whether to take on a new case. If the answer is yes, that attorney will be far less inclined to pursue the claim against your company. Therefore, you can generally consider the documented warning a cheap insurance policy to protect your organization from unwanted legal intrusion. That being said, a thirty-year employee may warrant additional corrective action beyond three steps. In such cases, an additional step like the decision-making leaves that we'll soon address in Question 35 may be appropriate.

Rule 2: Write in an objective manner.

When documenting the facts in the narrative section of the warning, be sure to write objectively. Remember that you're not only writing for the employee; you're also writing potentially for a jury some six to twelve months from now, so your documentation must be clear enough to stand on its own in the litigation arena. For example, turn the subjective statement: "You were disrespectful toward a customer" into something more objective and descriptive: "You were rude and abrupt with the customer when you told him you didn't care which loan program he picked. The customer complained that you rolled your eyes, placed your hands on your hips, and got up out of your chair in the customer's home to relay your frustration with his indecisiveness."

Likewise, "You appeared at the client's office under the influence of alcohol" is too subjective. Instead, write: "The client reported that he heard you slurring your words, saw you walking with an unsteady gate, and smelled alcohol on your breath from approximately two feet away." Documenting the objective nature of your findings is critical to creating corrective action documentation that will withstand legal scrutiny.

Rule 3: Document the negative organizational impact.

Document the negative organizational impact that resulted from the employee's substandard job performance or inappropriate workplace conduct. For example, you might write: "Your failure to meet yesterday's deadline will require that other members of the team work unplanned overtime, and we will need to hire a temp." A similar negative organizational consequence might show the impact of the individual's actions on you as his supervisor: "In addition, I had to work late for the remainder of the week to ensure that we closed our books on time by the month-end deadline."

Rule 4: Document your expectations.

Regarding step 2 of the written warning's content, the Performance Improvement Plan (PIP), always document your expectations in terms of what the individual needs to do to fix the problem at hand. For example, "I expect that no further incidents of misplaced or mis-delivered packages or orders will occur in your area. In addition, I expect that you will proactively communicate any concerns you have about not being able to meet a particular deadline or not completing your assignments in a timely manner so that we have an opportunity to dedicate additional resources before the deadline is upon us." After all, one of the fundamental elements of workplace due process is that the employee needs to know what to do in order to fix the problem.

Rule 5: Document training and supervisory direction.

Include any training and supervisory direction to be provided that will help the employee meet expectations. That's important because juries expect companies to do more than simply point out problems; they expect organizations to proactively rehabilitate their workers. Otherwise, a "failure to train" charge may be levied against the company in court, arguing that the organization failed to act responsibly because it refused to or failed to train the individual when management knew that the worker would fail without the training.

Therefore, always document the positive and proactive steps that you take to help your employees succeed. This could include in-house or outside workshops, one-on-one follow-up training, or providing the employee with a copy of a policy so that the individual knows what the company's expectations are (for example, when it comes to attendance and tardiness problems). Likewise, you could recommend that the individual enroll in an accounting class at a local junior college to refine his skills. This shifts the responsibility for improvement away from the company and back to the employee where it belongs. For example, a judge may ask:

> Mr. Smith, I see the company gave you a copy of the attendance policy, but the problems continued. Did you take the time to read the policy and, if so, did you speak with your supervisor about any questions you had?
>
> [Yes, I read it but I didn't have any questions, so I never spoke to my supervisor about it.]

> Ms. Jones, your supervisor recommended in this corrective action notice of January 16, 2015, that you enroll in a basic accounting course at a local junior college to familiarize yourself with the basics. Did you have an opportunity to enroll or do anything else to strengthen your core accounting skills?
>
> [No, your honor, I didn't.]

From these examples you can see how overall responsibility for fixing a problem shifts away from the company and back to the employee. That's one of the goals of effective corrective action documentation and how it can be used to protect your organization from unwanted legal challenges. More importantly, it's fair! These are adults, and no matter how much courts want employers to spoonfeed workers, it's your job in the corrective action process to raise expectations and hold employees accountable for their end of the bargain when it comes to fixing the problems at hand.

Rule 6: Include a closing statement.

When documenting part 3 of the written warning, the consequences, include a closing statement, such as:

> Failure to demonstrate immediate and sustained improvement may result in further disciplinary action, up to and including dismissal.

This tagline is essential in according the individual workplace due process. Again, remember that the fourth rule of workplace due process is that the individual must understand the consequences of inaction. If your consequence language is vague, a shrewd attorney for a plaintiff can argue that his client, your ex-employee, had no reason to fear that his job was in jeopardy of being lost. Therefore, generic consequence language, such as "Serious discipline will result if this continues" will make it very difficult for your organization to defend a wrongful termination claim because the plaintiff's attorney will do his best to convince a jury that "serious discipline" or some other type of generic or vague phrase didn't communicate the message that the individual's job was in serious jeopardy. Hence, he was denied workplace due process, and the termination was consequently illegal.

Rule 7: Include an acknowledgment statement.

Draft the acknowledgment statement of the corrective action document in a way that encourages the worker to assume responsibility for the problem at hand. Most companies use this line: "I have received a copy of this document." The employee signs (or fails to sign) but doesn't necessary assume responsibility for the problem. Instead, reinvent your acknowledgment statement to look like this:

> I have received a copy of this notification. It has been discussed with me, and I have been advised to take time to consider it before I sign it. I have freely chosen to agree to it, and I accept full responsibility for my actions. By signing this, I commit to following the company's standards of performance and conduct.

See the difference? Being written up shouldn't ever be taken lightly. Your expectation as a supervisor is that if it happens once, it's a big deal and shouldn't ever happen again. That's a cultural imperative that you'll want to enforce from day one with all of your team members. Unfortunately, many managers issue corrective action warnings without much forethought about the seriousness of being written up. So treat workers like adults, help them assume partial responsibility for the situation at hand, and use the corrective action engagement as a first step in correcting behavior, resetting expectations, and allowing the healing process to begin.

Further, in final written warnings, you might want to include language like this:

> In addition, I understand that this is my last chance and that my position is now in immediate jeopardy of being lost. If I fail to achieve the goals agreed to in this document, I will resign or be terminated for cause.

Can you see why treating employees like adults in your documentation—without a lot of drama or histrionics—can make a tremendous difference in their attitude toward work? This is the kind of language that will arguably keep people up at night, but they have to make a decision as to their commitment level. No one wants to be terminated, and a resignation on their own terms may be preferable to risking a termination for cause. What's important is that you're giving them a choice either to resign or to recommit to the job, with no judgment on your part one way or the other. That's fair and objective and will help employees make adult decisions about their future career with your organization by leaving the drama, apathy, or hostility and anger behind.

For more on the practical answers and approaches to tricky employee relations issues, in addition to disciplining and terminating probationary employees, union workers, and long-term workers who may require more than the standard "three-strikes-and-you're-out" steps of corrective action, refer to my book, *101 Sample Write-Ups for Documenting Employee Performance Problems.*

32 *Progressive Discipline: Appropriate Documentation for Addressing Inappropriate Behavior and Misconduct Issues*

Despite the "three strikes you're out" assumption, the rules of progressive discipline may not be applicable in addressing certain inappropriate behaviors or egregious misconduct issues, and instead the company may issue a final written warning, even for a first offense, or immediately terminate the employee. Many managers mistakenly assume that *all* problematic issues—performance, conduct, and attendance/tardiness—must start at the first level of corrective action. In actuality, managers have the discretion to skip steps or even progress to immediate termination when it comes to conduct-related infractions.

For example, certain types of grievous infractions are known as "summary offenses" that require no previous documentation to justify an immediate termination for cause, even for a first offense and even from a long-tenured worker with no history of prior corrective action. Theft, embezzlement, fraud, and certain cases of severe harassment may warrant immediate dismissal. Before moving to the summary offense decision, however, it's usually best to consult with qualified legal counsel to ensure that you've thought everything through correctly and filed all the documentation required in case this termination results in litigation.

Not all cases are as egregious as theft, embezzlement, and fraud, of course. Yet depending on the nature of the conduct-related infraction, your organization has the discretion of skipping steps in the traditional progressive discipline paradigm to accurately reflect the severity of the issue. How do you know when to skip steps? Well, if your company would somehow look irresponsible or remiss in not escalating the level of corrective action to match a particular offense, then it stands to reason that your organization's response to the problem should escalate to meet the severity of the infraction.

For example, if you've attempted to extend an olive branch in order to appease an aggressive manager who continues to mistreat employees or abuse the privileges of his leadership role, and your actions were rebuffed, then you have every right to document the issue formally. *How* you document the individual's attitude, however, becomes very important. Remember that this kind of document may be blown up on banner paper and presented to a jury months from now as evidence of your management style, so proceed with caution. Consequently, an objective writing style that paints a picture with words in the form of a written or final written warning will fare best:

> This morning you engaged in insubordinate conduct when you responded to my request to complete the Jones file by the end of business. Your initial response was to roll your eyes, sigh, and turn to me with your hands on your hips. You stated loudly in front of other members of the staff, "If you want that file completed by the end of the day, you can't ask me any other questions between now and then. I need to be left alone!" Such sarcastic and unreasonable comments are unacceptable because they are disrespectful and violate company standards of performance and conduct.
>
> First, you were aware of today's deadline for the Jones file over a week ago. Second, your concerns were shared loudly in front of three of your coworkers, and I received feedback that they were uncomfortable and embarrassed to have witnessed your actions. Third, you do not have the discretion to insist that all other job responsibilities be removed while you work on a particular assignment.
>
> In the future, I expect that you will never again voice your frustration in a rude and unprofessional manner. I expect that any future concerns that you have regarding the assignments on your desk will be shared with me privately in my office and not voiced publicly in front of others. Finally, I expect you to inform me any time that you are falling behind on any of your work assignments so that I have an opportunity to provide you with additional support or resources to meet any deadlines.
>
> Failure to demonstrate immediate and sustained improvement may result in further disciplinary action up to and including dismissal. Further, if you *ever again* demonstrate conduct or behavior that appears to be disrespectful, insubordinate, overtly challenging, or confrontational, you will be immediately discharged for cause.

Employees can be terminated for inappropriate workplace conduct and for attitudinal problems that appear to be difficult to measure; these fall under the category of insubordination. Documentation clearly describes the employee's actions in objective terms and spells out your expectations regarding the employee's behavior should another disagreement occur. In addition, it outlines the consequences of inaction should the employee violate the terms of this warning in the future.

The key to well-written, conduct-related documentation lies in describing the employee's actions accurately so that your documentation remains clear enough to convince a jury that you had cause to discipline or terminate. Whenever possible, quote the employee's exact words in the narrative portion of the warning:

> When I asked you where your equipment was, you walked up to me, stood approximately two inches away from my face, and stated loudly that you were "annoyed that I was asking you about the location of your equipment." You raised your voice using an inappropriate and disrespectful tone, and I perceived that you were trying to intimidate me.

> When I requested the file in question, you slid it across the table, and all of its contents fell out of the folder and onto the floor. Although you apologized for throwing the folder by saying, "Oh sorry" as it fell off the desk and onto the floor, you rolled your eyes and sighed as if you were annoyed with my request. Your actions were clearly insubordinate.

> When John asked you why you appeared to be so upset over a simple request, you pointed your finger at him and waved it back and forth shouting, "Don't tell me how upset I am! You don't know me, and you have no right to judge me!" Such actions were clearly inappropriate and unprofessional and violated company standards of performance and conduct.

Likewise, incorporate the employee's responses to your questions in the document whenever possible. For example,

> When I asked you after the incident whether you felt your behavior was inappropriate or disrespectful, you immediately placed blame on your coworkers. I then asked you to focus on the tenor and tone of your response—regardless of who was at fault for the missing equipment. You again placed blame on your coworkers without assuming partial responsibility for the problem at hand. As such, David, you do not appear to be holding yourself sufficiently responsible

for the conflict that arose as a result of your challenging your coworkers and me regarding the simple question that I asked you.

To be able to incorporate an employee's response into the disciplinary narrative that you draft, however, you have to meet with him first to learn his side of the story. And this begs the age-old question: Do I need to meet with employees before issuing corrective action, or can I simply issue the document first and allow them to rebut it afterward if they disagree with the findings?

In almost all cases, meeting with employees first to learn their side of the story—while also letting them know upfront that disciplinary action may be warranted—makes the most sense. First, it speaks to fairness: Everyone wants to be heard before they're judged, and as we've seen elsewhere in this book, mitigating circumstances can make a world of difference in terms of determining the appropriate corrective action to be applied. Second, and equally important, by incorporating an employee's feedback into the written warning itself, you show yourself to be a fair, patient, and wise employer. Juries look for companies that don't jump to conclusions and that delay disciplinary action to hear the worker's side of the story. Can there be times when you issue corrective action without getting the employee's side of the story first? Of course, but that should generally be the exception, not the rule.

Finally, when you speak with an employee about corrective action—whether for conduct, performance, or attendance—you gain a chance to reconnect. We all make mistakes, and sometimes the company has no choice but to document problematic behavior or performance. But you can ask what you can do to help, if there are any other resources that the employee needs, or if there's anything the individual wants to share that he's kept from you for some reason. Extending an olive branch at the time of discipline is an exceptionally wise way of leading others and will generally be appreciated. Sure, no one likes being written up, but if employees feel that their boss handled it fairly, then they can get on with their work lives.

Reconnecting with the employee also gives you a chance to re-emphasize that disciplinary action isn't what you expect to be doing with your employees and that you're looking for a commitment to avoid it in the future, which you'll typically get if this is handled appropriately. Also, you'll typically avoid the drama that occurs when employees refuse to sign or acknowledge that they received the document or, worse, submit a lengthy rebuttal to the CEO. Again, communication at the time of discipline goes a long way in ensuring that the behavior won't be repeated, which is the goal of this documented intervention.

This is a huge topic, subject to opinion and recent case law interpretations. For additional information and examples, see my book *101 Sample Write-Ups for Documenting Employee Performance Problems*.

33 *Writer Beware: "Codifying the Damage" or Documenting "Mental Element Qualifiers" Can Sink Your Ship in Court*

There are two common errors that leaders make when documenting investigations. In fact, these same errors are often committed when drafting performance reviews and progressive discipline. They're easy to avoid, however, if you're aware of them and understand the logic behind the damage they can cause.

First, be especially careful not to "codify the damage" when documenting your investigatory findings. Many a well-meaning supervisor has unintentionally placed the organization at risk by not thinking through the significance of their notes. For example, documenting that an employee has "sexually harassed" or "retaliated against" a coworker could later be used against your company as a documented fact. As a term of the trade, "sexual harassment" is a legal conclusion. If you confirm in writing that sexual harassment has indeed occurred, then your own investigational documentation may become prime fodder for a plaintiff's attorney looking to find proof of a supervisor's inappropriate actions. Similarly, if a loan administrator mishandles a pool of loans by failing to follow appropriate mortgage banking guidelines, then such documented information could become evidence of neglect and mismanagement on your firm's part if that pool of loans never gets sold on the secondary mortgage market or otherwise becomes discoverable to stock investors.

Therefore, instead of codifying the damage to the organization or to the recipient of a supervisor's inappropriate workplace behavior, adopt the practice of documenting such matters using language that is less concrete and more fluid in nature. For example, in the case of a harassment issue where it appears that a worker has violated company policy, write, "This individual's actions *appear to* violate company policy 5.30." You might also write, "The supervisor's actions *suggest that* he *may have* inadvertently created an offensive environment" and that, as part of your follow-up action plan, you would expect the supervisor to "never again engage in conduct *that could appear to diminish* a person's self-worth or sense of well-being." Similarly, in the case of the loan administrator's performance, you might write, "The loan administrator's failure to follow standard operating procedure *could have potentially jeopardized* an entire pool of loans."

Again, while certain documents may be protected by attorney–client privilege because you have need for legal counsel's analysis and guidance, *all* of your investigation notes will probably not be protected by the privilege (i.e., barred from consideration by the plaintiff's attorney). Since you most likely won't be able to protect all of your investigatory notes in a legal action—in fact, your notes will basically become the company's foundational defense mechanism to justify its actions—be sure to avoid codifying any damage done by being specifically vague in your documentation, which will prevent your own documentation from inadvertently benefiting a plaintiff's attorney's case against your organization.

Likewise, be careful to avoid documenting "state-of-mind offenses." In particularly egregious cases of inappropriate workplace conduct, investigators and supervisors sometimes mistakenly attempt to paint a picture of the severity of a particular offense by describing behaviors and attitudes using words like *deliberately, purposely, intentionally, willfully,* and *maliciously.* Such mental element qualifiers may indeed strengthen your message to the individual about having acted in a highly inappropriate way, but it isn't necessary to write this way. Instead, let the facts speak for themselves. It doesn't matter whether "John *deliberately* tried to offend Sally publicly in front of her whole team." All that matters is that "John offended Sally publicly in front of her whole team." The latter is an objective observation, while the former is a subjective judgment.

In the litigation arena, this becomes all the more relevant. Plaintiffs' attorneys will be quick to cast doubt on the validity of your "objective" investigatory findings if you pepper your notes with adverbs that speak to someone's alleged state of mind. In essence, you may end up making yourself vulnerable to a slew of legal challenges as plaintiffs' attorneys challenge your fact-finding skills and attack your credibility with questions about how you could have possibly known what was going on in their client's (your ex-employee's) mind at the time of the incident.

Simple solution: avoid words like *deliberately, intentionally, purposely, willfully,* and *maliciously* when documenting your findings during an investigation and, as a general rule, stay away from adverbs. To do otherwise would be a rookie mistake that could land your company in hot water.

34 *A Creative Alternative to Formal Corrective Action: Letters of Clarification*

Have you ever wondered if there was some sort of interim step between counseling an employee verbally and formally disciplining an employee in writing? You've no doubt been frustrated at times by employees whose problematic job performance or behavior falls just below the threshold of a violation of a specific company policy. And because you can't pin the problem to an existing policy violation, you tend to let it go or tolerate it for far longer than you should. That may no longer be necessary; you can write a letter of clarification as an alternative to formal progressive discipline.

Still, it's important to remember that a formal company policy doesn't have to be broken for you to address problems effectively with a member of your team. You've got a lot more discretion and flexibility here than you think, especially when dealing with an employee who is apathetic about his work, condescending toward others, taking advantage of a particular situation or personal relationship at work, or who speaks negatively about others on the team.

Addressing your concerns verbally is always the first step. Sharing your concerns in a constructive manner, alerting the employee to the issues at hand, and creating the beginning of a record that could later help the company justify the necessity for taking adverse employment actions like progressive discipline or termination are logical outcomes of verbal interventions. But what happens when your conversations don't work and you find yourself on a roller coaster, readdressing the same issue every few weeks or months? While you may have the discretion to issue a formal written warning, you may also be concerned that it's too heavy a punishment relative to the specific facts in the situation. In cases like these, write a letter of clarification as an interim step that confirms your concerns but is milder than formal progressive discipline (i.e., "being written up").

First, because it's in writing, it steps up the perceived level of severity and makes the employee realize that you're serious about the issue and want to escalate beyond verbal discussions. Second, letters of clarification are not part of your company's formal corrective action program. As such, they lack the "shaming" element that's so often associated with being "written up." In essence, you're escalating the matter without any of the negative trappings of progressive discipline.

What might a letter of clarification look like? While the technique can be used to address all sorts of job performance and workplace misconduct issues, here's a common example illustrating negligence and carelessness that might appear minor on its face but that, bundled together, paints a picture of an employee who's demonstrating a lack of interest in her role or who cares little about her coworkers:

Mary,

Over the past three weeks, I've shared with you my concerns regarding your overall job performance. Specifically, I've notified you that you are not handling patients' files correctly: Items are being misfiled, and files are being left around the office without being returned to the central filing area. In addition, a patient complained that you delivered a wheelchair to the patient pickup area that was still wet from the rain. Further, on multiple occasions, you have failed to use the magnetic location board to show that you were on break or lunch. As a result, the schedulers were not able to locate you in a timely manner.

This isn't a disciplinary document, Mary. It will not be placed in your formal personnel file and will not be shared with other members of management at this time. However, I have put my concerns in writing to impress upon you the seriousness of these multiple, smaller errors. My greatest concern lies in the fact that you appear to be less focused on your work or concerned about others' needs. You also appear to be apathetic about the outcome of your assignments, and several of your coworkers have noticed a change in your work as well and shared their concerns with me.

I want you to know that I'm here to support you in any way I can. However, I am also holding you fully accountable for meeting all hospital expectations regarding your performance and conduct. I recognize that you may have your own ideas for improving the situation at hand. Therefore, I encourage you to provide your own suggestions to turn around these specific performance areas as well as the overall perception of your lower commitment level.

Please sign this document to show not only that you received it but also that you agree to accept full responsibility for addressing these concerns and changing the perception problems that exist. Understand that if these issues are not resolved on an immediate and sustained basis, this document may be attached to a formal disciplinary notice in the future confirming our discussion today. Thank you.

_____   _____
Employee Signature   Date

Note the language in the sample above: While this isn't a formal disciplinary document and will not be placed in the individual's personnel file *at this time*, it "may be attached to a formal disciplinary notice in the future" as evidence that the conversation took place and that expectations were reset. Further, in cases of litigation, the letter of clarification is a formal part of the employer's record to show that the individual was aware of the problem and informed of the company's expectations. Therefore, the letter of clarification codifies the problem for the record and is typically used as an evidentiary element to demonstrate that the company acted responsibly in according the employee due process.

One note of caution about the use of letters of clarification, however: As practical as this tool may be, you won't want to issue letters of clarification every time someone does something wrong. If these letters become part of your active disciplinary practice and you issue them all the time, then you may end up inadvertently creating a new practice by turning your three-step corrective action process into a four-step process (i.e., by insisting that letters of clarification be issued prior to corrective action under *all* circumstances for *all* employees)— or so might argue a plaintiff's attorney in the wrongful termination litigation arena. But a letter of clarification, viewed by many employees as a precursor to formal discipline, typically has the same corrective effect as formal discipline without the negative trappings. Added to your performance management toolbox, this alternative could achieve the desired results without any of the drama or angst that comes from issuing formal corrective action.

35 *Decision-Making Leaves: Dramatic Turnarounds Without a Lot of Drama*

One of the greatest workplace challenges for supervisors and managers lies in turning workers around when their conduct or behavior consistently disappoints you. Maybe they're young and don't value the opportunity your company is offering them, or maybe they've been working for your organization for twenty years and suddenly have developed an attitude problem or entitlement mentality that makes them difficult to deal with. A "decision-making leave," otherwise known as a "day of contemplation," could be just what the doctor ordered to snap these people back to reality and make them realize how negatively they're coming across—without you, the employer, having to play the bad guy.

Decision-making leaves typically come into play in scenarios like these:

1. An early career worker demonstrates an entitlement mentality and consistently irritates others but hasn't been formally disciplined yet.

2. A long-tenured employee is due a greater amount of workplace due process because of her tenure, and you want to add a decision-making leave to the individual's final written warning as a way of impressing upon her that her position is now in immediate jeopardy of being lost.

3. A problematic employee with family ties to someone in senior management consistently comes close to breaching a formal company policy but never quite violates it, thereby avoiding formal progressive discipline but upsetting everyone around her in the process.
4. A top sales producer who performs his job well believes he can do whatever he wants because he "can't be touched" as long as he's the best performer in the group.

In the first case, you may not want to formally discipline the junior worker because he may not realize how he's coming across, or you may feel that formal corrective action might come across as too heavy-handed under the circumstances. In the second case, your goal in providing this once-in-a-career benefit to a long-term employee will be to help the individual understand the severity of the situation and also to protect your organization legally. (After all, the "three strikes you're out" method of workplace due process doesn't necessarily work as well for long-term employees because courts may reasonably rule that you owe the individual more notice than a few simple documented warnings.)

In the third case, you'll want to break the persistent track record that a problematic employee continues to demonstrate by getting him to assume responsibility for the problem at hand and stop the roller-coaster effect of his behavior—without upsetting the senior executive family member. In the fourth case, the employee only has it half right: he's responsible for both his performance *and* his conduct, and he needs to understand that performing well but failing to create an inclusive work environment or fostering a sense of teamwork leaves him failing overall; if he's meeting only the performance standards but not the conduct expectations, he's coming in at 50 percent—a failing score in most organizations.

To understand how a decision-making leave works, let's start with a definition: A "decision-making leave" or "day of contemplation" is a paid day off where an employee causing lots of grief is granted the opportunity to rethink his commitment to working at your company. Unlike a formal suspension, it isn't necessarily a step in your company's documented progressive disciplinary process. Also unlike a traditional suspension, the employee's pay is not docked for the time away from work. The worker actually *gets paid to stay home* for a day with pay and mull over whether working for your company is the right long-term career move for him.

If this sounds like too lenient a strategy that lets the worker "benefit from being bad," so to speak, don't be too quick to judge how effective this tool can actually work in the workplace. Here's why: Adult learning theory will tell you that when you treat people like adults, they will typically respond in kind. Unlike formal discipline, which tends to punish workers for substandard job performance or inappropriate workplace conduct, decision-making leaves are much more subtle. More important, they don't negatively impact a (nonexempt) worker's take-home pay, so there's no element of resentment toward the employer or embarrassment for having to explain to a spouse or family member why the paycheck is less that particular week.

This element of holding people accountable without issuing corrective action or negatively impacting their pay tends to trigger a guilt response rather than an anger response. *Anger* is external, and if you, the big bad employer, discipline workers and deduct their wages for any reason, they'll become angry and self-justify that you're the cause the problem, the Goliath to their David, the unilateral, punitive decision-maker hurting their career. On the other hand, *guilt* is internal—as a human emotion, it forces people to look inward and see themselves more honestly and objectively by assuming partial responsibility for the problem at hand. And that's the ultimate way to resolve conduct and attitude problems in the workplace: by helping workers look internally and introspectively at whether they want to recommit to the organization or resign.

More often than not, the events that will typically trigger the need for a decision-making leave revolve around employee conduct (as opposed to performance or attendance). In most cases, you, the supervisor, will want the individual's behavior to change, not only for your sake and for your staff's sake, but also for the good of the employee as well. In the case listed above with the long-tenured worker, you could add decision-making leave language to a final written warning by describing it like this:

> Mark, we've had a number of conversations regarding inappropriate behavior that you've displayed over the past four months, and you received a written warning for inappropriate workplace conduct on April 10, 2016. We initially addressed your over-mentioning your frustration with our organization being "cheap" and not paying fairly, which made some of your coworkers feel uncomfortable and prompted them to come and speak with me. Then we discussed your tardiness and, following that, your demonstrations of frustration that were evidenced by remarks like, "Who's running this asylum?" and "They've got to be kidding. Someone needs a Management 101 class around here."
>
> Yesterday you engaged in public altercation with a coworker that resulted in your screaming and using profanity in the lobby in front of visitors and vendors. At this point, you're being issued a final written warning because you don't appear to be taking this seriously, and your conduct is highly inappropriate and disrespectful. I'm also going to place you on what we call a decision-making leave for a day because this is your first job out of grad school, and I'm truly hoping to help you turn around this predicament that you're facing. This is how it works: I want you to stay home tomorrow. You will be paid. I want you to know that this is a once-in-a-career benefit that you should use to your advantage.
>
> While you're at home tomorrow, I want you to give some serious thought as to whether you really want to work here or not. If you come back to work the next morning and tell me that you'd rather resign and look for work elsewhere, I'll be totally supportive of your decision. You can tender your formal resignation, and there won't be any hard feelings. But if you come back to work and tell me that you really want to keep your job with us, then you'll have one additional assignment to complete while you're away from work tomorrow.
>
> Remember that I'm paying you for the day, so here's your homework: If you choose to keep your job, you'll need to prepare a letter for me convincing me that you assume full and total responsibility for the *perception problem* that exists in terms of your conduct and behavior. You'll need to convince me in writing that you recognize why there may be a perception problem and again convince me in writing that the problem will be fixed from this point forward and that we'll never have to have this type of discussion again.
>
> That commitment letter will be attached to your final written warning, and I'll be holding you to it. I'm considering this a very serious exercise and something that could be an incredibly important turnaround point in your career

development. However, if you violate the terms of your commitment letter, you'll in essence be firing yourself. Do you have any questions or concerns about this decision-making leave that you'll be taking tomorrow? Do you understand why I am taking this step with you now as part of your final written warning?

The value of this paid leave is that it forces the individual to be introspective and to engage in self-critical insight without the traditional trappings of formal progressive discipline. The worker won't walk away thinking, *I can't believe my boss gave me a final written warning and is docking my pay; she's a terrible supervisor,* but rather, *Wow, I can't believe I'm getting a day off to consider whether I want to continue working here or to resign. I'm shocked that she'd accept my resignation and that she'd be supportive of my leaving the company. I guess I'd better be good, and although I don't like any of this, I respect how she's handling it and realize that I need to turn things around.*

See the immediate paradigm shift in the employee's thought process? The value proposition of decision-making leaves is that they elevate employees in the process by empowering them to take control of the situation. And the hands-off nature of the exercise removes any semblance of judgment, replacing it with an objective, no-nonsense standard that the employee completely manages. In short, it's not about the company or the supervisor at all; it's strictly about the employee's willingness to reinvent himself in light of these issues being formally brought to his attention.

Even if this intervention doesn't work and the employee must be terminated nevertheless, you and your company still win. You'll demonstrate your reasonableness as a responsible organizational leader, and your company gains the advantage of creating a record that will minimize legal scrutiny should this ever turn into a wrongful termination or constructive discharge claim. (In a "constructive discharge" claim, the employee isn't fired but quits. The legal argument is that conditions at work were so bad that any reasonable person would have quit under similar circumstances. As a result, the damages sought for constructive discharge are basically the same as in a wrongful discharge case.) In essence, you'll have shifted the paradigm away from "irresponsible company did little to proactively rehabilitate a good worker with temporary performance problems" to "responsible corporate citizen went out of its way to help proactively rehabilitate a worker and communicate the severity of the problem as well as future expectations but employee refused to respond responsibly." Either way—as a thoughtful and caring frontline leader or as a legally sensitive organization trying to minimize potential liability—the company wins.

This decision-making leave strategy is a low-profile, low-drama type of employee intervention strategy that speaks volumes in its subtlety. As a tool in your management toolbox, it may be just the fix necessary to help others see things your way, keep them out of harm's way, and protect your company all at the same time.

One caveat about decision-making leaves: If your employees are covered by a collective bargaining agreement, then an unpaid disciplinary "suspension" may be part of your company's formal corrective action process, so adding a paid leave to an unpaid leave may not be necessary or make much sense. In any case, don't expect the union or an arbitrator to recognize this day of contemplation as a replacement for any formal step(s) in the disciplinary process outlined in the union contract.

Further, decision-making leaves are generally rare and should only be used in situations where warranted (as in our four examples listed above). And decision-making leaves shouldn't ever be used in cases where excessive absenteeism is the problem: the last thing the worker needs is more time off! Further, the goal is *not* to make a decision-making leave part of your regular corrective action process where, for example, no one gets terminated without a decision-making leave first. Used on a situation-specific, case-by-case basis, however, this tool can do wonders for turning around employees with attitude problems or otherwise protecting your company from the legal liability associated with terminating long-term workers.

36 *Structuring Terminations That Will Withstand Legal Scrutiny: Making Your Defense Lawyer Proud*

In the various courses that I've taught at UCLA Extension over the years and in the many workshops I've led at conferences, I've repeated one mantra: "Don't manage by fear of a lawsuit. Lawsuits are the cost of business from time to time in corporate America. Instead, simply make sure that if a lawsuit comes your way, you're getting sued *on your terms* and not theirs." Sage advice no doubt, but you may be wondering what that actually looks like.

First, let's look at its opposite so that we know where we don't want to go: When managers storm into HR and demand that an employee be terminated immediately, it's typically because some proverbial straw has broken the camel's back. The final incident usually isn't that grievous or egregious; the manager simply can't take it any more and wants the person gone. The HR representative pulls the personnel file and finds the following:

Number of disciplinary documents
   on record: 0

Number of performance reviews on
   record: 5

Actual performance review scores
   (on a scale of 1 to 5):   3 ("meets expectations")

And that's where the situation breaks down. After all, reasons the HR person, the manager hasn't done her job of holding the individual accountable for his performance, setting and enforcing expectations, and demanding higher quality products or services. Rather, the manager allowed the employee to drift, year in and year out, ignoring the multiple problems that she saw, avoiding the situation and simply hoping it would get better on its own. As a result, there's no documentation on file to justify and support a termination.

The HR representative reasons with the manager:

You're asking me to approve terminating this person because he failed to make himself available for your call last night at 8 PM? I understand you're frustrated because he said he would be available and because you emphasized how important this was, but there's no record to go into litigation with. In the eyes of the law, he's performed at a perfectly acceptable level for the past five years, hasn't once been censured by the company for any performance or conduct-related issues, and is now being terminated because he wasn't available for an 8 PM phone call on one particular night—probably because he'll say he had family emergency of some sort. Can you see how we'd look if this case went to court?" A plaintiff's attorney would argue that we are reactive hot heads and would likely prevail in court under a wrongful discharge claim because we failed to accord the employee due process in the form of progressive discipline.

No manager, no matter how angry or frustrated, could overcome the HR representative's argument here. So the manager is angry at HR, angry with herself, and irate that the system doesn't allow companies to fire employees who refuse to work hard and hold themselves accountable.

But if you've ever found yourself in this particular predicament, realize that you're not alone. Understand that the nature of the final incident is crucial to any termination decision because it justifies the company's decision to separate the employee. If the final incident is minor, however, and sounds like it might be difficult to sell to a jury of the worker's peers, then you might need to check your frustration and understand that your organization is not quite ready to pull the plug yet. More importantly, though, it doesn't have to be this way.

Instead, picture this: You've had ongoing communication with this employee as well as all the workers on your staff. You hold one-on-one quarterly meetings allowing them to check in with you and report on their progress and correct and adjust their goals as changes in plan dictate. You've had the opportunity to reset expectations so that employees can feel respected and able to make their own unique contributions to the projects at hand.

However, one employee doesn't work well with others. She may be burned out or bitter, may have an anger management problem, may present herself like a bully, and may make everyone feel like they have to walk on eggshells around her. Despite all your efforts, this person stands apart from the rest and refuses to put others' needs first, accommodate your needs as her boss, or otherwise make a positive contribution in the office every day.

Rather than avoiding these somewhat below-the-radar problems, you address them objectively and dispassionately when they arise. You provide the necessary verbal coaching and encourage this individual to reinvent her working relationship with her peers. You recommend that she assume partial responsibility for some of the problems she's having in getting along with others, and you hold her accountable for her own perception management in terms of raising her awareness of how she's coming across to others.

Still no success; she won't play nicely. You confer with HR or with your boss and create a united front so that she can't later "split the baby." You issue the first step of corrective action in your organization's progressive discipline program—a documented verbal warning. Unfortunately, there's little sustained improvement. A second incident occurs in which she is witnessed badgering someone from a different department who makes a formal complaint to her department head about this individual's overly aggressive behavior. That leads to the second step of progressive discipline—a written warning. You include the appropriate language that documents that the employee's failure to demonstrate an immediate and sustained improvement may result in further disciplinary action, up to and including dismissal.

Still no dice. Three weeks later, she's at it again, this time losing her temper with you and engaging in clearly insubordinate and highly disrespectful conduct. The final written warning is issued. Likewise, you offer the individual training, access to your company's Employee Assistance Program, and any other resources that may help her strengthen her interpersonal relationships and take better control of her temper. She refuses your offer. Lo and behold, it's time to issue your annual performance reviews, and you assign her an overall score of 2, "partially meets expectations." You praise her technical job performance but clarify that her conduct remains unacceptable and that her final written warning remains actively in place. She receives no merit increase or bonus.

With the final written warning and annual performance review in place, a final incident occurs one month later in which the employee demonstrates clearly unprofessional behavior that violates the terms of her final written warning. The company moves forward with the termination, and her coworkers feel relieved that the angst and tension will finally dissipate. They also respect your leadership in handling the matter in a straightforward and direct way because they could figure out on their own that the individual was being actively counseled and advised about her behavior. Now the group healing can begin.

But wait! The employee has filed a lawsuit for wrongful termination and discrimination. It alleges that you harbor some sort of animus against this woman because of her age and sexual orientation, and the law firm is making outrageous demands for a settlement. Understandably, you feel nervous about your decision to have terminated her months earlier. Well, fear not. You can't manage by fear of a lawsuit, and you can't be lured into analysis paralysis when dealing with substandard job performers or misconduct issues simply because the individual has threatened to sue in the past or may sue in the future. Instead, you think back to the standards you've set for your whole team. You reflect on how you've held everyone accountable on a consistent basis. And you realize that you could not have allowed this individual to wreak havoc on the rest of your team by making work a miserable experience for everyone else in the department.

Finally, you reason, *bring it on*! The progressive disciplinary documents are fair and cite concrete examples of inappropriate workplace behavior. The failed annual performance review invalidates an entire year's work because the individual was a net negative in terms of her overall contribution to the team. And the clean final incident that triggered the termination was incontestable in terms of the egregious nature of her behavior despite the organization's prior attempts at proactively rehabilitating this individual and resetting clear and consistent expectations.

Overall, you can be very proud of your performance, your team's support, and your management's agreement to terminate the employee for cause. After all, this individual may feel that she was terminated due to some prejudice on your part, but you realize she was never willing to assume any responsibility for the problems at hand. She intimidated and continually bullied others, and you had to stop such behavior using the tools and policies available to you as a corporate leader. You partnered with your boss and HR (or your in-house or outside counsel) appropriately, and you have nothing to feel bad about. In essence, it isn't that you terminated the employee; it's that she terminated herself. And you've got a clean record and clear conscience that will help withstand legal or ethical scrutiny.

As for the lawsuit, it's up to the attorneys to deal with it at this point. One thing's for sure, though: It's simple to file a lawsuit. All it takes is a one-time processing fee of around $100 or so, depending on where the lawsuit is filed, and a completed form or two, and an ex-employee is off to the races. But you've done an excellent job of treating the individual fairly and consistently. You've abided by your company's policies and procedures and issued corrective action and a failed annual review appropriately. And there were no surprises—this lawsuit was accounted for and defended against before it was ever filed. All because you, the immediate manager, took a responsible leadership position in managing the situation.

Whether the lawsuit will proceed is out of your hands at this point, but know deep down that you'll have mitigated much of the damage because of your documentation trail. You'll have protected your company legally and restored balance and harmony within your department. You won't judge this individual personally by any means, but you'll simply realize that the timing wasn't right for her to contribute to your organization in a healthy and meaningful way at this point in her career.

And you'll sleep well at night knowing that you mastered this process: you know how to manage subpar performance, both in terms of verbal coaching and formal corrective action, and you know you can do it again if need be. In short, you can be proud of yourself, despite the unfortunate circumstances involved. And you'll have made your defense lawyers' lives so much easier because it's rare that they have a case like this that's so well executed and easy to defend. Well done and congratulations—you're now a master in the game of leadership defense.

4 Avoiding Litigation Land Mines

LEADERSHIP DEFENSE is a topic that sometimes gets short shrift amidst all the media content relating to motivating and inspiring employees so that they experience total satisfaction and engagement in the workplace. While these sorts of seminars, books, and articles typically offer great ideas for improving employee morale and gaining stronger buy-in from the troops, the truth lurking beneath the surface can be less than pretty. Some employees are professional plaintiffs, looking for a reason to sue so that they can make enough money to get by without having to work. Union "salts" are still very real—posing as job applicants and getting hired by a company, only to identify and exploit leadership weaknesses that can then lead to union organizing efforts. Still others thrive on drama and will look for new ways of stirring the proverbial pot to alienate others, engage in power plays, and generally cause angst and tension in insidious ways.

As much as we tend to think that we hire the best and brightest, we can't X-ray candidates to see what's in their hearts. And while thorough interview rounds, pre-employment testing, criminal background checks, and, most importantly, reference checks, all play a critical role in making "high probability hires," there's still no guarantee that every person who joins your team will have altruistic and selfless motives to help you as their leader and the company overall to grow and thrive in a positive, healthy direction. Of course, not all problematic workers come from external hires. Managers sometimes inherit problematic performers via internal transfers or layoffs in other departments, and sometimes entitlement mentalities and victim syndromes simply develop on their own among legacy employees.

165

The point is, any employee at any given time may be facing severe personal problems or simply dislike working in your group or with certain members of your team. A perfectly successful worker from another department may resent the new challenges your department presents or have difficulty getting over past hurts or current perceived indignities. Whatever way such problems find their way into the workplace, you'll no doubt be required to deal with them at some point in your career. The goal, of course, isn't to judge anyone—it's simply to observe the situation and then remedy it professionally and respectfully. However, if an employee refuses to reinvent himself and his relationship to you and the rest of your team, then the leadership defense strategies discussed in this chapter should help in addressing the situation constructively and directly.

This chapter focuses on concrete, hard-core, practical leadership land mines that may await even the most well meaning or otherwise successful managers. Be sure to rely on these guiding principles so that you don't get caught in a snare that you didn't see coming. This isn't meant to make you a paranoid leader—it's meant to raise your awareness so that you come to rely more fully on your gut or that internal guidance system that we all have, often known as our intuition or sixth sense. You've got to make sure that you know how to follow these internal pulses when they tell you that something may be going wrong. Equally as important, you need to know when, how, and to whom to disclose your concerns so that you build successful alliances within your company and create the proper record when problematic employee performance or conduct may occur in your group. Consider this chapter *Visceral Leadership 101*, and make every effort to master these best practices in leadership defense strategies to protect both you and your company.

37 A Brief Employment Law History Primer to Show Why Documentation is Critical—Even for At-Will Workers

One nagging issue remains unresolved in the world of leadership and management: Why do we have to provide documented corrective action when workers are employed at will? First, understand that in the

United States, employment "at will" means a company may terminate an employee without incurring legal liability at any time and for any reason—except an illegal one. Likewise, an employee is free to leave a job at any time for any reason or for no reason without any type of adverse legal consequences. In many other countries, employers can dismiss employees only for cause. It's this interplay between "with cause," "without cause," and "illegal reasons" that causes much of the confusion surrounding the employment-at-will relationship and its consequences in the workplace.

Understanding the legal dichotomy between employment-at-will and its opposite, the termination-for-just-cause-only standard, will shed light on how these mutually exclusive concepts apply in a court of law. Understand, however, that the concept of employment-at-will only exists in the courtroom—not in the workplace. So trying to terminate someone at work by arguing that she's employed at will is completely out of sync with reality; instead, any arguments that someone was terminated due to her employment-at-will status will only occur at the hearing stage of the litigation process, as we'll soon see.

There are three factors in U.S. employment history that will shed light on this: (1) the 18th-century employment principles of England, which our forefathers relied on during the nation's founding; (2) the Great Depression of the 1930s and the subsequent creation of the employment-at-will legal concept; and (3) the 1980 California court case that introduced limitations and exceptions to employment-at-will theory. Let's briefly discuss these three critical factors for a broad overview of how we got where we are today.

In the 18th century, at the time of our nation's founding, the "job as property doctrine" stated that the right to work was so fundamental to U.S. citizens that it shouldn't be taken away arbitrarily or without just cause, as later codified in the 14th Amendment to the Constitution. This "termination for just cause only" standard was borrowed from English law and basically made working a "property right" of all American citizens.

That all changed, however, at the time of the Great Depression in the 1930s, when capitalism and free enterprise were deemed to be at risk. Congress passed a series of drastic measures that resulted in severely limiting U.S. workers' rights and gave companies the power to terminate workers "at whim" in order to keep their doors open. In the Great Depression, hundreds of unemployed workers would line up outside a factory door waiting for a plant employee to be injured or to make a mistake and get fired, thus creating an opening for a new worker. It was workplace mayhem, plain and simple, but "employment at will" became the law of the land in the 1930s, and as a result, a fundamental shift occurred where employers' rights to terminate at whim replaced workers' right to due process. In essence, a fundamental shift occurred where working became the "property right" of employers, not of workers.

When World War II began, the employment-at-will debate was sidelined. It wasn't coincidental, however, that labor unions saw their massive rise from the late 1940s, when the war ended, through the 1970s. Why? Because union organizers could sell prospective member workers on the idea that if you're represented by a union, then your employment would not be at will; the collective bargaining agreement would revert to the "termination for just cause only standard" that was established in the 18th century. Workers flocked to unions as a result, if only to have a modicum of job security and be given advanced notice if their positions were in jeopardy prior to being terminated. (The right to collectively bargain for wages and benefits was another big reason to join unions, but that was typically secondary to the advantages that greater job security offered by not being held to the employment-at-will standard.)

But wait; there's more. Employment-at-will took a major turn in 1980, when a California court ruled that there could be exceptions to the employment-at-will doctrine. California Chief Justice Rose Bird ruled in *Tameny vs. Atlantic Richfield Co.* that a long-term employee couldn't be fired under the employment-at-will affirmative defense for refusing to engage in unlawful activities (in this case, price fixing) on the employer's behalf. Once the employment-at-will veil was pierced, the public policy exception was born, and tort law became part of the legal landscape.

Today, four key exceptions to the employment-at-will doctrine are generally recognized thanks to the *Tameny* precedent:

1. Public policy exceptions (e.g., in the Tameny case, where whistle blowing or otherwise engaging in protected, concerted activities eliminates a company's ability to terminate at whim under the employment-at-will affirmative defense)
2. Employment contracts (including collective bargaining agreements)
3. Implied contract exceptions and implied covenants of good faith and fair dealing (especially pertaining to potential promises made in employee handbooks)
4. Statutory considerations (e.g., protected classes, like those outlined in Title VII of the Civil Rights Act of 1964, which prohibits discrimination on the basis of sex, race, color, religion, and national origin)

With such broad exceptions to employment at will now in place, you, the employer, can't know without a crystal ball what type of spin a plaintiff's attorney may apply to a particular case if your company gets sued at some point in the future. Therefore, you can't rely on the employment-at-will affirmative defense as an absolute and exclusive measure against a wrongful termination claim—there are just too many exceptions that plaintiffs' attorneys have at their disposal. Instead, you must be able to demonstrate that your company had "good cause" to terminate. Here's why:

When it comes to understanding the freedom to terminate when an employee is hired "at will," you'll need to look at the anatomy of a lawsuit by distinguishing between hearings and trials in the litigation arena. Employment at will only exists at the hearing stage. Your company's defense attorney will argue that the individual was employed at will and that your company did nothing to abrogate the employment-at-will relationship. Therefore, your defense attorney will request a "summary judgment" (i.e., immediate dismissal of the case) using the "employment-at-will affirmative defense." If your company prevails, then the case is dismissed and everyone can go home.

However, the plaintiff's attorney will argue that the case should not be summarily dismissed at the hearing stage and should continue to trial, where it can be judged on its own merits because the company arguably engaged in some form of unlawful activity that justifies an exception to the employment-at-will relationship. If the plaintiff's attorney prevails and the judge agrees to hear the case at trial, then there's no such thing as employment at will anymore. (Remember, employment at will only belongs at the hearing stage.)

Once the case proceeds to the trial stage, then the 18th-century concept of "termination for just cause only" becomes the only standard available, so your company must show that it had good cause to terminate. And most judges and arbitrators will rule that if nothing was written down (i.e., in the form of corrective action), then the performance problems may not have been serious enough to warrant termination. In short, your organization could be left trying to defend its actions without the supporting documentation necessary to prove that it had good reason to terminate the plaintiff.

Unfortunately, you won't know in advance if your defense lawyers will be successful in prevailing at the hearing stage by winning a summary judgment (i.e., immediate dismissal) of the case. Therefore, you'll always want to have progressive discipline in place to defend and justify your company's actions should the case proceed to trial. When it comes to employment at will and corrective action, it's not one or the other—it's *both*. You want to protect the at-will relationship to give your company the greatest chance of winning a summary judgment at the hearing stage, but you'll want to rely on your documented corrective action at the trial stage to prove that the individual was accorded due process and that your company had good cause to terminate.

Progressive discipline is the way a company demonstrates that is has "good cause" to terminate and is therefore a necessary part of performance management, regardless of a worker's employment-at-will status. Relying on employment at will as a sole defense (as opposed to a fallback measure) in terminating workers provides far too many employers with a false sense of security. Don't fall into this trap. Your company should never rely solely on employment at will to make wrongful termination charges magically disappear. Understanding how the two concepts are actually applied in the courtroom should help to highlight the simultaneous benefits of maintaining an employment-at-will relationship with your workers as well as the necessity for documenting subpar performance prior to termination.

38 *The Fine Art of Playing Employment Defense: Avoid "Pretaliation"*

So what does or should a solid defensive game plan for leadership look like for you as a manager in corporate America today? First and foremost, you should have a greater sense of awareness of how sophisticated workers have become in using the system against their companies. Second, acknowledge that you can't do this alone—you've got an affirmative obligation to disclose certain matters to HR, your boss, the legal department, an ombudsman, or some other compliance officer when certain facts arise that require assistance from a third party, impartial observer, and witness. Third, you need to create a record—both verbally and in writing—to ensure that the company is positioned in the best light possible should litigation later arise.

Let's assume, for this discussion, that all workers may be tempted to sue their employer at some point in their career. Statistically, one in four managers will become involved in some form of employment-related litigation during their careers, and that's an awfully high percentage, especially if you live outside of high litigation states like California or New York. Therefore, your ability to spot problem issues, escalate them appropriately, and resolve them fairly on the spot or prepare the appropriate record for litigation becomes a critical leadership attribute that, once mastered, will benefit you for the rest of your career.

Workers are sophisticated consumers, and whether they figure this out on their own or get tips from plaintiffs' attorneys coaching them on the sidelines, just waiting for the person to get fired so they could initiate litigation, it's your responsibility to spot issues and involve the appropriate internal parties to support you from the very beginning. For example, if workers seek legal counsel to complain of harassment, discrimination, or retaliation, attorneys might typically ask, "Are you aware of anyone else who's suffering under these same conditions or under that same supervisor?" They'll also ask hourly employees, "By the way, have you ever had to skip breaks or meal periods or work unauthorized overtime?" Clearly this may have nothing to do with the initial claim that brought the prospective plaintiff into their office, but as we'll see in Question 49, class action wage and hour lawsuits are on the rise because of the fees that plaintiffs' attorneys can charge.

But what if a worker is seeking legal counsel because she's afraid she's going to be fired or suspects that her boss is somehow out to get her? Workers have been known to reach out to lawyers under those circumstances where they feel vulnerable just to see if they have any legal protections, and that's where plaintiff lawyers' advice and counsel can get really interesting: "Well, I probably can't help you until the company takes some adverse action against you, like termination, but let me ask you this: Do you know who your internal HR representatives are? Have you spoken with them about your problem, and if so, what did they say?" This question seems fairly straightforward and benign, the assumption being that the employee should try to resolve the matter internally with HR before hiring an attorney to sue the company.

But there's more to this question than meets the eye: In many instances, attorneys instruct a potential plaintiff client (i.e., your employee) to initiate a "preemptive strike" against the supervisor by complaining about the supervisor's conduct *before* the supervisor has a chance to take further punitive action regarding the employee's performance. The result of such "pretaliation" is that workers who are performing poorly can potentially "reverse engineer" the record and put the company on the defensive. With that record in place, it becomes much more difficult for the company to terminate the individual because such actions may appear to be retaliation. Here's what it looks like in chronological form:

1. Employee senses she's about to be disciplined or terminated for substandard job performance reasons and reaches out to an attorney for help.

2. Attorney encourages employee to complain to HR about the supervisor's conduct, specifically using words like *hostile work environment, harassment, intimidation, bullying,* or *retaliation.*
3. Company has a more difficult time terminating the employee due to the recent harassment claim that the employee initiated against the supervisor.
4. The plaintiff's attorney wins either way: If the termination is delayed for the time being, a strong trust builds between the lawyer and the client because the attorney gave great advice that benefited the client; if the termination goes through, the attorney has another arrow in her quiver to shoot back at the company in the litigation phase in the form of retaliation.

The supervisor, of course, may be acting in good faith in disciplining the individual, only to find himself the target of an investigation from HR because of the employee's complaint.

This situation occurs again and again in corporate offices, with managers inadvertently stepping on land mines and not realizing until after the fact that a bomb went off. Here's how you'll know when this situation is at hand: HR receives a employee complaint about a manager's conduct and calls a meeting with the manager and the manager's boss. The HR person opens the meeting by saying, "Joe, we've received a complaint of harassment from one of your employees regarding how you manage them, and we need to explain the nature of the complaint and also to learn your side of the story."

The manager asks who lodged the complaint and is told it was Heidi Jones. He becomes furious and replies, "It was Heidi? You've got to be kidding! I was just about to come to HR to discuss placing her on a final written warning because she's such a poor performer. She comes in late, leaves early, and . . ."

Boom! The land mine just exploded. The employee—either on her own or under an attorney's guidance—figured out that by launching her claim first about her boss's conduct, she could turn the tables on the record that was being created. She engineered a perfect scenario for a retaliation claim later, and the manager didn't even see it coming. The lesson? Don't fall prey to a preemptive strike. When your gut tells you that there's a problem with someone's performance or you sense the person may be speaking with a lawyer, contact HR right away.

After all, whoever gets to HR first gets the ball rolling in terms of how HR conducts its investigation: If you initiate the matter with HR and focus on your subordinate's substandard *performance*, then HR moves in one direction. But if the employee meets with HR first to complain about your *conduct*, then HR moves in a different direction in terms of the investigation it conducts. Timing, it turns out, is one of the most critical elements in determining what type of record is made in many employment-related situations.

It's clear from the example above that management is no longer an individual game: it's a group sport. And you've got to know who's there to support you when a problem arises. In the past, leaders felt that they should be able to handle their own employees without anyone else's help; going to HR was like "taking a matter outside the family," and managers never wanted to see that happen. They reasoned that if they need HR's help, they're not doing their job. That's no longer the case; with preemptive strike incidents drastically on the rise, managers need to know when and how to escalate. Further, they have an *obligation* to disclose matters that they believe may ultimately result in some form of employment-related litigation. As such, your HR representative should be seen as a true business partner who can help you create the right record from the beginning. And the sooner you get to HR, the greater the chances that you'll be able to protect yourself and your company from unnecessary litigation by partnering with an internal resource that can help you establish the appropriate record.

Finally, as I stated in Chapter 3, don't manage by fear of a lawsuit. Lawsuits are part of the cost of doing business in corporate America from time to time, and managing by fear rarely has positive results. Instead, just be sure that if a lawsuit comes your way, you're getting sued on your terms rather than theirs. The most successful way to do this is to act professionally, demonstrate respect for those you supervise, and enlist the services of internal support teams (like HR) that are there to help you through these very types of situations. You'll find that a winning strategy like this will allow you to thrive in your career without any of the angst, drama, or histrionics that plague certain managers who opt to go it alone.

39   *Policies (the Letter of the Law), Codes of Conduct (the Spirit of the Law), and Past Practices*

Have you ever wondered why companies have so many documents addressing employment in the workplace? Policy and procedure manuals, employee handbooks, business conduct statements, and mission, vision, and value declarations serve different purposes, and it's important that you understand their function. What's more important, however, is to understand that *practice trumps policy*. In other words, what your company actually does with its policies is more significant in a court of law than what a handbook or policy and procedure manual says you're *supposed* to do.

Therefore, don't rely completely on what your handbook or policy and procedure manual tells you that you may do in specific instances. Generally speaking, you have to look at the totality of events involved in any given situation and at your organization's past practices. (You'll generally get that information when escalating the matter to HR or your organization's legal counsel.) For example, if a supervisor complains to you that a team member told him to "f--- off," your first reaction might be to terminate that individual, with no questions asked. But what if the manager used that very same phrase on the employee first? Would you still argue that the subordinate should be fired? Or should they both be fired? And what if everyone on the team uses that expression while kidding around with one another? Is it justifiable to take one instance in isolation and out of context and then terminate someone for gross insubordination?

The lesson is that you've got to look at how your company has handled similar situations in the past. Looking at any one event in isolation—no matter how egregious—could show that you didn't do your homework before reaching a conclusion about the case. Remember that there are two sides to every story, and acting on only one side may leave your company vulnerable and exposed when it comes time to explain the rationale behind your final decision to terminate in light of the incomplete investigation that your organization conducted, or so reasons the Equal Employment Opportunity Commission (EEOC) or the plaintiff's attorney. Again, bear in mind that the policy exists as a guideline, but it's only valuable if it is consistently enforced across the board.

Workplace policies, in comparison, are important because they prescribe how to go about dealing with particular employee challenges in the office or on the shop floor. Antidiscrimination, overtime, substance abuse, and other policies provide you with the steps necessary to successfully manage problems that arise. As a rule of thumb, though, whenever you sense yourself reaching for the employee handbook or departmental policy and procedure manual, make a quick call to HR, in-house legal counsel, or other similar resource to see how the company has handled similar situations in the past. First, you'll soon realize that you're not alone in experiencing this type of problem and that HR has probably dealt with similar situations in the past. Second, you'll get a quick overview of how your company's past practices have played themselves out so that you're not basing your decision exclusively on what the manual says you're supposed to do. Third, remember that most companies practice the "rules are meant to be broken" adage from time to time under extenuating circumstances, so a quick call to HR is in your and the company's best interests to see how closely your organization has historically followed that particular policy or standard operating procedure.

If policies outline the *letter* of the law, as your company defines it, then codes of conduct, otherwise known as corporate ethics statements, address the *spirit* of the law. Corporate ethics statements are not intended for line-by-line interpretation; instead, they're designed to cast a much broader net that speaks to worker ethics, morals, and appropriate workplace conduct. Such business conduct statements emanated from the passage of the Sarbanes-Oxley Act of 2002, or "SOX," which came out of the "tech bust" financial crisis of 2000, when publicly traded companies knowingly falsified financial statements rather than disclose the falling value of their company stock prices. And while financial compliance, internal controls, and reforms in corporate governance standards make up a majority of SOX initiatives, documented codes of ethics are also a mainstay of the Act.

To comply with the new law, publicly traded companies are required to publish a code of conduct and ethics, often referred to as a business conduct statement. This statement defines and addresses conflicts of interest that are incompatible with, or had the potential of adversely affecting, the organization's financial reporting requirements. From there, the ethics required by SOX spread naturally to other employee behaviors, including nondiscrimination, harassment, retaliation, and the like.

The point to keep in mind is that, unlike with policies, ethics statements cast a much wider net in terms of capturing employee improprieties. The old excuse, "Well, I didn't read that in the handbook" goes out the window in an environment where workers, and especially leaders, are held to much higher behavioral standards. For example, a supervisor who dates a subordinate but fails to disclose that fact could—under a typical business conduct statement—be deemed to be acting outside the course and scope of his employment and could potentially warrant immediate dismissal if the subordinate claims quid pro quo harassment: "I had to sleep with my boss if I wanted to keep my job and I had no choice. I feared retaliation if I said no, but I just can't take it any more."

Similarly, the typical code of conduct stipulates that managers have an obligation to be aware of what's going on in their purview and have an affirmative obligation to escalate and disclose perceived incidents of harassment or retaliation—even if those activities are occurring in someone else's department. Corporate leaders no longer have the discretion to say, "I'm not getting involved." If they knew, or *should have known*, what's been going on and failed to disclose it appropriately, they could be individually disciplined for their lack of discretion and failure to abide by the company's code of conduct.

Likewise, if an employee falsifies his dates of employment on a private record for his own personal benefit, it potentially speaks to character and could likewise result in an immediate dismissal from the company. Falsification of a verification of employment record for a home loan application might not be addressed specifically in a hand-book or policy and procedure manual, but depending on the cir-cumstances, the ethical misjudgment may cast enough doubt on an individual's overall morals to justify a corporate punitive action like termination, even for a first offense. In short, SOX has teeth, so learn and memorize your organization's business conduct statement and be very careful about potentially bending ethical rules.

40 Differentiating Between Performance and Conduct Issues: A Critical Distinction

Organizations typically refer to their standards of performance and conduct as a general catchall for their policies, procedures, and work-place expectations and guidelines. But there's a tremendous difference between a performance infraction and a conduct violation, and it's critical that you understand how they are treated in the workplace.

Performance infractions typically refer to substandard produc-tivity in the areas of quality, quantity, speed, customer service, and attendance/tardiness (although many companies don't include at-tendance in the broader "performance" category in their progressive disciplinary action policies). When problems occur in these areas, companies are expected to provide workplace due process as outlined in their employee handbooks and policy and procedure manuals. Spe-cifically, a progressive system of increased consequences gets docu-mented each time an additional infraction occurs, and each step contains some added element indicating the severity of the situation if it isn't remedied immediately.

After that final written warning is issued, a "clean" final incident will typically justify termination of employment. There can be excep-tions, of course. A new hire may be terminated within the first ninety days without prior written documentation or may receive one docu-mented warning just to protect the company before being dismissed. (It depends on the company's tolerance for risk: Some organizations feel that the one written warning will serve as an insurance policy of sorts to keep plaintiffs' attorneys from suing because "Did you ever receive documented corrective action before you were terminated?" is still one of the first questions that plaintiffs' attorneys ask when considering whether to take on a new case.) On the other hand, a thirty-year employee may be accorded greater workplace due process because of his years of tenure. As an example, the individual may be given a letter of clarification or a decision-making leave as incremental, additional steps that document the problems without escalating the formal corrective action chain that leads to termination.

Whatever the case, when it comes to performance and attendance infractions, the general expectation is that the company follows its policies and accords workplace due process in the form of progressive corrective action notices so that the worker understands what the problem is, what he needs to do to fix the problem, and what the consequences will be if he fails to demonstrate improvement within a reasonable period of time.

Not so with conduct infractions: Conduct infractions may lead to immediate dismissal even for a first offense where there is no prior corrective action on record. And even if a company opts not to terminate on a first offense, the organization may arguably proceed straight to a final written warning and stop just shy of termination—even for a first offense.

If an employee engages in theft, he would be terminated, even if it is a first offense. In such cases, the issue drives the outcome, meaning that the company doesn't have the discretion not to terminate (even if it wanted to). It simply has to terminate for the sake of the record that's being created and in order to avoid creating an unwanted precedent. After all, if you don't terminate one employee for stealing, how could you justify terminating another employee at some point in the future without looking like a discriminatory employer? The same goes for embezzlement, fraud, egregious cases of sexual harassment, and the like.

This makes sense. If someone stole from the company, he should expect to be fired, so you, as the manager, probably wouldn't have too much trouble justifying termination for someone on your team who took cash out of the till. But what about someone who demonstrates disrespect or contempt for his supervisor or coworkers? What about someone who constantly demonstrates a "bad attitude" and has a

detrimental effect on workplace camaraderie and departmental morale? Many employees mistakenly assume—as do their supervisors—
that as long as their performance is acceptable, the company can't do
anything to them to address their poor conduct.

Not so! That's a very serious mistaken assumption on the employee's part, and a key blind spot for supervisors who don't realize
they have discretion to escalate through the progressive discipline
process to address the problem. All employees are responsible for
both their performance and conduct; they don't simply get to focus on
one and not the other. Everyone is responsible for performing at an
acceptable level *and* ensuring that their coworkers feel welcome and
comfortable working with them.

Therefore, think of the performance and conduct as two halves
of the same whole. You can't have one without the other, and when an
investigation reveals that someone is bullying, confrontational, condescending, or otherwise vexing to his supervisor and teammates, remember that you have the discretion to move straight to a final written
warning—even for a first offense, if necessary. Again, supervisors
often have a lot more discretion than they think and should never feel
that they're being held hostage by good performers who otherwise
conduct themselves poorly.

In fact, you can explain this simple conduct rule to employees on
the back of a napkin: Draw a circle, put a line through its center, and
write "Performance" in the top of half of the circle and "Conduct" in
the bottom half. Explain that while their performance isn't an issue
(i.e., the top half of the circle), the bottom of the circle—their conduct—
remains a challenge. And until that's fixed, they're only operating at
fifty percent, which is a failing grade since they're only meeting half
of their overall expectations. Such a simple visual can go a long way
in pointing out a problem and resetting expectations.

41 *Sameness Versus Consistency: Looking at the Totality of Events*

Supervisors and managers often make the mistake of assuming that
everyone has to be treated exactly the same when, in fact, it's *consistency* they're looking for. They have more discretion in many circum-

stances than they realize, and simply trying to treat every infraction exactly the same misses the point. Let's look at an example.

Sleeping on the job is a serious infraction in any situation. But does it warrant a first written warning, a final written warning, or outright termination? As with many workplace investigations and employee relations issues, it depends. Has the individual who was caught sleeping at his desk done this before? How long was he asleep? Did his falling asleep cause some negative organizational impact that warrants an immediate termination, on the one hand, or little if any corrective action at all, on the other?

Don't look only at the issue of sleeping: it's also about the conditions and circumstances surrounding the act of sleeping that play an important role in rendering an appropriate decision. Here's how companies have ruled in the past:

1. An insurance claims adjustor caught napping at her desk received a *first written warning* for inappropriate workplace conduct.
2. A charge nurse on the night shift of a hospital's intensive care unit caught sleeping at the nurses' station console was issued a *final written warning*—even though it was a first offense—since patients' safety may have been jeopardized.
3. An anesthesiologist who fell asleep during surgery was *terminated* outright, because the patient's life was endangered by his actions.

As you can see, it's not the sleeping per se that drives the outcome: it's the circumstances surrounding the sleeping that must be considered, and the potential negative organizational consequences typically drive the employer's decision to act in a certain way. So the company in the first incident acted appropriately when it issued a written warning to the claims adjuster. Similarly, issuing a final written warning to the charge nurse in the second incident, and immediately dismissing the anesthesiologist in the third incident were appropriate under the circumstances. Therefore, the sleeping issue in and of itself doesn't drive the company's response: it's the circumstances surrounding the employee's sleeping at work that does.

One size doesn't fit all in the world of workplace investigations and employee relations, so remember to look at the totality of events rather than at isolated behavioral acts. As always, the best way to determine what an appropriate company response should be comes from speaking with HR, the legal department, or the department in your organization that deals with employee issues. Just remember that there may be more to this than meets the eye. Ask employees for their side of the story before rushing to judgment, and get the appropriate internal support before making a termination decision.

42 *Stopping Attitude Problems in Their Tracks*

It is frustrating when certain workers on your team intentionally withhold their best efforts or otherwise work against you by influencing their coworkers to hold back or by instigating negativity and distrust. You need to address this situation swiftly and wisely. When substandard job performers also become bullies, it is time to establish the appropriate written record and verbal communication trail to focus on that individual's performance and conduct problems and eliminate his or her negative influence.

How do you know when you're dealing with bullies who may be launching preemptive strikes to divert attention from their substandard job performance? There are certain signs to look for: Sometimes a loud brash personality dictates "who's really in charge around here" and intimidates others or publicly humiliates them. At other times the threats are veiled, as when individuals imply that they have an attorney or may be otherwise keeping track of any offenses against them in a notebook. And sometimes it's more of a group effort: several senior people on your team appear burned out and constantly frustrated, spewing their discontent openly with anyone who will listen.

Where does that leave you, the organizational leader, in terms of creating a friendly work environment for the team members? Doesn't everyone on the team have a right to work without fear of being sued? And why should it be that everyone on the team has to feel intimidated by this one individual's unwillingness to work cooperatively? When these types of issues arise, it's critical that you take control of the situation, and the most important way of doing that is by revamping the written record in favor of the company.

When dealing with employees who have a negative attitude, your intervention needs to be swift and definitive, so as to deter your good employees from resigning. You'll want to enlist the services of your HR department (or an objective third party if you don't have an HR department) to conduct an impartial investigation and gather the whole team's feedback. Assuming everyone seems to get along fine with one another except for this one individual, who threatens to sue or otherwise aggressively confronts others who might challenge her, then you've got an excellent opportunity to meet with the individual in a private setting (with the HR investigator) and outline the feedback you received in very objective terms. You don't need to name names in terms of who said what, but you could simply share specific feedback without assigning attribution.

Acknowledge that there are two sides to every story, of course, and explain that you'd like to hear this individual's side of the story as well, but based on the feedback that the investigator received, there's clearly a breakdown in *perception*: "Perception isn't right or wrong, it just is. And right now it appears that you have a serious perception problem on your hands because all fingers are pointing to you. My initial question to you is, Does anything that HR heard from the others on the team appear to warrant merit? Can you see why others may feel that way when working with you?"

Perception is a powerful word to use under circumstances like these, especially when dealing with he-said, she-said issues or with facts and circumstances that are open to interpretation. Perception is reality until proven otherwise, but it's not about judgment: It's about observation because you're simply relaying feedback and facts. And when people feel that they're not being judged and are simply being engaged as adults to participate in solving a problem—even if it's their own problem—they're more likely to listen openly and not feel defensive.

Assuming the individual will acknowledge at least partial responsibility for the problem at hand (as most will if the informational findings are shared appropriately), you can move forward with this

intervention as planned. Of course, if the individual denies all culpa-
bility despite all fingers being pointed at her from the group, you'll
want to adjust your approach as outlined below. Now is the time to
reset expectations in this private setting so that the individual has a
chance to reinvent herself and start over. You might want to try a discussion like this:

> First, you're no longer allowed to threaten coworkers with a lawsuit. While you
> have every right to file a lawsuit against anyone you want at any time, you're
> not to threaten anyone because you may be creating a hostile work environ-
> ment, which violates company policy.
>
> Second, you're not allowed to carry around your "little black book" that others
> have come to understand as a record you're keeping against them should you
> ever choose to sue them in the future. You can keep a book like that if you
> want, but you're not allowed to show it to others or keep it out in the open
> where others can see it. That may be creating a hostile work environment, and
> we can't allow employees to engage in such conduct.
>
> Third, as a result of the ongoing behavioral concerns we've learned of, you'll be
> receiving corrective action in the form of a final written warning for what we
> consider egregious misconduct. This is serious and your position will be in
> immediate jeopardy if any type of behavior or conduct like this occurs again.
>
> Finally, I want to hold a group meeting tomorrow to reset expectations re-
> garding how we treat each other, how to escalate complaints and use internal
> resources appropriately—whether that's HR or our department or division
> head—should this type of behavior occur in the future from anyone on the
> team. I want you to be part of that meeting and support this new turn in direc-
> tion from this point forward.
>
> If there's anything you need that will help you be more successful in this role,
> let me know. But right now all fingers are pointing to you, Michelle, and I'm
> planning on treating you respectfully and holding you fully accountable for
> your own perception management. Does that sound like a fair approach, and
> do you have any questions or recommendations at this point?
>
> [Yes.]

With that problematic individual's advanced buy-in, you're now at
liberty to address the entire team. You can reset your expectations verbally with the group and allow the healing process to begin. You're
no longer going to be held hostage because you've got the right disciplinary record in place regarding Michelle's behavior and you've reset
verbal expectations for the rest of the group.

In my experience, the outcome of these types of interventions is that the team feels re-energized, satisfied, and motivated because the matter is being proactively acknowledged and addressed. The bullying employee or negative influencer often behaves for several months and then quietly resigns once she's found other employment. And that's okay: Some people really do thrive on drama and chaos, and once you've taken the wind out of their sails, they'll likely want to pursue opportunities elsewhere. The victory, however, lies in the fact that you've addressed the matter constructively and confidently and avoided potential turnover and even lawsuits. "Let them be successful elsewhere" is a healthy strategic approach toward workers who opt not to participate in your team's newfound success.

43 *Performance Appraisal Bombshells: Delivering Bad News for the First Time During the Annual Performance Review*

One of the biggest mistakes that managers at all levels make is inflating annual performance reviews. To minimize hard feelings in the office, many managers give "meets expectations" scores to underachievers or workers with poor behavior records. But that score will most likely preclude terminating the employee for cause, should the need arise.

Why so? Well, as a supervisor and leader in your company, you'll have created a written record for one or more years documenting that the employee's overall performance was acceptable. With no other progressive disciplinary documentation on file to break that chain of positive performance evaluations, you likely won't be able to demonstrate cause should you be sued for wrongful termination. Therefore, as a general rule, if you expect to terminate someone in the upcoming year, only give a performance review with a final grade of "does not meet expectations." That baseline foundational review will very likely provide you with a lot more discretion to terminate at some point in the future.

And don't make the mistake that too many managers make in the performance review process. They give one employee on the team lower *relative* scores in individual performance categories than everyone else. Still, if the *overall score* at the very end of the review states that the individual "meets expectations," then employees have little reason to believe that their employment is in serious jeopardy of being lost (or so argue their attorneys). This isn't a game of relativity; it's a game of absolutes. It's not how employees rank relative to their peers; it's the final grade at the end of the review that counts.

When you suspect that substandard job performance or inappropriate workplace conduct may preclude a long-term employment relationship with an employee of yours, call in HR as soon as possible. Many HR departments will have the resources to help you construct an annual performance review or progressive disciplinary warning that documents substandard work. HR can also help you document a performance improvement plan, the company's expectations, and "consequence" language that is clear and incontestable in its intent. In certain cases, HR will also be able to coach the employee or offer outside training services that help your company demonstrate its willingness to rehabilitate flagging performers.

Documenting new, negative information at the time of the annual review should always be the exception, not the rule, because you don't want your employees to feel blindsided at the time they receive their annual feedback, merit increase, and bonus. But sometimes you'll have to share negative information for the first time at the annual review. When that's the case, be sure to assume responsibility for your shortcoming as a leader in not sharing this negative feedback earlier. Here's what it might sound like both verbally and on paper:

> Roger, I recognize that we haven't formally discussed over the past year the problems you have in getting along with the other team members, but I felt it appropriate to bring this issue to your attention during the annual performance review because it's so serious and such a critical aspect of your overall contribution to the department. In fact, it could have a significant impact on your career potential if it's left unaddressed.
>
> I also owe you an apology: I realize that I should have shared this with you at the time these incidents occurred, but I was guilty of avoiding the confrontation myself and hoping the problem would simply fix itself, and that wasn't fair to you. That being said, I can't avoid the issue any longer. This performance review window is the ideal place to discuss my concerns—even though I realize that you may feel blindsided by my doing so.

Specifically, I believe you're suffering from a perception management problem: Regardless of your intentions, people tend to avoid you. You come across as being angry much of the time, confrontational, and condescending, and other team members—myself included—tend to cut a wide swath around you and do the work themselves rather than come to you for help. That's damaging the overall morale and camaraderie in our department, Roger, and you're responsible for creating a friendly and inclusive work environment, just like I am and everyone else on our team is. In short, your behavior is negating your overall performance contributions.

I'll make a commitment to you now to bring these matters to your attention immediately whenever I notice them in the future, but my main message to you in this performance review is that you're not meeting company expectations overall because of this significant detriment. Again, I apologize for not addressing the matter on the spot in the past, and I'll commit to you that I'll bring this to your attention whenever I see it from now on. But it's significant enough to formally document now and to reset expectations going forward.

Remember that annual performance reviews carry an awful lot of weight in the eyes of the law. Disciplinary measures aside, if you pass someone with an overall score of "meeting expectations," you'll end up validating their entire year's performance—despite any documented corrective action that you may have issued during the performance year. And when it comes to making a clean record of workers being accorded due process, your corrective action documentation and your annual performance review must be in sync. Remember, it's all about alignment of the overall documented performance record, and in areas where employees received mixed messages—for example, where acceptable performance reviews follow final written warnings—any ambiguity will be interpreted against you in court. Avoid this very common mistake to remain two steps ahead of the game in terms of evading litigation land mines.

44   *"If I Can't Fire Someone, Can I Lay Him Off Instead?"*

Managers who want to avoid the confrontation associated with progressive discipline and termination often opt for a no-fault layoff because it seems to provide a quicker solution to ending employment. However, there are certain guidelines that you will need to follow when considering a layoff. Specifically, you'll need to consider how long you'll have to wait before you can refill the position, and what could happen if you were legally challenged for having improperly laid someone off.

First, keep in mind that you eliminate positions, not people. In other words, your written records must reflect that a position needs to be eliminated because of a lack of work or other financial constraints, and the individual who currently fills that position will now be impacted because there's no longer a job to report to. If removing a problem performer is your goal, then eliminating that individual's job may be a big mistake. After all, you'll still need to get the work done.

Second, it can be difficult to determine which employee should be separated once you've established that there is a legitimate business need to eliminate a position. Remember, you can't arbitrarily select someone for a layoff simply because she is your weakest performer or because she happens to be sitting in the seat that's being eliminated. Instead, you must identify the least qualified person in that classification or role to assume the remaining duties. The least qualified person on paper, however, may end up being your best (albeit newest) performer.

Let's look at an example to clarify these concepts. Let's say you're looking to eliminate one of three secretarial positions in your marketing department. Since there are three individuals that currently fill the role of administrative assistant in marketing, you've now got a selection pool to choose from, and your company will be required to conduct a "peer group analysis" to see which of the three current individuals is the least qualified to assume the remaining job responsibilities once the position is eliminated.

To do so, first develop a list of all employees in that group with similar titles or responsibilities. This would include the three administrative assistants in marketing but might also include an office manager, an administrative specialist, an office coordinator, or even other administrative assistants outside of marketing. Second, review the nature of the remaining work to be done after the position is eliminated. For example, if the secretarial position that supports market research is being considered for elimination, then document the responsibilities that will remain in the unit after the reduction in force. (Job descriptions can be very helpful for such comparisons.) In this case, answering a heavy volume of phone calls, coordinating travel arrangements, supporting data collection, and developing PowerPoint presentations that focus on new products may be the key tasks left to be done after the reduction in force.

Third, determine which of the three secretaries in marketing is the least qualified to assume these remaining duties. In essence, you'll be comparing all three employees' essential job responsibilities, skills, knowledge, and abilities. In addition, consider the employees' annual performance reviews, tenure, and history of progressive discipline in creating an appropriate written record. It would also make sense to review their work experience prior to joining your organization so that tenure alone doesn't outweigh other considerations.

Finally, once you have documented the comparison of the three employees who could potentially qualify to perform the remaining work, then it's time to determine who is the least qualified individual. If that individual is the person you originally targeted for the layoff because of her ongoing performance problems, then it may be safe to end her employment. But it's rare that it works out that way. It's more often the case that the underperforming employee is arguably not the least qualified individual (based on your review of all relevant criteria, including performance evaluations and other written records). Since your records don't support separating the problematic employee in question, then you'd have to lay off one of the other two secretaries. Of course, that would mean that a layoff would no longer be a viable alternative for you since you can't use it to separate the one administrative assistant who's causing all the problems. Therefore, you'd have to revert to managing that individual's performance via documented progressive discipline.

It's a bit different if the person you select for layoff is in an individual contributor role where there is no comparison pool. In such cases, the layoff option would likely be easier to justify, especially in the case of straightforward position elimination. However, if you are *repurposing* the job (for example, downgrading from director to manager or focusing on, say, government affairs rather than community relations for a public relations director), then you may want to permit the laid off individual to apply for the new role. Check with HR or with legal counsel to determine if permitting the impacted individual to apply for the repurposed role might be a wiser strategy or make for a better record than not allowing the individual to apply.

There is yet another key consideration when determining if a layoff is the appropriate employer action when dealing with underperforming employees. Courts and juries have certain expectations about employers' responsibilities when eliminating positions and laying off workers. The logic is simply this: If a company has a legitimate business reason to eliminate a position, then it probably shouldn't have a need to re-create that position in the near future. If the company were to do that, it could appear to a judge or jury that the company's original action was a pretext. In other words, the court could be persuaded that the so-called "layoff" was really a termination for cause in disguise. This could damage the company's credibility during litigation.

How long does the position need to remain unfilled? That depends on state law. There is usually a one- or two-year statute of limitations on wrongful termination claims, so filling that position in less time becomes legally risky unless you have a legal release from the ex-worker that precludes a lawsuit for wrongful termination. What if an employer were willing to gamble and fill the position after, say, six months? Well, if the ex-employee learned that his previous position was filled and he then engaged the services of an attorney to pursue the matter, the damages sought would be similar to those in a wrongful termination claim. If you were held to a for-cause standard of termination, you could be burdened with providing documentation to show that you had reason to terminate the employee because of substandard job performance, inappropriate workplace conduct, or excessive absenteeism. And that's not an easy threshold to meet if you laid off someone who has no corrective action on file.

As a result, an out-of-court settlement would probably need to be reached. Damages could include reimbursement for lost wages, compensation for emotional distress, attorneys' fees, and, in egregious cases of employer misconduct, punitive damages. Thus, progressive discipline is the optimal way to deal with substandard job performance or inappropriate workplace behavior. A layoff may seem easier to implement, but it could leave your company vulnerable to litigation. So don't look at the layoff option as an easy way out. While it may indeed be viable under certain circumstances, it tends to be an undisciplined way of conducting business and exercising leadership because it short cuts the due process system.

If there's a performance issue with an employee, address it. Don't tiptoe around it by trying to lay the person off after eliminating his position. It may have initial appeal because it appears to be a tidy and efficient way of separating someone from the company, but you owe your employees more than that. Hold yourself to the highest leadership standards and address critical performance or conduct issues head on. That's how the system was designed, and it's what great leaders do when faced with adverse employee performance situations. It's also healthier for your organization overall because it's honest and transparent, and employees respect their companies more when they feel that matters are treated above board, especially in difficult situations like these.

45 "If I Can't Fire Someone, Can I Give Him a Separation Package Instead?"

"Separation packages" typically mimic severance packages in terms of the structure of the offer—two weeks of pay for each full year of service, for example. However, with a separation package, there's no position elimination involved. Instead, the company simply opts to give a separation package to an employee to entice the individual to leave the company. A release is signed, and the company is held harmless to move forward with hiring someone else for the position.

It sounds like a tidy solution, but much like the layoff option, it poses a number of challenges that aren't necessarily evident at the outset. First, let's assume you've got a director of finance who continues to have ongoing performance problems. A recent error was so significant that it had to be escalated all the way to the CEO, causing embarrassment to both the vice president of finance and the chief financial officer. These executives then make their way to HR to request a "package" to move this individual out of the organization, since the proverbial straw has now been broken on the camel's back.

Unfortunately, HR soon discovers that none of the problematic performance issues were brought to the director's attention over the past five years since he joined the company. Performance review scores met or exceeded expectations, and no corrective action was to be found on file. The request to separate the individual now with a separation package therefore poses two significant challenges for the HR team:

1. What if the employee refuses to accept your offer?

   If your company offers three months of lump-sum salary in exchange for his signing a release, for example, and he demands six months, you'll be betting against yourself. Since you have no leverage in this negotiation other than an intense desire to have the person leave, you have little choice but to meet his demands for a six-month separation package if you want him to sign and go.

2. What if the company threatens to fire the individual if he doesn't accept the release package?

   You certainly have the discretion to make it a take-it-or-leave-it offer, threatening termination if the employee doesn't accept the package and sign the release. However, many sophisticated consumers will reach out to an attorney to find out if the "deal" you're offering is better than what they could get in litigation. And if the attorney senses that there is a potential case not only for wrongful termination but also for other causes of action like harassment and discrimination that carry punitive damage potential, then you may find yourself in court with little if any defense. (After all, you won't be able to demonstrate cause for the separation.)

As far as the finance director is concerned at this point, either he gets six months or he won't sign the release agreement. And now you're in a quandary because he's holding all the cards and you need that release agreement to avoid some form of post-termination legal action. Since you can't know upfront whether someone will sign a release according to the initial terms that you've outlined, this may not be an optimal strategy.

Further, if he refuses to sign and you opt not to terminate at that point, you've now "showed your hand" and revealed your intention to remove the individual from the workplace. Therefore, as soon as you take legitimate action steps to document the director's substandard performance in the future, your actions will likely be interpreted as retaliation by an attorney who could argue, "Once he didn't voluntarily accept your severance package, you made up reasons to terminate him for cause." You can logically expect the attorney to argue that reasons for your progressive discipline were either based on pretext or were downright bogus.

Yet there's a practical solution here as well: Don't begin separation negotiations or offer any type of separation package without having leverage in the game. And you guessed it—that leverage comes in the form of documented corrective action that places the individual's job at risk. Here's what it might look like in reality: Depending on the nature of the infraction above, a significant performance error may result in a written or even final written warning (especially if it included negligence or exceptional carelessness on the executive's part). Assuming you opt to issue a written warning for the recent infraction, you can have the following "negotiation" discussion with the individual:

> Pete, this issue is serious, and something on par in significance with this in the future could result in your receiving a final written warning or even being terminated outright. I know that's not what you want to have on your record, whether you remain with the organization or look elsewhere. You've worked too hard over the past five years to get to a point where your job could be in jeopardy, and it may make sense to look at some options.
>
> I just want to make sure that you've got some choices and flexibility at this point, but make no mistake—this is strictly up to you. I'll need to prepare the written warning on my end, but this could have just as easily been a final written warning. There was some significant debate about the level of corrective action in light of the severity of the issue. If you want me to look into some sort of separation package for you, I can do that. I can't make any promises,

of course, but if that would help you transition out of the organization with your head held high and your dignity and self-respect in tact, then it may be something that I could convince senior leadership to consider.

I'll only go ahead and ask about that if you want me to, and I know they don't do this frequently, but I'm guessing I could ask for a three-month separation package in exchange for your signing a release. You can sleep on it and let me know what you think, but just make sure you're looking at this clearly so you're making the right overall career move for yourself in light of these recent challenges. I'm here to discuss this whenever you're ready, so can you get back to me by the end of the week?

[Yes]

The beauty of this negotiation is two-fold: First, the pending written warning serves as a leverage point because the finance director realizes that his job may be in jeopardy. Second, you've now set up the negotiation so that *he's asking you* for the package, and you're offering to look into it to help him. No guarantees and no promises, but you now have him asking for your help because it's for his own good. And even if he doesn't want to pursue the package option right now, you'll have quietly established that escape option should the need arise in the future.

No, this won't provide you with the ultimate solution you were hoping for: separating the individual immediately. But you also have to assume partial responsibility for not necessarily having managed the situation appropriately in the past. After all, if Pete is such a problematic performer that you wish he would simply disappear from the workplace, there were likely opportunities in the past where you could have documented those issues formally on performance reviews or in the form of corrective action warnings.

As in all successful negotiations, the transaction must be a win-win for both sides. But you've got to have some form of leverage to rely on. Corrective action documentation will save you every time—whether it comes to justifying who gets laid off when a position gets eliminated or how to leverage a separation package if need be. Keep your documentation tight and avoid recommendations that attempt to make people magically disappear overnight. Those typically won't work because you have very little control of the outcome, and you won't want to expose your organization to unnecessary liability under circumstances that are otherwise within your control. Besides, you owe your people more than that.

46 *Whistle Blowers Versus Character Assassins: Dealing Appropriately with Anonymous and Mean-Spirited Employee Complaints That May Lack Merit*

Most companies grant their employees the discretion to escalate matters anonymously, and well they should. Whether the company is publicly traded (i.e., where a SOX code of ethics is required) or privately held, organizations want employees to have immediate and direct access to senior leadership, often including the board of directors or heads of the organization in most instances. After all, if the company isn't aware of a problem because an employee doesn't know how to escalate a claim and bring it senior management's attention, then the C-level (e.g., CEOs, CFOs, and COOs) won't learn of a problem until it's potentially too late. That's why many privately held companies ascribe to the code of conduct mantra, even though they're not legally required to. It just makes good business sense.

But there can be a downside to such openness and transparency. Allowing employees to complain about managers and supervisors anonymously may inadvertently open a Pandora's box of unfounded allegations that allows workers to engage in character assassination with apparent impunity. Likewise, because employees have become savvy about the whistleblower protections contained in many companies' written policies, they have figured out that engaging in the proverbial preemptive strike—"I'll complain about my boss's *conduct* before she has a chance to complain about my job *performance*"—can provide them with a cloak of protection in the form of a retaliation charge against the company should the organization later come back and attempt to dismiss, lay off, or otherwise discipline them after filing a complaint.

So how do you, as a responsible corporate leader, handle it when you suspect that the nameless voice behind an anonymous complaint is actually engaging in character assassination against a targeted supervisor? How do you appropriately respond to an unknown member of your team who is spouting unfounded rumors and gossip? It's a fine line between the individual privacy rights of complainants and mean-spirited slander toward the alleged wrongdoer (often the supervisor). This fine line places every department head and HR executive in an ethical quandary and places the company in a compromising legal position. Attacking workplace problems like this directly and appropriately poses exceptional challenges to even the strongest companies and most confident leaders alike, so an approach that combines both legal guidance and common sense will work best.

For instance, a workplace escalation matter that alleges that someone is engaging in embezzlement of company funds or timecard fraud is fairly simple to investigate and verify. But what about an anonymous letter that alleges that Supervisor X is sleeping with his subordinate? And what if that anonymous complaint appears in the ombudsman's mailbox at the same time that the supervisor's wife receives an anonymous text message alleging that her husband is sleeping with that same subordinate? That's when things can get ugly and personal, and the targeted supervisor will often feel he's being attacked at work at the same time that he's attempting desperately to repair his relationship with his wife. It's a classic situation of the gun being pointed at the employer's head from two different directions—from the anonymous complainant who may be alleging discrimination, harassment, and potential retaliation and from the supervisor who's threatening a defamation lawsuit.

To resolve these types of character assassination attempts, first ask the anonymous complainant (who typically makes the company aware of the problem via email from a made-up address) to make himself known so that you can work on finding a solution together. If that doesn't work, follow up by asking who should be interviewed to verify the allegations. At the initial stage of the investigation, the anonymous complainant is clearly calling the shots, but your attempt to involve the person is both the right thing to do and the most practical solution from a legal standpoint.

What happens next depends on your initial findings. If you can identify little if any corroborating evidence to substantiate the initial anonymous complaint, it might make the most sense to conclude the investigation quietly. Notify the complainant via the same email address that was used to initiate the complaint that you've completed an initial investigation and can't find merit to the claim, so after checking with the HR, Legal, and Operations departments, you're opting to conclude the investigation with a "no findings call." That is, unless the individual opts to emerge from the shadows and provide you with additional information.

But even if you're unable to corroborate or find any merit to claims that attack someone's character, it's important that you address the matter, take appropriate action, and close the loop—both for the sake of the legal record and for the employees' right to know. As is often the case in these types investigations, the claims raised can be exaggerated, taken out of context, or appear to assign some form of ill intent to the supervisor's actions when there was none. When a claim appears to have little if any merit, don't ignore it once you've concluded your investigation and found no merit. It makes more sense to address the matter openly so that it can be resolved.

Consider addressing the matter as follows: First, ask in-house or outside counsel for legal advice in phrasing your findings and your conclusion. Second, ensure that the wronged supervisor supports your intentions of addressing the matter openly with the rest of the team in the supervisor's presence. You could then set the stage for a group "investigational wrap-up" meeting with HR and a member of the senior leadership team present as follows:

> While I'm not planning on going into detail about the investigation that HR has been conducting for the past two days, I want you all to know that we've fulfilled our commitment as a responsible employer to conduct a thorough investigation in a timely manner and to reach a reasonable conclusion.
>
> However, I'm not comfortable just closing out this investigation without addressing the issue. We don't know who filed the original allegation, and that's

fine. But I want to remind you all that real damage can be done to someone's career and personal life when anonymous complaints are made behind the scenes with apparent impunity.

I'm very disappointed in how this matter was escalated: The allegations appear to have been grossly exaggerated, the witnesses couldn't support the allegations, and this felt like a very personal attack against John. In addition, I've invited the anonymous complainant multiple times to disclose him- or herself and work with me and with HR to get to provide more details, but to no avail: the anonymous complainant did not come forward. What he or she said about John was unjustified and mean spirited, which is why I invited John to this meeting. John, I want to apologize to you on behalf of the team for what occurred here. I think you deserve to hear that publicly, and I'm very sorry.

As for the rest of the team, if you have legitimate issues and concerns, feel free to raise them openly or file your complaints anonymously—but please remember that there are real people whose careers may be placed at risk, and I expect you all to act in a more responsible manner in the future. This investigation is officially concluded. But I have higher expectations of you as a team than you've displayed here, and I hope you all take the time to consider how this might have felt to John and other members of the team.

With this public apology to the wronged supervisor in place and an opportunity to reset group expectations, you stand the greatest chance of healing the wound while enforcing your company's escalation policy and whistleblower protections. Addressing the matter openly and honestly will provide a healing touch that will go a long way in preventing future mean-spirited and anonymous attacks while allowing your team to rebuild fractured relationships and reinstitute a healthy sense of camaraderie.

47 *Vetting the Record Before Recommending Termination: The Importance of a "Clean Final Incident"*

Terminating an employee is necessary occasionally. Before doing so, make sure that you're accounting for the key issues that any plaintiff's attorney will consider in evaluating a case and determining whether to bring suit against your organization. In terms of the individual being considered for termination, review the following before recommending any termination action:

Termination Checklist

- Date of hire
- Length of tenure
- Age (there are key protections for employees of ages 40 and above)
- Ethnicity
- Gender
- Corrective action history
- Most recent performance review score and overall performance review history
- Open workers' compensation claim(s)
- Open intermittent Family and Medical Leave Act (FMLA) claim(s)
- Disability status: for example, is the company currently engaging in the Americans with Disabilities Act (ADA) "interactive process" with this individual or otherwise granting some form of protected leave or reasonable accommodation?
- Pregnancy
- Possibility of a retaliation charge for having lodged a good faith complaint against the organization ("whistleblower" protection)
- Supervisor's age, ethnicity, and gender (to counter any potential claims of discrimination)
- How long has the supervisor managed this employee?
- Did the supervisor originally hire the employee? (If so, a discrimination claim may be more difficult to prove)
- Specifics regarding the final / most recent incident that could justify termination

---

Armed with this short list of guidelines to practical workplace investigations, you can then objectively determine whether a "clean final incident" justifies a termination for cause. The nature of the final incident that triggers termination is exceptionally important. The more specific and concrete the violation, the stronger the justification to terminate. For example, if the newest incident clearly violates the terms of a final written warning, you should be safe to terminate. Similarly, if the incident stems from some form of egregious misconduct like theft, embezzlement, or fraud, you should likewise be safe to terminate as a "summary offense" (meaning that no prior corrective action is warranted because the one-time occurrence justifies outright dismissal).

In comparison, avoid *de minimis* (i.e., minimal) final incidents that could appear insubstantial or otherwise appear to lack objectivity. For example, if the record you're relying on to justify a termination appears as if you were looking for a reason to fire the person, then your credibility could be challenged. So could the validity of your decision to terminate the individual. The best yardstick: Ask yourself, "If one of our best employees engaged in a similar infraction, would discipline be warranted?" If the answer is no, then the final incident may not be substantial enough to warrant dismissal. But if the answer is yes, you can feel more confident that you're being consistent in the application of your own rules and that the termination decision will withstand legal scrutiny. When in doubt, check with qualified legal counsel. With HR's or your attorney's review and approval, you'll be much better prepared to address exceptional situations not only with the confidence that comes from knowledge but also with the wisdom that comes from experience.

48 *Don't Rush to Judgment: Learn All Sides of the Story First*

Line managers often mistakenly insist that a termination decision be made without asking for the accused person's input: "It doesn't matter what they say—there's nothing they can say to undo the damage that was done" goes their logic. And that may be true—but you won't know until you ask.

Let's assume it was reported that $200 in cash was missing from the petty cash drawer. The video camera footage shows that the branch manager took this money last night at the close of his shift. Should you terminate at that point strictly based on the video footage? While taking money without authorization is tantamount to theft, and theft is a "summary offense" (meaning that it's not subject to corrective action—termination for a first offense is warranted), you have an obligation to hear the individual's side of the story. What if the employee admits it and states that his regional manager gave him prior authorization to take the cash to buy office supplies? Would that be a terminable offense? What if the employee admits that he took the funds but states that he only needed it overnight to buy milk and sundry items for his newborn baby? In fact, he put an I.O.U. note in the safe stating that if anyone opened the safe that night, there would be $200 missing that he would return promptly in the morning before the branch opens. Is that a terminable offense?

The point is, you can't know if there were any extenuating circumstances unless and until you ask. Even if the individual in the example above left an I.O.U. note, you would probably still move to termination. But at least you'd have a better understanding of his motives and would be more informed about your recommendation. In short, you should always learn both sides of the story before moving to termination. That's a fundamental element of workplace due process, and it's a fair and objective practice that doesn't limit your discretion in any way; it simply helps you make more well-informed decisions and maintain positive employee relations while protecting your company legally.

49 *Wage and Hour Quagmires: Employee Classification and Overtime Considerations*

No discussion of litigation land mines in the workplace would be complete without addressing wage and hour challenges. Managing overtime properly can be quite a daunting task for managers who may not be aware of some of the intricacies and traps that await them on this issue. There are a number of interesting twists and turns in this particular area of employment law, and you can't be armed well enough in terms of protecting your company from wage and hour liability because of its class action potential.

Exemption status will always be your first hurdle. It's your company's responsibility to pay overtime to nonexempt workers for hours worked in excess of forty a week (or in some states like California, in excess of eight hours a day), and it all begins with classifying your employees properly. Most companies don't have any problems identifying their CEOs and vice presidents as "exempt" from the protections of the Fair Labor Standards Act (FLSA) of 1938, which established overtime during the Great Depression as a penalty to employers for "stretching out" their existing clerical or manufacturing workforce and not adding new employees to the payroll. Employers understand that clerks, receptionists, and laborers are indeed nonexempt. In other words, they're paid for their time, protected by the FLSA, and docked when they come in late but paid overtime for hours worked in excess of forty a week.

But where this gets dicey is with "wobbler" job categories like coordinators, analysts, specialists, and administrators (and, in some cases, assistant managers). Some companies classify these paraprofessional and junior management positions upward into the exempt category, while others place them downward into the nonexempt, overtime-eligible category. The decision is up to you and your company, but just understand that if you're ever audited, the government will expect you to pay overtime whenever there is any doubt as to an employee's classification.

If you choose not to pay overtime and instead opt to classify these wobblers upward into the exempt category, then the burden will be on you and your company to prove or otherwise demonstrate that they're indeed exempt from overtime pay. And if you're wrong, you could end up with a massive back wages tab on your hands that governs the entire class of workers. Remember, all else being equal, the government wants companies to pay overtime whenever possible so that workers aren't exploited or otherwise denied the additional overtime pay.

In terms of paying overtime correctly, it's important to understand that overtime premiums must be paid for all overtime worked, including unapproved overtime. In fact, you're allowed to discipline an employee for working unapproved overtime, but you're not allowed to withhold the overtime pay. That would be a classic wage and hour violation.

Reciprocally, you have the right to instruct employees to work overtime as the workload demands. That's a basic right of any supervisor, and employees who fail to make themselves available could likewise be in violation of workplace conduct standards. Of course, before proceeding to disciplining someone formally for insubordination (i.e., failure to follow a reasonable workplace directive), be sure to look at more practical issues like the reasonability of your request, the amount of notice you've given the employee, and how you would treat any and all similarly situated employees under the same circumstances. This will avoid perceptions of favoritism, bias, and potentially discrimination in the workplace.

The problem with wage and hour violations is that they lend themselves to class-action lawsuits. In fact, plaintiffs' attorneys often question prospective nonexempt clients who come in looking for representation to pursue discrimination and wrongful termination claims to see whether they worked unpaid overtime hours or skipped lunches and breaks without pay on a frequent basis. If the answer is, "Yes, it was expected of us," you could very well see a class-action wage and hour claim attached to your ex-employees' other legal charges. And costs add up quickly. Calculations typically go back several years, and it's not uncommon for damages resulting from unpaid overtime plus attorneys' fees to reach the seven- to eight-figure range, depending on the size of your company and the number of workers in the class.

The lesson here? Don't panic if one of your nonexempt employees misses a break or lunch period on occasion. However, don't become known as a company where skipped meals and breaks become the norm or where working unpaid overtime occurs on an "expected" basis. If you steer clear of developing that type of reputation by respecting the law and treating your nonexempt workers fairly, then occasional, nonsystemic lapses probably won't pose much of a serious legal threat.

That being said, you should encourage your nonexempt team members to get away from the office (or at least their desk) during lunch and rest periods. If taking lunch at the desk becomes the norm or expectation, it will be assumed that your hourly staffers were expected to pick up the phone if it rang, keep an eye on email, or attend to other matters of business. And that, unfortunately, violates the definition of a true rest or meal period. After all, courts will generally rule that if *any* work was conducted, the entire meal period was invalidated. Oh, and if you and your employees don't have a record of all the times they skipped their breaks and meal periods, then the courts or the Department of Labor will gladly share their calculation tools and tell you how much your company owes in back wages and attorneys' fees based on their estimates. Just remember that for nonexempt, hourly employees, breaks and lunches are for breaks and lunches—not for work. There's no need to surprise your organization with a class-action wage and hour lawsuit because you failed to adhere to the law in this very fundamental respect.

5 Inspiring Employee Engagement

HOW DO YOU MOTIVATE your team in the face of tight merit pool caps, limited promotional opportunities, and daunting workloads that demand high levels of discretionary effort? What about when layoffs loom: How do you keep your staffers engaged when a sense of gloom pervades the workplace? More importantly, how do you, as a manager, foster respect and loyalty, and exhibit role model behavior for others in light of the many challenges facing your company? Becoming a leader who inspires team members by example and who creates an environment in which people can motivate themselves stems from building trust, respect, and camaraderie in the workplace. The keys to motivating and engaging those who report to you lies first in assessing your relationship with your employees, engaging in "stay interviews" with your top performers to ensure that they're energized and in tune with your department's and company's overall goals, and helping your team members build their skills and success profiles to prepare for their next move in career progression—whether at your organization or elsewhere.

Yes, you read that right: whether at your organization *or elsewhere*. Successful leaders know that the key to developing employees in light of your organization's changing needs lies in making them feel that they're making a positive contribution at work (for the company's benefit) while developing their own skills and building their résumés (for the employees' benefit). Selfless leadership, also known as servant leadership, requires putting your team members' needs above your own and expecting them to respond in kind. There's no doubt, however, that garnering loyalty and getting people to fall in love with your company stems not only from engaging their heads but from piercing their hearts. True motivation is inspirational and emotional—not necessarily logical or cognitive. Knowing that there are ways to win people's hearts as well as their minds will provide you with a special formula to foster respect and loyalty throughout your career.

Whether you're an introvert or extrovert, a driver, an analyst, or a people pleaser, the following steps foster greater employee commitment and dedication:

- Getting to know your team members individually and personally
- Giving meaning to their work
- Demonstrating respect and trust in all you do

The key question, of course, is how do you do this with the members of your team? How can you reach a level of engagement where people feel valued, garner the appropriate amount of psychic income that comes from the workplace experience, and feel that they're making a positive difference and that their opinion matters? On the one hand, this isn't as hard as you think if you apply certain principles and guidelines to engage and motivate winning teams. On the other hand, it can appear to be a most daunting task if you feel responsible for motivating others or otherwise making them happy and satisfied in their work situations.

As a leader in corporate America, you're not (technically) responsible for motivating others. Motivation is internal, and employees must motivate themselves. However, as a leader in your organization, you *are* responsible for creating a work environment where people can motivate themselves. There's a tremendous difference between creating the right working conditions versus crawling inside your team members' hearts and hoping to make them feel a certain way. But by understanding your opportunities and limitations when it comes to motivation, you can gain a much clearer picture of your role in influencing others. And as we'll see in this chapter, you must understand yourself first—your style, your expectations, and your limits —before you can create a work environment that is both motivational and respectful.

50 *Developing a Blueprint to Inspire and Motivate Your Team*

Senior executives, middle managers, and front-line supervisors face significant challenges in inspiring and motivating their teams due to the ongoing challenges their companies face in this new era of disruption. Technology and globalization trends continue to cause massive corporate consolidations, layoffs continue in many sectors while others go begging for talent, and employee loyalty gets chipped away as a sense of disengagement, disenchantment, and disconnectedness creeps in. Where does that leave you in terms of your responsibility for delivering day in and day out the functions that lead to your organization's success? You're a leader, but you're also an employee yourself. How do you motivate yourself in light of these many changing priorities and demands? How do you assume responsibility for your employees' well being? How can you insulate them from the vagaries of the global marketplace that have made your local workplace so much more demanding, exacting, and challenging?

It all boils down to what you believe about yourself. What kind of leader and people manager are you? Who do you wish to be in terms of influencing others to do their best work every day, inspiring them to thrive in their careers, and building a cadre of future leaders who will ultimately thank you for the opportunities you've given them through the gift of your time? There's no simple approach to motivating and inspiring others. Like many of life's challenges, it depends on how important this is to you and what you want to make of it. The fact that you're reading this book, however, is a step in the right direction. So have faith that your new tomorrow is right at your fingertips when it comes to leading and inspiring others, with only a few twists and tweaks to your sponsoring thoughts about who you are and who you choose to be in light of the challenges and demands that corporate America may throw your way.

The blueprint that we're proposing in this book focuses on your getting to know your employees. It espouses recognizing the opportunities and limitations in this activity we call "work," delegating to your team as a means of professional development, and ultimately preparing less experienced team members to replace you at some point in the future, both for their own good and for the good of your company. It encompasses motivating team members when you have limited financial resources to do so, preserving restless top performers, and recognizing burnout and engaging in turnaround situations to help your employees get back on the right track. Finally, it entails becoming a leader who puts your staff's needs ahead of your own for the benefit of those who report to you and feel loyal to you. This chapter discusses strategies and techniques to lead and motivate more successfully and consistently.

51   *The Nature of Motivation: Rules and Myths that Inform Your Reality*

Engagement is vital to any organization. Inspired employees produce better results, find new ways of adding value, and sense a greater loyalty—if not to their company then at least to their immediate boss. The end result is increased retention, a hallmark of leading companies with strong employee-oriented focuses. Fixing the engagement issue that plagues workers from time to time is no simple task, but it doesn't have to be as complicated as people make it. Top managers consistently engage individuals and their teams by creating a culture of transparency and open communication. They acknowledge and recognize good work because work that is performed well is inherently noble and deserves respect. These are foundational beliefs and sponsoring thoughts to help leaders thrive and excel among their peers.

In contrast, suspicion, lack of trust, an unwillingness to share information, micro-management, and the imposition of rules suffocate creativity and free spirit and de-motivate employees. Creating a culture of compliance will only get you so far; if people operate out of fear or focus only on avoiding mistakes, their contributions and the team's output will stall. On the other hand, treating employees with dignity and respect, fostering a greater sense of inclusion, demonstrating recognition and appreciation, and infusing your team with a spirit of career development and self-education all breed loyalty. In today's hypercompetitive marketplace, what's good for your employees tends to be good for your customers, suppliers, and the community. The quicker you can get to this reality of enlightened leadership, the more you'll reap the benefits of managing a motivated and engaged team.

To succeed in this arena, however, you'll need to understand that motivation isn't solely about money. It isn't even solely about promotional opportunities and vertical career trajectories. Millennials (i.e., those born roughly between 1980 and 2000) will make up more than half of the U.S. workforce by the year 2020, so we can look to this new and upcoming generation's values to understand how to set the course for the coming decades. Interestingly enough, Millennials typically want many of the same things that other generational groups in the workforce want as well: a company that articulates a healthy mission, benefits from establishing and practicing the right values, makes a difference in its community, and serves as a responsible and benevolent corporate citizen.

General Rules of Motivation

To be a successful leader, focus on the following three rules, which garner positive results by their simplicity and selflessness:

1. What you want for yourself, give to another.
2. Beingness trumps doingness.
3. Giving the gift of your time to those who work for you and report to you is the ultimate in recognition and appreciation.

Regarding rule 1, what would you like to see in your relationship with your boss and your company? How can you find a way to create that very same experience with those who report to you? It is by giving to your employees that you'll always receive the highest rewards—spiritual or otherwise. The metaphor of work being a Darwinian jungle where only the fittest survive may be legitimate to a certain extent, but it's only one aspect of our careers. The greatest gift that the workplace offers, in comparison, lies in growing and developing those who are following in your footsteps and helping them excel and grow in their careers.

Rule 2 is a spiritual concept that states that who we are—not what we do—is the most important aspect of what emanates from us. Too many people are busy *doing things* and running themselves ragged in the process while trying to prove their worth. In reality, true inspiration comes from who we are as individuals, what values we espouse, and the level of character and integrity we demonstrate. As such, effective leadership often runs softly and quietly, demonstrates the appropriate values that define who we are, encourages others to follow our example, and allows others to follow in our footsteps.

Regarding rule 3, you must find the time to get to know your team members more personally and foster their professional development. While it's true that many workers—yourself included—may feel overwhelmed by the harrowing pace of change in the workplace these days, remember always to focus on activities that provide the greatest return on investment for your time. The highest activity that leaders can engage in is getting to know their team members more closely, helping them in setting and achieving their goals, and supporting them in realizing their career ambitions while making your company a better place.

Myths and Other Blind Alleys

There are several ideas about motivation that don't hold up under scrutiny. Thus, I call them myths. Here are some examples:

- Until we pay our workers "at market," we'll never have happy workers or a stable workforce.
- With merit budgets so low and bonuses not being paid out at 100 percent, you can't blame employees for being disengaged and disenchanted.
- Until the company invests in more headcount and slows down this frantic pace and this "evolutionary change at revolutionary speed," we can't thrive and prosper.

While it's true that these and other challenges may make it difficult to catch your breath at work, focus on completing one project or task at a time and permitting workers to feel a sense of control over their surroundings. The speed of change will only increase over time and become the "new normal." Likewise, merit and bonus restrictions or headcount reductions are part of the new reality for all organizations globally, so to simply use this as an excuse for employee disengagement and dissatisfaction is a copout that permits you to deny reality or otherwise vent your own frustration. Instead, help your employees understand the broader picture and adjust to these changing realities by finding new ways to succeed in today's business model.

Setting a Course to Meet Your Goals

The rules of motivation are important guidelines and parameters that will help you set a course for the right goals and support your staff. Think about your own favorite bosses; can you emulate them and become the kind of power source for your team members that your bosses were for you? To accomplish this, you must do the following:

- Listen actively and demonstrate that you really care about what each individual member of your team has to say.
- Help others find their own solutions and creative approaches to challenges that come their way in the workplace.
- Help others plot their course for career growth and development.
- Hold others to very high standards while remaining fair and consistent in the application of company rules and guidelines.

This is all within your reach, but only if you believe it's a priority and are willing to reinvent yourself in this critical aspect of your own career development. Remember that the key to enlightened leadership is setting up people for success and then getting out of the way, allowing them the freedom to gain traction and excel in their own personal and individualized style. Likewise, look to the wisdom that allows you to follow a "less is more" approach to leadership, appreciate the value of creating a culture where workers can motivate themselves, and become a best-in-class organization (or department) that invites people to fall in love with your company every day.

52 *Creating an Environment in Which Employees Can Motivate Themselves in Light of Your Organization's Changing Needs*

The first rule for creating a motivated and engaged workforce is to practice open communication and transparency. The second rule is to provide recognition and appreciation to your staff as an integral part of your organizational strategy. While this may sound like common sense, common sense isn't often common practice. What stops leaders from creating an environment where workers can feel fully engaged, self-motivated, and comfortable? Here are some excuses that managers typically use for not recognizing and rewarding their employees consistently:

1. "I don't know what to do."
2. "It's not an important part of my job."
3. "I don't have the time."
4. "I don't want it to go to people's heads."
5. "The company doesn't support or care about this."
6. "It costs money and takes too much time."

While these excuses may be valid under certain circumstances, they provide a smoke screen or an easy out that ignores the needs of the workers. In contrast, to develop a good reputation and to achieve success by respecting your team members, you need to practice open communication and transparency and to educate and train your staff to understand the broader picture. Thus, successful leaders do the following:

- Practice MBWA (management by walking around)
- Know members of the company by name (to the extent possible)
- Go out of their way to make others feel welcome, included, and heard
- Provide new recognition opportunities based on employees' particular needs
- Praise in public by instituting "applause" bulletin boards or "wall of fame" photos for special achievers
- Invest in experimental incentives, such as going-green initiatives, finding new ways of giving back to the community, and instituting health and wellness programs
- Emphasize a continual focus on career growth and development
- Model the behavior they expect others to follow

Successful leaders also practice open-book management (OBM), which entails sharing specifics about the company's challenges in an attempt to get everyone on board with practical solutions to help the business. John Case of *Inc. Magazine* first coined the OBM phrase and began using the term in 1993. At its core, the basic tenet of OBM is that employees empowered with information and intelligence about the company not only perform their roles better but also gain a stronger understanding of how the company operates as a whole. The goal is to make employees partners in the business, offering solutions to challenges that may not even be in their purview. Yet who better than those in the trenches to recognize and flag potential problems in product manufacturing, service delivery, and the customer experience?

Further, when employees are given access to information and are involved in finding solutions to problems, they experience a greater sense of trust in the company and confidence in their roles. What better way to build and develop staffers than by educating them about your organization's challenges? What better way to keep people engaged and focused than by encouraging them to solve problems and suggest alternatives? Furthermore, employees can be encouraged to learn about the financial drivers of organizational success and to help improve company performance. They can then ultimately share in the company's success.

To do this, you must first create an environment built on trust where it's safe to volunteer new ideas. Second, there must be a respectful and inclusive work environment where all workers are valued regardless of pay grade or title. Third, there must be some kind of critical measurement that's fairly easy to explain and that all employees can work toward. Whether you're sharing financial statements, feedback from an employee opinion survey, C-SAT (customer satisfaction survey) results, KPIs (key performance indicators) or scorecards, the more you inform, the more you educate. And the more you educate, the more people feel inspired to participate in finding solutions.

Start by picking a small task and introducing it as a new challenge. Discuss opportunities for influencing the critical measurement that's identified upfront, and encourage the sharing of ideas publicly. There are no right or wrong answers in this type of work environment —only suggestions for improvement. It may take the form of recruiters seeking to lower their hiring costs, insurance adjusters seeking to shorten the time it takes to complete a claim, or organizations seeking to minimize their unemployment or disability claim activities. But it's not just about efficiency and lowering costs. It's also about finding opportunities to increase revenue and introduce new marketing ideas. Are the employees the first users of new company products? Can your team members become due diligence experts and learn what competitors are advertising in their neighborhoods? Are there opportunities to reinvent the way your organization does business, from the smallest detail to the largest initiative?

You'll only know if you ask. You can only ask if people feel truly safe to speak their minds and volunteer new ideas. But the art of employee retention is no longer strictly about job satisfaction: it's about true employee engagement. Involving employees in problem solving, trusting workers to participate in activities or decisions that are beyond their immediate pay grade, and creating a learning environment where those in the trenches who are closest to the customer experience have a voice and can express their ideas will garner the highest results. That's the margin of difference that helps individual teams and entire companies stand out from their competition.

Foster a healthy sense of curiosity. Recognize that intrinsic motivation means that the interest comes naturally from within and that your job as an effective leader is to encourage that sense of inquisitiveness and help others tease out answers to challenges that require collaborative thought. As with many things in life, what matters is how you set things up and how you establish and communicate expectations. It's okay to start small and measure progress incrementally. Now the only questions are when do you start and what do you choose to share.

53 *The Nature of Motivation: Five Steps for Quick Turnarounds*

When you ask people why they work, common responses are "Because I have to" and "For the money." But the people who respond this way tend to be those who hold "jobs" rather than build "careers." That may be okay for some people. But readers of this book are likely dealing with employees who are looking to build careers and stand out among their peers. The adage "If you love what you do, you'll never have to work a day again in your life" speaks to a kernel of truth: At its core, work is meant to fulfill us, engage us, and provide a certain amount of psychic income that goes beyond paychecks and bonuses. It gives us an opportunity to define who we are, to be part of a greater whole, and to contribute to making a difference.

For most of us, even a moderate amount of self-examination and career introspection will reveal that we want to make a difference; we want to learn, grow, and develop new skills; and we want to help others develop according to their talents so that they can feel fulfilled and experience satisfaction in defining who they are and what they want to be. To truly understand the nature of motivation and how to create the right kind of workplace that allows others to gain traction and define themselves relative to the challenges posed by the workplace, you've got to look at your own thoughts and assumptions about human behavior.

For example, if you believe that work can benefit the employee, the manager, and the company, then creating an engaged workforce is a noble goal. Likewise, if you feel that people will exercise self-direction and self-control in the service of projects and goals they've committed to, then you recognize that the key factor in motivation lies in setting up people for success and then simply getting out of the way, allowing them to find their own creative solutions to the problems at hand. Workers want to assume responsibility, share recognition, and exercise a high degree of imagination, innovation, and creativity in the solution of organizational challenges. If you believe these things, then you're looking for a way to channel people's energies so that they experience more success for themselves and others.

Since the time that social scientists seriously began studying the nature of work in the 19th century, there's been an ongoing debate between two competing schools of thought:

1. Workers naturally shun work, do as little as they can get away with without being disciplined, and must be closely watched and guarded, lest they take advantage of the company and hasten its demise with little regard to others who run it or otherwise make their living there.

2. Leadership's responsibility is to create conditions that make people want to offer maximum effort, help others succeed, and excel by standing out among their peers.

You know the end to this particular debate: In a knowledge economy, encouraging workers to find their own individualized solutions to workplace challenges is far preferable to imposing a system of controls that need to forced upon workers who either don't understand or don't care to learn more about their roles and responsibilities.

Rewarding people for achievement, it turns out, is far more preferable to punishing them for failure. Allowing people to assume greater responsibilities is better for them and for the organization because no one knows the work or the customers better than those on the front line who deal with them every day. Creating an environment marked by innovation, creativity, and imagination can only come from an enlightened workforce with the right incentives and recognition programs in place.

How do you motivate workers through tough times? How do you lead different generations? And how do you change your organization's culture? You do it one day, one person, and one step at a time. No single manager can change the course of history, turn villains into heroes, or reinvent a company's culture. But you're the first domino in the row. You can make an impact in your unit, department, or division that can alter your team's output and trajectory. You can find new ways of motivating your top producers and making work fun again by simply changing your sponsoring thought about who you are and what you do. It all stems from the respect, recognition, and, most importantly, trust that you sense and share with your team members every day.

Here's a quick recap of how to create a healthy work environment where team members can find new ways of motivating and reinventing themselves in light of the newest challenges:

Praise and recognize hard work.

By far, the most dramatic and immediate change in your organizational culture will stem from your willingness and ability to praise employees and recognize their achievements. Recognition need not be monetary. In fact, many consulting firms that specialize in reward and recognition programs will tell you that research shows that public praise and recognition scores higher in workers' minds than a cash card or a check. There are many simple and effective ways for leaders to recognize their employees. Sometimes it's as simple as a handwritten thank-you note. Encourage your team members to follow your lead in recognizing others for a job well done. Share praise openly, and consider organizing recognition events to honor bigger accomplishments, especially those reached by a team working closely together.

Help employees fulfill their career goals.

Career development is a key driver of employee engagement. Your strongest performers will always be résumé builders, and providing opportunities for talented individuals to do their best work every day, combined with training and educational opportunities, will go a long way in helping people achieve their career advancement goals. Become an organization known for having a commitment to professional development. Provide networking opportunities for your staffers to meet leaders from other parts of the organization over team lunch meetings. Serve as a mentor and coach to your employees by asking them about their long-term goals and how you can help them get there. Show that you're interested in the whole person, not just the one who shows up at work. You'll likely find that people will respond in kind to the heightened dose of positive attention they're garnering.

Move dissatisfied employees out of the organization.

Some workers are simply unhappy people. They look for reasons to prove you wrong or constantly focus on shortcomings within the organization. They may suffer from "victim's syndrome" or some type of entitlement mentality that kills camaraderie and teamwork. Often they find their outlet in inciting union activism, threatening lawsuits, or repeatedly being absent. Whatever they do is negative for themselves, their peers, and the organization as a whole.

Removing these unhappy souls from the workplace, while difficult to do, will often improve the engagement of the other workers and increase their enthusiasm for their work, as they experience an immediate sense of relief that they no longer have to walk on egg-shells around that person. Removing obstacles is key to developing a motivated team, and sometimes these obstacles are other workers.

When you've identified someone who refuses to be motivated, refuses to get along with others, or spreads misery despite your best efforts to look for the best in people, find a way to remove the person —respectfully but lawfully (as these individuals will often be the first to sue). Remind yourself that 3 to 5 percent of your workforce will fall in this category at any given time, so work closely with HR or your immediate supervisor to "help the worker be successful elsewhere."

Plug leaks.

On many employee opinion surveys, "Employee Relationships with Management" and "Working Environment" are two of the top five categories that are most important to employees. Respectful treat-ment of all employees at all levels, trust, open communication, and the relationship with the immediate supervisor will typically cover the majority of questions found on a typical survey. Why? Because the relationship with the immediate supervisor, more than anything else, determines the individual's success and potential long-term viability. Relationships with coworkers, teamwork, and the meaningfulness of the work itself round out the broader categories of how the individual worker feels as part of the broader team.

Plan ahead.

All employees want some sense of job security regarding their future with the company. They likewise want to understand how their ef-forts contribute to the organization's larger goals, mission, and vision. Share information generously. Ensure that people understand the *why* of your directives so they can tie their recommended solutions to the broader picture. Help them learn about your organization and build upon their knowledge by collecting data in scorecards, dashboards, and other forms of data intelligence gathering. Likewise, honor the annual performance review process—the one hour per year dedicated to each individual worker as a culmination exercise over the previous twelve months (i.e., the 2,080 hours typically worked).

Conduct mid-year or quarterly reviews with team members to update their performance goals and year-to-date progress. The more you can tie them in to your organization's future and bind their career to the organization's focus areas, the greater the chance of long-term retention. Remember that best-in-class companies are recognized by long-term tenure because of the sheer amount of institutional knowledge that's retained over time. Helping employees plan ahead and understand their role within the organizational context of the company's future challenges is a positive way of binding people to your company for the long haul.

54 *Delegating as a Means of Professional Development, Not of Offloading Work*

Employee performance falls on a bell curve: 20 percent of your staff members will be outstanding, 10 percent will demonstrate performance or conduct problems, and 70 percent will perform consistently and responsibly but not necessarily with distinction. How do you manage and develop the 20 percent who are your superstars and the 70 percent who are your average performers and have development potential? How do you motivate, manage, and develop people when most companies continue to face layoffs, tight merit pool caps, or hiring freezes due to mergers and acquisitions or in light of global competition and technological disruption?

The key to developing staff in light of corporate America's changing needs lies in understanding your own leadership style. Before you can address delegating to people's strengths in an effort to build their skills and help them find new ways of reinventing themselves, you need to assess your own management style as well as your workers' talents and abilities. Let's do this in the following steps:

Step 1: Define your own management style.
Here's the exercise: A headhunter calls your best employee saying that he has an excellent opportunity with a competitor firm and wants your employee to sit down with that company for an hour to see if that organization could offer her a better career opportunity or compensation package. How would you initially respond when you heard about this?

1. "I'd want my employee to stay with me out of loyalty, and I certainly wouldn't want to have to rehire someone and have to train a replacement."

2. "I'd expect that my employee would want to stay with me because I've trained her, respect her, and truly enjoy working with her."

3. "I'd want my employee to pursue the opportunity if it is indeed a better career move, and I'd help her get that step-up in her career even if it meant losing her and having to find and train a replacement."

If your answer is either 2 or 3, then delegation may be a strategic tool for you in terms of motivating and developing your staff. On the other hand, if your answer is 1, then you view delegation as more of a "task" as opposed to a strategy for growing and developing people, and you despise turnover simply because of the burden it adds to your job in the short-term.

Delegation, in its highest sense, requires you to give up something that you're comfortable with or enjoy doing. For example, if you're a finance manager who enjoys budgeting for expatriate relocation assignments overseas or a legal department head who enjoys conducting your company's code of conduct training, then you might not want give up those responsibilities. Likewise, if you see your highest value to your company in your ability to care for the needs of your senior management team and you pride yourself on the relationships you've built, then it might be somewhat threatening to integrate a subordinate into your network. That's why it's critical that you assess your own strengths and management style before undergoing an exercise like this. Be sure you're aware of what you'd be willing to delegate before making any commitments to your staff.

Step 2: Rank-order your staff.

Wanting to delegate to people is both a natural inclination and a learned behavior, often depending on the corporate culture and degree of nurturing that you've personally experienced. But you can't delegate until you understand who among your subordinates is ready to accept the opportunity to learn new skills. Remember that as a leader, you're not striving for *sameness* in terms of how you lead;

you're striving for *consistency*. That means that you have every right to spend more time with your engaged and self-motivated employees who may be looking for additional duties and responsibilities. "Challenging the superstar" is a practical approach to effective leadership, although it typically implies that you'll be spending more of your time building on the strengths of a smaller subgroup of people rather than doling out your time in even increments across your team despite different levels of talent, engagement, and capability.

Begin by rank-ordering your employees into the following three categories: (1) top 20 percent, (2) middle 70 percent, and (3) bottom 10 percent. Then subdivide your staff so that you identify the top individuals in each of the first two categories. Next, divide and conquer: Set up a meeting with your short list of selected employees to discuss the importance of delegating as a means of developing talent, and ask them to think about what that might look like in their particular circumstances. Your goal, in essence, is to work collaboratively to define the right outcomes and then allow each person a way to find his or her own route toward that outcome. You're looking to empower people to create their own success their own way, and to balance motivation, talent, and goals in a way that leads to a customized and personal outcome. You can later extend this exercise to people who weren't selected for this first cut.

Step 3: Monitor what you've delegated.

Remember that the core responsibilities of leadership include selecting the right person for the right job, setting expectations, and then monitoring the results. The key step in delegating then lies in selecting the appropriate assignment or project to mentor or oversee, such as technical, managerial, or administrative assignments or special projects. However, it's not simply a matter of passing along responsibilities and then forgetting about your staff. The delegating itself becomes the focus of the exercise. It binds your subordinate to you throughout the period of implementation. So set the expectations at the point you delegate, by asking the employee the following questions:

- "What exactly are your expectations in overseeing this project? What's your initial plan of attack in assuming responsibility for your new project? What parameters or boundaries would you place around this project if you were to accept it?"

- "How often do you plan on keeping me informed with status updates, and how would you prefer to communicate your progress?"
- "What are the measurable outcomes so that we know that you've achieved your goals?"

With this information in hand, you'll be able to determine what to delegate to whom. The goal of delegating, after all, is to pass along skills and opportunities that will help the employee prepare to replace you one day, as all managers have a responsibility to their company in terms of succession planning. And if you're developing staff to learn the skills that you've mastered in your career, then you'll develop loyalty because you'll be placing others' needs before your own.

There are limitations to using delegating as a motivational staff development tool. Don't ask subordinates to volunteer information regarding their career goals if you're not prepared to give up some of your current responsibilities. You probably already have a general idea about what they might request. If you believe that information is power and that it's your best form of job security, so you're reluctant to share it, then avoid this exercise. Delegating as a tool of individual development may not be right for you at this point in your leadership career. Instead, you can simply continue to delegate tasks as a means of sharing the workload and getting work done.

Don't overload your staff. Delegating makes your job easier because you share your workload, but it must be managed carefully. If subordinates perceive your efforts as self-serving or if they are afraid to say no to anything you assign them, then you may not be ready to use delegating as a career development tool. There must be a foundation of trust and mutual respect in your working relationship before you initiate delegating in the professional development sense.

When staff members develop new skills and feel respected and recognized by their bosses, they stay in their jobs and find new ways of improving the workplace. In essence, your up-front investment in assessing your staff members and taking the time to learn about their motivations will make your job easier and save you time, and there are few opportunities in the workplace that allow you to work in that smart a fashion. Such are the elements of enlightened leadership and proactive management.

55 The Holy Grail: Motivating Staff Without Money

They say there are two kinds of employees who quit companies: those who quit and *leave*, and those who quit and *stay*. We've all experienced working with and leading employees who wish they could be somewhere else. Their dissatisfaction or apathy shows in all aspects of what they do. Turning around employees who have lost the motivation to make a positive contribution to the team will always be your toughest job as a supervisor.

Let's start with one basic assumption: it is not your job to keep people happy, especially in today's business climate. Few companies have had opportunities to promote people internally; many have withheld promotions and equity adjustments and even annual merit pool increases because the bottom line has been squeezed so tightly. More importantly, there exists an underlying tension in corporate America that as the economy improves and hiring increases, employees will leave in hopes of making up for lost time career-wise.

Therefore, now is the time to look at the latter half of the "recruitment and *retention*" equation. Retention programs and incentives tend to go by the wayside when the market is flat and no one has anywhere to go. For retention programs to be effective, however, they need to be in place for a year or so in order for employees to have time to buy into the program and experience its benefits. The time to begin recognizing, appreciating, and motivating your staff, therefore, is now. That doesn't mean you have to be a corporate cheerleader. There are, however, several relatively simple ways to create an environment in which people could motivate themselves:

Increase the competition between your company and your competitors.

More companies adhere to the philosophy of minimal communication rather than open book management (OBM). Senior executives often assume that the less their employees know, the better. "I want them to come in and do their work, not busy themselves learning about our organization's profit-and-loss statement" goes the old-fashioned logic. Even if your senior management team adheres to this closed communication style, practice OBM with your own staff: Whenever possible, research your organization on an Internet search engine like *Google* or social media site like Glassdoor.com. Send several members of your team to the library to find content from leading journals, research databases, and trade publications in the *Reader's Guide to Periodical Literature, Zack's Investment Research, Hoovers, Morningstar Investment Research Center, SEC.gov, Dun & Bradstreet, Bloomberg Business Week, Value Line, Guide Star,* and *Charity Navigator.* (Your librarian will likely have additional suggestions.) Likewise, assign a small team to review the Bureau of Labor Statistics' *Occupational Outlook Handbook* to investigate specific roles and career paths found in your department and their ten-year projection in terms of job growth.

In essence, you'll develop your own "corporate futurists" who can research trends and patterns in your industry or sector and have a chance to better understand your competitors. Little does more to stimulate interest and competition than pointing employees to the right tools where they could educate themselves (and the rest of your staff). Knowledge is power, and the Internet and library make for free resources of invaluable information.

Set up a quarterly achievement calendar.

Encourage your team to focus on developing an achievement mentality with the help of an Excel spreadsheet or a departmental share drive. All the team members should have access to the document to track their key projects, upcoming milestones and deadlines, and completion notes. This way everyone can see what everyone else is working on, allaying any sense that "I do all the work around here and no one else works as hard as I do." It keeps your people in the know about their peers and your department's key initiatives. And most important, accomplishments will be easily codified for everyone to see, and achievements can be publicly celebrated. Achievement calendars are a very simple tool to increase communication, raise accountability, and increase awareness about others' priorities. It also helps people fill in for vacationing team members or for those who are away from the office for any other reason.

Start a book of the quarter club.

To stimulate your team members and challenge them to think outside the box, suggest a relevant book for everyone on the team to read. Assign each member a chapter, and have that individual discuss the merits of the chapter in your weekly staff meeting. The real challenge will lie in getting your employees to apply the theoretical knowledge from the book to the day-to-day workplace. The company should pay for the books, but that will be money well spent, with a terrific potential return on investment.

Set up intermittent rotational assignments.

Some Fortune 500 organizations have very formal job rotation programs that may last several years and include assignments in other countries that require relocation and foreign language acquisition or knowledge of immigration law (think visas, green cards, work permits, and the like). These programs strengthen the overall employment experience and the individual's long-term value to the company. Smaller organizations can also expose key employees to other areas of the business at the same location to increase their awareness and knowledge.

Staff rotations, on an occasional, limited basis, allow employees to learn new skills and develop new perspectives on their work. Intermittent rotational assignments could begin with half-day assignments to other departments, listening in on calls, or accompanying field employees to customers' residences or places of business. Rotations help people broaden their knowledge about their own career interests as well as gain a comprehensive perspective of the organization's operations. Having an insurance adjuster sit in with an underwriter, a budget analysis sit in with an international finance person, or a recruiter spend a half-day with an employee relations specialist can be an excellent way to help people broaden their outlook and gain exposure to other parts of the business.

Encourage workers to attend outside training workshops.

Your best employees may be résumé builders who will stay long enough to prove their worth so long as they're on the fast track. But once they feel blocked from upward promotion, they'll look elsewhere rather than forgo their personal goals. The key is to allow all your employees a chance to make a difference. People are much more inclined to feel that they're making a positive contribution to your organization if they're learning. So even if you can't promote them because of hiring freezes, you could indeed encourage them to challenge themselves.

Training organizations like the American Management Association (AMA) offer short offsite workshops as well as onsite seminars on everything from business writing to team building to supervision for first-time supervisors. The costs are reasonable and because prices are relatively low for the value of the education you're getting, the real issue becomes the opportunity cost of having your employees out of the office for a few days. The AMA and many other training organizations offer hundreds of situation-specific seminars via Web-based e-learning self-study courses like finance for non–financial managers, foreign language acquisition, and software certification. Two or three outside seminars or in-house training courses per employee per year may add very little to your overhead budget and allow employees an intermittent "sabbatical" to reflect on their careers as well as to reinvent themselves in light of your company's changing needs.

Also, many states offer tax advantages for funding employee development programs like these. For example, California offers employment training panel funds that will allow your company to tap monies set aside for employee development via payroll taxes. Such training panels look to return these monies to the participating companies in order to encourage the retraining and retooling of American workers. Contact your local unemployment office for more information. Sending your employees to outside training and then finding the funds to reimburse the company for these workshops could make you a hero to your superiors and subordinates alike.

Insist on quarterly (or midyear) performance and goal reviews.

Finally, remember that people want to learn, contribute, and make a difference at work. They'll do this better if they feel a direct connection with your company that benefits their own careers. Even if it's not time to do annual performance evaluations, encourage your employees to conduct their own out-of-cycle reviews. These won't be tied to merit increases, which typically happen only once a year at specific times. However, it's a chance for your workers to grade themselves so that you can both compare notes. It's also important that you set aside one-on-one time for this; even if the meeting lasts only fifteen minutes, it provides a chance for the employee to be heard, acknowledged, and recognized.

It's a simple exercise, but until you know what's important to your people, you can't lead effectively. And you won't know unless you ask. People are, after all, motivated by very different things. If you could build a program at minimal cost that provides these motivational opportunities, then kudos to you! In a business environment often marked by scarce resources and few payroll increases or promotional opportunities, you'll have provided your staff with the two key elements of any retention program: professional development and recognition for a job well done. Then when the employment marketplace opens up again, you'll have accustomed your staff to an environment that encourages and fosters individual growth and institutional learning.

Remember, employees don't leave companies solely for money; money is typically fourth or fifth on the ranking scale. The top three or four slots are reserved for open communication, recognition for a job well done, career progression opportunities, and the ability to make a difference at work. This approach to reinventing your working relationship with your teams could become part of the glue that keeps your top performers with you and your company. In the end, you'll have done your organization a great service and will have made your life easier in terms of building tomorrow's leaders who are helping you lead more effectively today.

56 *Salvaging Restless Top Performers by Instilling a Greater Sense of Career Engagement*

Poll after poll reveals that some 50 to 75 percent of employees say they would leave their current companies once the job market starts heating up and they have a greater sense of job security overall, and members of your staff may be no exception. How do you identify subordinates who may be vulnerable to becoming "recruiter's bait," and more importantly, what can you do now to stimulate their loyalty to your company so they don't leave when temptation calls?

First, remember that it's not so much employee *satisfaction* that's at issue as much as employee *engagement*. Keeping subordinates engaged in their work, helping them feel that they make a true difference, and helping them build their résumés and skill sets are the goals of great leaders. In fact, the glue that binds an employee to a company is the learning curve. Help them to better themselves while benefiting your company, and they'll be both satisfied and engaged. Happy cows do indeed produce more milk, and when employees are engaged and firing on all pistons, no amount of money (within reason) will likely be able to entice them away.

Employee disengagement, however, can be insidious and can seep into your workplace over time. No job, after all, is great enough for the human spirit. That being said, some labor pundits believe that people are most amenable to learning when they are moderately dissatisfied. That seems to be the push necessary to force people to step up to the next level in their careers. However, too much dissatisfaction can be paralyzing. Once an "us-versus-them" entitlement mentality takes hold, it can be difficult to counteract it. In such cases, the grass tends to become a lot greener anywhere other than at your company, and by that time it may be too late to turn things around.

People remain engaged when they receive recognition and appreciation for a job well done. They're satisfied when they experience open communication and a sense of trust with their immediate supervisors, and they excel when they believe that they've got long-term opportunities available to them in the organization. In short, there is *psychic income* at work that makes people feel socially accepted and respected.

Disengagement, on the other hand, may show itself in a number of common ways, both subtle and overt, including a sudden 9-to-5 time-clock mentality, an unwillingness to participate in social events outside of the office, or a tendency to "fox hole" oneself apart from one's peers. It becomes most noticeable when someone who was previously outgoing and enthusiastic suddenly has nothing positive to contribute. Sometimes it shows itself quietly with raised eyebrows and sighs of apathy, and other times it results in open challenges to authority or shouting matches with peers. Whether the change is obvious or intuitive, assume that you may be vulnerable to losing your superstar once opportunity comes knocking because working in your office just isn't fun, rewarding, or exciting for that individual anymore.

Reengaging the superstar isn't difficult if you, the supervisor, have the desire to do so. There is a myriad of books available on tips for motivating your employees, but Marcus Buckingham and Curt Coffman sum it up best in their bestselling *First, Break All the Rules: What the World's Greatest Managers Do Differently* as follows:

> But the best managers have the solution: Ask. Ask your employee about her goals: What are you shooting for in your current role? Where do you see your career heading? What personal goals would you feel comfortable sharing with me? How often do you want to meet to talk about your progress?
>
> Find out about her taste in praise: does she seem to like public recognition or private? Written or verbal? Who is her best audience? It can be very effective to ask her to tell you about the most meaningful recognition she has ever received. Find out what made it so memorable. Also ask her about her relationship with you. Can she tell you how she learns? You might inquire whether she has ever had any mentors or partners who have helped her. How did they help? [p. 152]

How true: the most effective strategies focus on the individual's needs. Ask yourself if there is *trust* in the relationship. It's one thing to say you *like* your boss and it's another to say you *respect* your boss. But *trust* is the third and most critical element: If a strong bond of trust exists, then assume you could fix just about anything. If it's missing, however, then you may be best off allowing the employee to leave the company and start looking for a replacement.

Assuming that trust is indeed present in your relationship, the first move will be yours as the supervisor to raise the subject this way:

> Joe, I wanted to meet with you to discuss your level of satisfaction in your current role and with our company in general. I think it's important to do these sorts of pulse checks occasionally, especially with our best workers and most valuable contributors. I'd like to discuss what I can do to support you in your

career growth and development. I don't mean to push you or otherwise take your eye off your current workload, but I really want you to give some thought to my role—not only as your supervisor but also as your mentor and coach—in terms of what I can do to help you achieve greater satisfaction in your career with our organization. You're one of our top performers, and it's important that I understand what your needs are so that we can both engage in a plan that keeps you highly satisfied and performing at your best.

I want to keep you with our company, and I want to make sure you're satisfied and feeling engaged with our organization and your role in it. I see you as an integral part of the future of this company and our department. I realize we may not have any promotional opportunities for you right now, and I can't tell you what our year-end merit budgets will look like, but I can tell you that I want to help prepare you for greater responsibilities within the firm, and I'd like to speak with you now about how to do that.

With such a solid verbal commitment (and an equally solid performance review and development plan on file), it's time to get creative. This creativity will be a function of your industry, location, and company history as well as your subordinate's personal interests, but let's take a look at an example from the discipline of HR management.

Your director of staffing is doing a stellar job identifying talent and closing offers with difficult-to-find job candidates, but you suspect competitors that know of his reputation may recruit him. Besides, you believe that he may feel that his position is becoming less challenging and more of a "maintenance mode" type of job. Maybe this individual wants to eventually run his own HR department, or maybe he prefers to remain in the sub-discipline of recruitment over the long term. Following are creative alternatives that could motivate this individual to stay with your company for his own good despite an onslaught of job offers that may come his way.

Scenario 1:

Joe, I realize that your next move in career progression will be to move beyond recruitment into more of an HR generalist role so that you could ultimately head up your own department. Let me tell you where I need your help as I pursue new initiatives within our group.

First, it's time for us to take another baseline look at our entire department—from compensation and benefits to training, employee relations, and HR systems. I'd like you to spearhead that fact-finding initiative, work closely with all the group heads to benchmark their current practices, and then develop a market comparison so that we know where we stand relative to our peers and competitors. By the end of this six-month project, you'll be as savvy about the overall HR operation as I am, and at that point I could show you line-by-line how that audit will provide us with tremendous opportunities for operational improvements and increased efficiencies.

I'll also ask you to present your findings to our senior management team. It'll be a very time-intensive task, and it will no doubt take you away from your immediate recruitment responsibilities fairly often, but I guess my question to you is, Would you be motivated and excited to pursue a project like this? And are you up to the task and willing to join me in this new initiative?

Scenario 2:

Joe, I realize that you enjoy recruitment and you're certainly stellar at it, but I'd like to see you move in some new directions that will really complement your overall approach to staffing and selection and give you a much broader appreciation of your specialty.

First, the biggest trend in HR's future lies in international expansion. Although our firm has no overseas operations, I'm going to recommend that you enroll in an international HR course at the local college so that you can gain an appreciation of recruitment practices in Europe, Asia, and Latin America. Once you see how staffing as well as other HR generalist functions are performed abroad, you'll gain some greater insights into the work you do here for us domestically.

Second, once you've completed that international HR course, I'd like to spend some time with you reviewing our organization's financials and human capital metrics. One of the things I've benefited most from in my career is my understanding of enterprise valuations, income statements, and balance sheets, because once you understand what to look for in these kinds of financial statements, you become much more astute at forecasting workforce planning needs. Combined with an HR scorecard to see how we're increasing the efficiency and effectiveness of our organization's HR operations, you'll be able to drive your career to new levels of achievement.

Finally, while you've focused most of your recruitment efforts up to now on mid-level professional openings in finance, legal, and marketing, I'd like to work with you on giving you broader exposure to the executive search function here at our company. You'll be able to partner with me on a few select searches so that you can gain broader exposure to the intricacies involved in executive salary negotiations and other considerations. How does that sound in terms of your career interests? Also, what else could we add or subtract to this menu to help you progress in your career?

By making individual commitments like these to your key "keepers," you'll be helping them gain skills, knowledge, and competencies that they didn't formally possess. You'll also identify skill gaps and developmental opportunities to motivate them and enhance your own reputation as a true leader and career coach. It's a win-win for all because your proactive outreach will have kept a top performer from leaving. In addition, you will have saved the company the time and expense of having to recruit and train a replacement, and you will have reengaged someone who, consciously or not, may have simply been cruising along unaware of his own career desires and needs.

Is there risk that you'll be encouraging the employee to make unrealistic salary and promotion demands? After all, Joe wasn't complaining to you outright; you simply suspected that he might be feeling disengaged and insufficiently challenged by his current level of responsibility. So there is a slight risk that you'll inadvertently raise Joe's expectations and create a morale problem by not offering him more money and a promotion along with these other activities. But if there's trust in the relationship to begin with, this shouldn't be an issue. Besides, if you preempt your conversation by telling him this is about career development and not about immediate salary or promotional changes, you'll set expectations correctly so that your praise and recognition of his work doesn't immediately go to his head.

In essence, you'll have initiated a "counteroffer negotiation" before it was ever needed and in a much friendlier light. Challenging your employees to reengage in their roles and reinvest in their careers, and creating new career opportunities for them will no doubt make your own career a lot more rewarding and fun.

57 *"Stay" Interviews Trump Counteroffers Every Time*

Top performers and career drivers will always have the most options available to them should they opt to pursue opportunities elsewhere.

And who can blame them? Many workers feel that they've been treading water career-wise for a number of years but fear changing companies for reasons of job security. How do you get ahead of this natural curve in a top performer's career trajectory and keep your best and brightest motivated and engaged? And how do you obviate the need for a counteroffer discussion once the employee you count on most comes into your office with a letter of resignation?

Once a letter of resignation is submitted, the employee has already made a mental break with your organization. And you don't want to be forced into discussions that sound like this: "Oh, I didn't know you were unhappy! Why didn't you tell me you wanted more? Let me know what your new title and salary are and give me a few days to see if we can put together a package that will keep you happy. Just promise me you won't make a decision yet until you hear what we have to say."

Unfortunately, this real-life scenario is playing itself out more and more in organizations throughout the country. But could it have been avoided? Was there something the manager could have done proactively to evade this snare? The answer of course is yes; surprises regarding your best performers are avoidable if you're in tune with their career needs and long-term goals. So if you've been taking this for granted and haven't had this type of conversation in a while (or ever), now's your opportunity to open up the lines of communication and go through a "resignation drill" to ensure that your best and brightest are fully engaged, excited, and in some sort of learning curve that keeps them motivated and committed to your team and company.

"Stay" interviews don't only have to focus on your top performers—the top 10 or 20 percent of your workers who set the standard for performance and productivity and make your life so much easier. They can just as easily apply to the 70 percent of your workers who populate the middle of the bell curve performance-wise. But starting with your top performers makes inherent sense. Communicating your appreciation of their contributions and demonstrating interest in their future career development within your organization in general and on your team specifically is critical. This type of engagement exercise shouldn't ever seem artificial, superficial, or insincere, but it may be something that your team members aren't used to or otherwise expecting from you. Therefore, here's a way to ease into a conversation with employees you'd hate to lose to another organization should an opportunity come their way.

First, some background context: If a headhunter approached one of your top employees with an enticing opportunity at a competitor firm, the headhunter might ask the following questions:

- "Why do you want to leave your present company?"
- "What would have to change in your present position for you to stay?"
- "What's your next logical move in career progression if you stay with your current employer, and how long would it take you to get there?"

How would your top performing workers respond? A typical response from an unhappy or otherwise disengaged employee might be, "Well, there's really no room for growth at my current company. I don't see myself learning anything new; I'm just doing more of the same work that I've been doing for the past few years. And I just feel that I'm treading water career-wise. There's very little opportunity here, either in terms of dollars or new responsibilities." So if you suspect that one or more of your key players might respond to a headhunter's call in similar fashion, it's time for you to talk with them and get to know more about their current level of job satisfaction and engagement. In other words, use this starting point as entrée into deeper discussions about their ideas for improving the workflow in your area, building their own careers while remaining at your company, and finding new ways of reinventing themselves in light of your department's changing needs.

Start your discussion by asking the staffer how he'd assess his experience at your organization in terms of how happy, engaged, and rewarded he feels. Also, does he feel that he gets to do his very best work every day? If he asks why you're asking, just tell him that you want to raise the engagement level of the people on your team. However, you're starting with your star players first to get a gauge on how they're feeling and how they think the rest of the team might respond to similar questions.

Ask the employee to rate his job satisfaction on a scale of 1 to 10, with 10 being extremely happy and 1 being extremely unhappy. Expect an answer of 7 or 8. After all, it's only natural that most employees are discontent to some degree at any given time, but most won't volunteer that type of feedback directly unless they are asked. And when you ask, they typically won't give a score lower than 7 for fear that you'll think they're unmotivated or otherwise looking to leave. Likewise, anyone who defines themselves as a 10 probably is "blowing smoke" rather than being totally honest with you (barring any recent promotions or special events that really benefited them). If the employee answers with a score of 8, first ask, "Why are you an 8?" Follow up their initial response by asking, "What would make you a 10?"

The goal here is to find out, in a subtle and sincere way, where the employees stand relative to your organization and how receptive they might be to a headhunter's call. To drive the conversation even further, ask,

> Which of the following six categories hold the most significance for you career-wise at this point:
> 1. Career progression through the ranks and opportunities for promotion and advancement
> 2. Lateral assumption of increased job responsibilities and skill building (e.g., rotational assignments in other areas, overseas opportunities, and the like)
> 3. Acquisition of new technical skills (for example, via external training and certification)
> 4. Development of stronger leadership, management, or administrative skills
> 5. Work–life balance
> 6. Money and other forms of compensation

While almost everyone will initially comment on the money/compensation invitation—after all, who wouldn't want more money—most will quickly shift to one of the other five areas, which are the real drivers in terms of their motivation to remain with or leave your organization. Use this conversational format to launch into more in-depth discussions about your key performers' needs, wants, and desires, and then ask for suggestions in terms of how to get them there. Yes, you run the risk of eliciting pie-in-the-sky wish lists, but in a one-on-one setting, the risk of hearing such unrealistic requests diminishes. Instead, ensure that you understand what's driving your top performers and how vulnerable you and your company might be to losing them.

If your approach is sincere and selfless and comes from the heart, your employees will respect the effort that you're making, and that alone could go a long way in strengthening your working relationship. Of course, you have to be prepared to follow up on requests for promotions, equity adjustments, and the like, but you can always clarify upfront that you can't make any promises or necessarily control the budget constraints that the organization is facing. Explain that the purpose of your conversation is not only to gauge how they're feeling about the organization but also to remind them how much you value them and appreciate their contributions. Tell them outright that you wouldn't want to lose them to a random headhunter's call, and this kind of "stay" interview is far more valuable than an exit interview after the fact.

Finally, confirm that you want to encourage them to develop a realistic and customized development (a.k.a. retention) plan that will help them prepare for their next move in career progression and that you're willing to support and sponsor. Likewise, ask for their input on what can be improved, made more efficient, reinvented, or re-created within your department and how you both can partner as co-leaders to make things better for the team members by increasing their confidence level and their willingness to take on new challenges.

Start the conversation now. Make your key performers a critical part of the team's performance turnaround. Listen to what they're saying and look for new ways of helping them build their career within your organization—whether vertically, horizontally, or via a renewed learning curve. Engaging your best and brightest before they're lured to new opportunities elsewhere is a healthy and proactive measure to avoid counteroffers after the mental break has been made, and "stay" interviews and resignation drills are a practical and smart approach to raising both key employee engagement and retention.

58   *If You're Going to Make a Counteroffer, Make Sure You Do It Right*

If "stay" interviews represent the proactive side of keeping your employees engaged and tuned in so that they have no need to look for new opportunities elsewhere, counteroffer discussions, while sometimes necessary, are more reactive and dramatic in nature. Counteroffers, generally speaking, should always remain the exception, not the rule, because once employees go through the mental separation process of terminating their employment, an attitudinal break typically occurs that can't easily be undone. In addition, appearing to throw dollars at people to stay aboard once they've committed themselves to another employer could be perceived as a desperate move on the company's part and poor career management on the individual's part. Ask headhunters if counteroffers work, and they'll quickly tell you that in a majority of cases, employees who accept counteroffers will likely be gone within six months because the underlying reasons for their dissatisfaction don't often change.

Barring sincere management intervention, therefore, the additional cash from a counteroffer may simply delay the inevitable, and employees who accept counteroffers out of a fear of change or a sense of guilt eventually come to realize that if the original reasons they were considering leaving didn't change, then leaving still makes sense. Add that to the fact that companies that engage in counteroffers on a regular basis run the risk of creating a moral hazard with the organization; coworkers watch the pattern play itself out time and again and come to believe that the company is cheap and won't do anything for you to keep you happy unless you give notice. Not a good strategy at all, and in fact this can serve as a trap for employers who throw money at workers this late in the game to convince them to stay.

That being said, there may be times when a counteroffer makes sense in dealing with an employee's resignation. The key lies in knowing how to structure the counteroffer to help the individual reconnect with the organization and regain a sense of value—both in terms of his impact on the organization and his ability to build his career there.

It takes honesty and transparency on the part of both the company and the worker to make the outcome successful. Both sides must readily admit their shortcomings in allowing the situation to rise to this crisis stage, and both must be willing to make a sincere and conscious effort to correct the situation. Then the healing process can begin, and the individual can go about reinventing his relationship with the organization from a fresh perspective.

Here are two simple guidelines to follow if you, the employer, think that a counteroffer would be effective in dire circumstances where an employee has tendered his resignation. First, if you are truly committed to hearing what this individual's issues are and partnering to correct the core problems that caused the individual to look for work elsewhere, there's a chance that an honest employer intervention in the form of a counteroffer could work. But it's got to be sincere, selfless, and focused on the individual's needs. Throwing money or a title at a problem and then forgetting that it ever occurred is a formula for disaster because it simply delays the inevitable. And that's not fair to your employee who may be walking away from a great opportunity elsewhere.

Second, prepare for the exercise as if you had no money or title changes available to offer. Would you still be able to make a compelling argument as to why this individual might want to remain with your company? What else besides money and title could change, and what would that renewed relationship look like? True, you arguably wouldn't extend a counteroffer without trying to meet the demands of the new opportunity that's been offered, but if you're not looking at this holistically and in a broader sense than simply in terms of dollars and titles, you may be missing the point of the whole intervention. In short, if you're not willing to engage and invest in a "hyper-care" opportunity where you'll dedicate yourself to this individual for the next three to six months to ensure that everything remains on track in terms of the agreements you're making now, then forgo the counteroffer and wish him well in his new job. It's true engagement that's required here, and that includes ongoing partnering and follow-up.

Here's what a genuine counteroffer discussion might sound like:

Laura, I was surprised to hear that you're considering leaving us. You joined us just as the economy was beginning to tank, and there have been so few opportunities available internally. We haven't been able to promote people, make market equity adjustments to their pay, or otherwise find concrete ways to reward our key employees financially or in terms of internal career growth opportunities. But I want you to know that you are indeed a key employee. The management team in our department considers you a "keeper," and we certainly would do whatever we could to make you happy and have you stay with us.

I respect the fact that you may ultimately decide to leave us and take your chances of finding greener pastures elsewhere, but I'd like to ask what prompted you to consider looking elsewhere. Also, if you wouldn't mind, would you share some of the specifics regarding your proposed title and salary? I'd like to know more about what you're considering.

After listening to the employee's explanation, continue this way:

I can't make any promises to you during this meeting; this is simply meant to be a fact-finding mission for right now. Still, it's important for me to relay to you, on behalf of the management team, that we'd like the chance to provide you with some of those same opportunities here. I recognize that this is about more than money, but if we were able to come close to matching your proposed salary, title, and/or new responsibilities, we'd like you to consider remaining on board with us.

Even though I can't promise anything at this point, I hope that you will consider allowing us to explore this avenue with you. If we can't develop an overall career development strategy and growth trajectory that would motivate you to stay with us, then we'll certainly support your transition to the new company. Losing key employees isn't ever fun, but we're always happy to see people thriving and growing in their careers. On the other hand, we might be able to carve a path to newer responsibilities within the organization. Would you be willing to engage in those kinds of discussions with us?

Such an honest and selfless approach to engage in counteroffer discussions will almost always be met with flattered acceptance. After all, the employee will see that your company understands the importance of *career* rather than the immediate lure of *money*. This broader approach to career building will also help your company avoid the main error that organizations make when engaging in counteroffers: assuming that money or title alone is the issue. Many disgruntled

workers have walked away from a current employer's insincere attempts at keeping them on payroll by responding: "They just don't
get it. Why are they throwing money at me *now*? If I'm that good, they
should've offered me that money two years ago. They always cry
poverty, but all of a sudden they can find $15,000 in the budget to get
me to stay. No thanks."

More likely than not, your proposed counteroffer will not meet
the terms of the new company's offer. Your salary budget may not
enable you to bridge the gap, your internal equity matrix won't allow
you to award the salary increase even if you had the money in your
budget, or a promotion in title won't be available until someone else
in the organization leaves and frees up the headcount. Those restrictions being what they are, you'll need to structure your counteroffer
more creatively and include other benefits that the individual may not
have considered. For example,

Laura, we've looked at the opportunity that you've been given by XYZ Corporation, and we'd like to discuss some of the ideas that we've come up with.
First, I just wanted to let you know that I'm sorry if I've let you down. I never
meant to take you for granted or fail to recognize your work and your contributions to our department. That may have been how you interpreted things in
light of the financial challenges that our company, like all other companies,
has been facing, but that was certainly never my intention. I guess I may have
gotten so busy with the workload that I ignored other key areas, like developing the staff and creating new opportunities for career growth.

"We can't match everything that XYZ Corporation is offering you. I need to
tell you that upfront. Based on what you've told me, they're offering you a director title at $95,000/year with a staff of six. If you remain with us, you would
have to retain your current manager title, we could raise your salary from
$73,000 to $78,000 without breaching any of our internal equity guidelines,
and we could transfer one employee to your staff, for a total of four people.

In addition, we would consider enrolling you in a two-year university extension program and gaining a marketing certificate program at the company's
expense as well as assigning you to the corporate headquarters office in New
York for two 1-week trips next year to help you build your internal network.
And don't forget: As a three-year employee, you're only two years away from
being fully vested in the company's defined benefit pension plan. Of course,
you'll have our commitment that as any internal opportunities arise, you'll be
the first in line for consideration. And you won't have to be as concerned about

LIFO considerations at the next company, if the "last in, first out" formula comes into play for new hires in cases of layoffs or reductions in force. After all, you've proven yourself here and have a strong record to match your existing tenure. We would politely ask that you think about this, discuss it with your family, and then get back to us in a day or so. What are your thoughts?

With such a respectful, selfless, and well thought out counteroffer strategy lined up, you'll no doubt have a chance at retaining this individual. Even if you're not successful, you can at least rest assured that word will get out that you handled the whole matter professionally, that you put the individual's career interests above your own needs, and that you were very "cool and classy" about the whole thing. The outcome may be beyond your control; the strategy that you employ, however, will make you feel good personally and distinguish you as a true leader within your company.

59 *Recognizing Burnout and Reengaging Your Employees Based on Their Individual Needs*

Workplace burnout is a state of emotional or physical exhaustion that is brought on by long periods of stress and frustration. It's an all-too-common result of ongoing pressure, stress, and fear about job security, individual performance, the company's health, and the like. With roller-coaster job markets resulting from massive upticks followed by significant downturns, workers at all levels feel the pressure inherent in managing a career in corporate America. Perhaps you feel the emotional drain as well from constantly trying to keep your employees engaged and happy. Whatever the case and however you and your employees got here, the results aren't pretty: shorter tempers, snappy and condescending responses, excessively long evening and weekend work hours, loss of a good work–life balance, and feelings of disengagement.

Whenever you sense that one of your team members may be suffering from career burnout or work overload, start by recognizing where those feelings are coming from. If working long days with no breaks is the problem, then scheduling time away from the office may be a simple and effective remedy. Yes, that means that work will likely pile up pending the individual's return, but maybe you could help with that by assigning new incoming work on a rotational basis. Do this for all your employees and give them all a much-needed break.

If everyone's eating lunch at their desk on a regular basis, then it may be time to address that issue: Start slowly by establishing a group lunch one day per week where you all go out to eat together. Likewise, make it a priority to go for a group walk around your building or through your neighborhood. A 20-minute midafternoon walk is healthy for everyone, including yourself, and gives you a chance to bond with one another and breathe some fresh air. You could even consider it a form of team building if you can come up with an exercise to engage in while you're walking.

Remember that even a small change can make a big difference. For starters, limit the number of incoming emails that you're all sending one another. Email inboxes are filled with unnecessary messages; instruct your team members not to send emails that merely say "Thank you" or "Much appreciated." Make it a rule to limit email length to one screen without scrolling down your smart phone screen with your thumb (i.e., about two to three sentences). For anything longer than that, the final sentence should read: "If you'd like more background, please see below." But at least you'll train your people to provide you with snapshots of data so that you can get the main message without reading through a five-paragraph missive that leaves you to tease out the key points.

Since we're talking about email challenges that lead to employee burnout, instruct your staffers to use the Subject line more effectively. A subject line that reads "FYI" doesn't help much because you have no operational context to prioritize. On the other hand, if the subject line reads: "Change in California Paid Sick Leave calculation (90-day look-back required)," you'll have a much clearer understanding of the resolution required before you even read the message.

Besides massive email volume contributing to employee burnout, the second largest frustration factor typically has to do with the number of meetings that workers must attend during the day. If everyone's in meetings six or seven hours a day, then those emails can't be read until after hours or on weekends. Therefore, scour your meeting lists, see which ones can be combined or eliminated, and challenge the purpose of all but the most critical. Too many meetings simply causes information overload, and it's not true that everyone needs to know everything all the time. Informational meetings are helpful, but not if they take people out of circulation to the detriment of the work they're doing or the team they're leading.

Remember as well that burnout may be the result of being over-worked, underappreciated, bored, or otherwise depressed. It's easy to feel under-stimulated in a work environment where career pro-gression has been stymied at most organizations due to the ongoing downsizing that continues to mark the landscape in corporate Amer-ica. Vertical career progression isn't necessarily a thing of the past, but there are relatively fewer opportunities for promotion now than there have been historically due to ongoing changes from technology and globalization. In cases where you suspect that people may feel de-pressed about the daily nature of their work or their inability to get ahead, a simple solution may lie in limited rotational assignments or job shadowing exercises where employees can spend an hour, a day, or a week working side-by-side with other members of the team to learn about new roles and focus areas. Maybe you can "lend out" a staffer to help another team with a particular project, with other mem-bers of your team covering for the individual during the temporary period of absence.

In short, if your employees dread coming to work on Monday mornings or are otherwise crabby with one another and short with you, then you've got to step in and find out what the key drivers of their dissatisfaction are. And you'll only learn if you ask. Ask all team members individually where they stand on a scale of 1 to 10 in terms of feeling overworked or undervalued. Ask what they would like to see the team doing differently or what they would focus on if they could change one thing about how the work gets done in your office. Ask the team members to develop three ideas for lessening their work-load, relieving their stress, or adding exercise breaks to their day.

Lack of enthusiasm, isolation, decreases in productivity, and over-all apathy or apparent frustration won't lend themselves to a quick-fix solution. In most cases, real and significant changes will need to be discussed, evaluated, and implemented. But this is your shop, and as the leader, you have enormous influence in these areas to make things happen. You have it within your power to reshape people's work lives, to turn around lackluster performers who may be feeling burned out by the workload, under-stimulated by a lack of career progress, or otherwise underappreciated for what they contribute. As with most things in life, however, your experience is created internally. Change your perspective and you'll change your perception. You can change your mind any time about how something affects you. Use this opportunity to turn around your team, focus on opportunities that are important to them, and move everyone forward in a healthy and renewed spirit.

60   *Motivating Your Team After a Layoff or Termination: Healing the Wound*

We often think of motivating and engaging our staff members in the most positive light possible: How do we get people to feel good about themselves and the company? What can we do to spike morale? How can we liven things up in the workplace and create more of a spirit of camaraderie and creativity? And all those questions are noble in their intent. After all, creating an environment where people can motivate themselves and feel better about helping the company, the department, and their coworkers is what motivation should be all about. But what about creating the appropriate role-model behavior in times of stress and anxiety? When times are tough and everybody at work is nervous, managers have to help workers stay engaged, focused, and motivated. That's motivation of a different sort—indeed a more difficult and challenging kind—but it's equally as important, if not more so, in leading your troops successfully through adversity.

A common occurrence where things need to be talked about (and not swept under the rug) occurs at the time of employee separation. Coworker separations (resignations, layoffs, and terminations) can make the remaining employees feel uncomfortable, and restoring workplace confidence can be exceptionally challenging. How do you communicate difficult news so that your team members can heal the wound left by the departing employee? This kind of "motivating from the negative" speaks volumes to your leadership style and willingness to make yourself vulnerable and, in a very real sense, human. *How* you communicate your message in a way that allows employees to recoup from the loss of a friend or a coworker is the key to your approach.

Communicating a Termination for Performance or Attendance Problems

Terminations for performance or attendance problems typically don't occur in a vacuum. Employees receive corrective action notices that convey that their job may be in jeopardy, and it's not uncommon for workers to share this with their peers in frustration and disappointment, either at themselves or at their boss. The cases where progressive discipline leads to termination for cause are typically not a surprise because the person's coworkers are often aware of the situation. In fairly straightforward situations like these, it's okay to make a general statement to the team that John Doe is no longer with the company. The key is to keep it simple, respectful, and short. A straightforward announcement might sound something like this:

> Everyone, I just wanted to call a meeting to let you know that John Doe is no longer with the company. John was with us for the past 2½ years, and we appreciate all his efforts over that time. But his separation became effective yesterday, and we'll discuss filling his position and temporarily reassigning some of his responsibilities to keep things moving while we recruit to fill his position. If you have any questions, please see me privately. Finally, out of respect for John's privacy, I'd ask you all to please keep this fairly quiet so we can ensure a smooth transition for everyone involved. Thank you all.

Notice that the reason for the employee's departure isn't given for the sake of the individual's privacy as well as to demonstrate respect. This is fair, transparent, and above board, and that's a nice way of allowing the team members to heal and get on with their business.

Sharing News of a Termination for Egregious Misconduct

Conduct-related infractions include harassment, bullying, discrimination, violence, gross insubordination, theft, fraud, embezzlement, falsification of records, and substance abuse. The resulting termination can be more shocking because people don't know the specifics, and they might make incorrect assumptions. Therefore, the announcement, while similar to the scenario above, should focus more on instructions and guidelines rather than simply "healing the wound." For example:

> Everyone, I called this meeting to let you know that Lucy Brown is no longer with the company. I'm not at liberty to discuss specifics with you, and out of respect for Lucy's privacy, I'll ask you not to engage in speculation regarding her leaving the company. What I want you to know is that we treated Lucy very respectfully, we listened carefully to what she had to say, and we took appropriate action based on our findings. What I'd specifically ask you to do is to refer all calls for references regarding Lucy's performance to HR. I'll remind you that we have a policy and active practice of not sharing references with outside third parties like prospective employers or headhunters, and violating that policy in this case could have grave consequences for both you and for the company. Further, out of respect for Lucy's privacy, I'm formally instructing you all to avoid any gossip or banter about Lucy or her separation from the company. Do I have your commitment?

While your message may appear to be shrouded in mystery, it's important that you remind everyone on your team not to engage in third-party reference checks under any circumstances. Doing so could open your organization to claims of breach of privacy and defamation (slander) and potentially hold the referent as well as your company liable for damages relating to lost wages due to a rescinded job offer. In other words, defamation claims have teeth, and no one on your team will want to see their names listed in a lawsuit that the departing employee files against the organization and specific individuals within the company because a poor reference killed her chances at landing a new job.

Announcing a Layoff

Layoffs are very different from terminations for cause. In a termination, individuals are separated from the company for something that was under their control: failure to meet quality standards, to arrive on time, or to reach certain productivity thresholds, for example, that others are able to accomplish. In layoffs, in comparison, positions are eliminated and the people filling those positions are let go (often due to no fault of their own).

After an individual member of your team is laid off due to a position elimination, meet with the remaining members of your team to openly address and acknowledge what's occurred:

> Everyone, I called this meeting to let you know that we've unfortunately had a position elimination in our department, and Laura Smith has been laid off. I know it's always unnerving to hear these kinds of things, which is why I wanted to bring us all together to discuss this. First, I want you to know that Laura handled the news very professionally and said she'd be okay. She understands that she can be rehired in the future because she left the company in good standing. We've treated her with respect and dignity, and she responded in kind, so we're all on good terms. Therefore, there's no need to feel uncomfortable if you should see her outside of work. Finally, we have no further plans of laying off anyone else after today. As a next step, we'll all take a close look at Laura's responsibilities, as they'll need to be divided up among the rest of us. As always, I appreciate your support.

This is a respectable and professional way of handling messages about individual position eliminations because it answers the immediate questions that people have: "Will Laura be well taken care of? Are our jobs in jeopardy now as well?" In short, answer the group's questions honestly and openly but refocus them on what's important—that they're all still employed and have a job to do. The company is relying on them more than ever. And you need their support to let the healing begin and reinvent yourselves as a group in light of this new and unexpected challenge.

61 Leading and Motivating Through Extreme Adversity: When Your Job Is on the Line

Downsizing, right sizing, outsourcing, off shoring, restructuring, transformation, reductions in force: there's no shortage of euphemisms for shedding people in corporate America these days. And maybe that's understandable seeing that payroll-related expenses are one of the highest costs on a typical corporate profit and loss (P&L) statement.

When revenues fall, expenses must fall accordingly. But now you're responsible not just for your own potential job loss and career transition but also for your staff members, who are looking up to you for help and guidance as well.

How do you keep yourself and your team motivated through such a devastating period? How do you balance your own needs as well as the career needs of your staff in light of the company's requirement to forge ahead with its mission despite the news of your own pending position elimination? Most importantly, what legacy will you leave behind as the manager of a small group of individuals who may all face the same fate?

These are not easy questions, and the answers vary based on how the company handles delivering the news and caring for its soon-to-be-let-go workforce. Perks like outplacement career services, "stay" bonuses, and generous severance packages certainly help, but even under the best of circumstances, the task looks daunting because it's not just about you anymore—it's also about your responsibility to your subordinates. Too many times you'll see employees bear ill will toward senior management for something clearly out of the senior management team's control, and that resentment will show itself in demonstrations of anger, defiance, or apathy. Instead, managers and supervisors who are about to lose their own jobs and who are saddled with the responsibility of continuing to get work done through their own staff members for a predetermined time period need to concentrate on keeping their subordinates focused on strengthening their references at work while preparing for their next move in their career progression at another company.

Here's how it's done: Unstable times call for lots of information and communication. Granted, you might not have a tremendous amount of updates on any given day, but when it comes to communicating with your staff, assume that you can't give enough feedback at times like these. Keeping a focus on balance—both of the company's goals and your team members' personal career needs—will keep everyone calm, in the information loop, and objectively focused on executing the appropriate action plan. Remember, where a gap in communication exists, people will tend to fill it with assumptions and misinformation from an overactive grapevine.

Your daily (or at least weekly) staff meetings might sound like this:

> Update time, everyone. We were given sixty days' notice two weeks ago, which leaves us with about six weeks of work ahead of us while we're simultaneously pursuing our own career needs. We know that there doesn't appear to be opportunities at other company locations in town or opportunities for transferring to the corporate office, so let's keep each other informed about any new events. Have any of you heard anything since we met on Monday?
>
> I'd propose that we strike a balance between the company's needs and our own. First, thank goodness, we were given sixty days' notice. I'd much prefer to have that run time than be given same-day notice, which I know is pretty common these days.
>
> Second, remember that I'll need at least 24 hours' notice if you need time off for an interview at another company so that we can cover your work while you're out. We're a team, and we're going to stick together and support each other right through to the end, both from a company and team standpoint.
>
> Third, this company has kept our families fed and roofs over our head for a number of years, and as much as I'm going to hate to see this plant close, we're still obligated to earn a good day's pay for a good day's work. That means that our production goals and our productivity targets still need to be met. However, we'll get that done in a more flexible manner than has been done in the past. Are you all on board with me? Do I have your support?

Notice that such informal get-togethers give all members of the team a chance to voice their opinions, share news, and ask questions. There's little more that needs be done. Keeping everyone focused on their efforts (both work- and job search–related) will build camaraderie and a shared sense of accountability. But there's more to it than that: Loyalty and productivity to the bitter end give individual workers a huge leg up when interviewing at other companies.

A typical question that arises during an interview is, "What is your reason for leaving your current or last position?" Many job candidates fill out the line on the application form with a simple, one-word response: "Layoff." While technically true, the value of the answer lies beneath the surface, and your current employees who are about to become job candidates will be better served by amending their response: "Layoff; currently meeting all performance and productivity goals and standards through our sixty-day notice period."

Such a written response begs for more information and discussion on the interviewer's part and clearly enables the job candidate to put an unpleasant situation in the most positive light. Furthermore, job candidates should expect interviewers to qualify the layoff by asking for more details about the reasons for the plant closure, the effectiveness of management's communications, and company expectations regarding individual performance. Watch how this could play itself out in a typical interviewing scenario:

> Interviewer: "Rob, I see that you're looking to leave your current position because you're in a sixty-day notice period, but I really like how you jotted down that you're meeting all your preassigned performance and productivity goals. Tell me about that."

> Candidate: "Well, our manager came to an agreement with us that we could all work together to find a balance between our job-finding needs and the needs of the company for the two-month notice period. Our manager asked for 24 hours' notice whenever we line up an interview, but he also wants us to 'protect our references,' so to speak, and keep the company's needs first and foremost in our minds, even as we approach our separation date."

> Interviewer: "Do you feel that's a fair request on his behalf under the circumstances?"

> Candidate: "Absolutely. We're all sad and nervous about our jobs ending, but I want to be the one who turns the lights off. I want my reference and my official record or legacy at the plant to say that I worked to the end as a loyal and productive employee. I appreciate the opportunity I've been given to work at that plant for so many years, and although I'm sad that it's ending, I choose to walk away feeling grateful and appreciative for all I've been given and for all I've had a chance to do there."

And therein lies the true value of finding that balance between company and career and encouraging employees to end their employment relationship with their heads held high. The candidate's response above shows clear business maturity—appreciation, commitment, and loyalty despite the pending position elimination. And as critical as it is to ensure that workers protect their references and turn a negative event like a layoff into a positive outcome in future interviews, the most important factor is that the manager allowed for healing to take place. Affected workers were given a chance to communicate their frustration, anger, angst, disappointment, and anxiety in a safe environment. They were then refocused on their responsibilities in light of the company's changing needs and allowed to address both issues—career and company—responsibly.

Remember that anger, disappointment, or apathy expressed in any worker's notice period—whether two weeks or sixty days—creates the final impression left behind. No one should work for a company for years, only to leave a bad taste in everyone's mouth at the finish line. The truth is that companies change; they shed employees quickly these days. Group layoffs are no one's fault; they happen regardless of performance. But a layoff doesn't mean that all the goodwill you've built over time, the positive relationships you've developed, and on-the-job accomplishments you've earned are forgotten.

In fact, it should be just the opposite: Help your subordinates find the cathartic effect and peace of mind that comes from knowing that they worked hard over the years and gave the company their loyalty and commitment. In essence, help them change their perspective about what's happening to them. Then all of you will walk away from a potentially devastating event with a positive attitude and a sense of accomplishment that will help you stand out as a leader and help them stand out as loyal and consistent performers.

The loss of a position is an objective reality that happens through no fault of our own. *Who you are* in light of this position elimination is what's at stake here, and as a manager who balances your staff's individual needs with those of the company, you'll have an opportunity to demonstrate true leadership. In addition, you'll teach those who look up to you how to deal with adversity in their lives from a positive perspective. That gift goes well beyond the scope of the workplace and will do more than anything else to help your staff members come to terms with this unexpected change and gain peace of mind through an otherwise exceptionally trying time. You may also just find that you'll have changed your role as supervisor and manager into that of coach and mentor in the eyes of your subordinates, and that your personal stability, consistency, and care are critically needed to offset the tremendous changes that unfortunately are part of the new business landscape.

62   *A Broader Shift in Corporate Mindset: Putting Your Employees First, Even Above Your Customers and Shareholders*

Organizational reward systems—employee of the month, anniversary awards, "applause" bulletin boards, "Wall of Fame" photos, and on-the-spot special recognition awards—are great. But this chapter's focus has gone beyond those activities and programs to address a soft skill that's arguably one of the most critical drivers of business success—recognition of employees at the individual level, which is an integral part of your organizational strategy.

A motivational work environment rests upon:

- Developing open and honest relationships through communication
- Building a positive team spirit
- Sustaining a continued focus on career growth and development

As such, it recognizes that the single most important variable in employee performance and productivity hinges on the quality of the relationship between employees and their supervisors. Further, workplace wisdom suggests that besides supporting their families, work allows employees an opportunity to make a difference. They want to understand how they fit in with the company's vision and how they can contribute.

On a more practical basis, therefore, placing your focus on employee engagement over customer satisfaction will likely yield happier, more loyal customers. That's why organizations often create mission statements that reverse the traditional order of placing employees at the bottom of the pecking order (i.e., behind customers, products, and shareholders). Organizations realize that their most important assets are their employees. To generate excellent customer service strategies, organizations need motivated employees who deliver the customer experience.

Vineet Nayar, CEO of HCL Technologies and author of *Employees First, Customers Second: Turning Conventional Management Upside Down*, writes that your employees are the gateway to customer satisfaction, and if they aren't happy, the customer isn't going to be happy. Richard Branson, CEO of Virgin, famously stated, "The formula is very simple: Happy employees equal happy customers. Similarly, an unhappy employee can ruin the brand experience for not just one, but numerous customers." And Southwest Airlines consistently emphasizes the philosophy behind its employee-centric approach to doing business and creating long-term value.

The Gallup organization has been measuring employee engagement for years and found conclusive evidence that the level of engaged employees a company has is directly proportional to their profitability levels. Implementing an employee-first culture builds trust, holds people accountable, and rewards companies financially because of their ability to attract and retain the best and brightest. Besides, they're more fun and creative. If customers are the life-blood of your company, then your workers are the veins. Showing that you care for them—even more than you value your customers—sends a message regarding your priorities and your workers' well being. At that point, you can unleash all those happy cows to produce more milk because they want to, not because they have to.

6 Putting It All Together

WHEN IT COMES to achieving the model workplace it's the path to your destination that counts most: it's all about managing the trip along the way. This chapter offers practical advice and guidance—not theory or wishful thinking about how things could be in an ideal world. Effective leadership, which entails getting people to fall in love with your company and become loyal to it, is within your grasp. But it's details and nuance that matter, such as how you treat the most vulnerable, isolated, or marginalized employees, and how you create a workplace based on respect and trust. Create that healthy environment that invites everyone to perform at their best and reach their highest self in terms of creativity, innovation, and teamwork.

Let's look at some of the ways you can make small differences that can have a profound effect—not just on those immediately impacted but for the team members who are witnessing your leadership style. You can be the nicest and most caring boss in the world, but it will only work if you set high expectations and hold people accountable for their actions.

63　Achieving the Model Workplace: Productivity, Loyalty, and High Performance

Throughout this book, we've discussed the following principles:

1. Motivation and engagement stem from knowing your employees on a more personal level and demonstrating that you're listening and that you care.

2. Creating an environment where people can motivate themselves is the greatest responsibility and opportunity for all leaders.
3. Practicing selfless leadership and expecting others to respond in kind creates an ideal work environment where self-expression becomes the norm, employees feel safe to customize solutions to the challenges they face, and personal and career development complement the contributions that people make to the company.
4. Setting and communicating high expectations allows you to challenge your superstars and get everyone in sync in terms of your department's priorities and goals.
5. Removing problematic employees who are either unwilling or incapable of assuming good intentions or otherwise supporting their leader, department, or company is as important as creating a healthy, motivating, and engaging working environment for the rest of the team.

All these factors combine in an ever-changing, dynamic matrix that requires constant oversight, focus, and fine-tuning.

We've demonstrated throughout the book what tools, tactics, and strategies you have at your disposal to lead effectively though change: quarterly achievement calendars, self-reviews, intermittent rotational assignments, proactive "stay interviews" to gauge the level of employee engagement and satisfaction, constructive approaches to communicating bad news, alternatives to corrective action, and the like. But how do you know you're approaching a working environment where people are genuinely happy and firing on all cylinders? How can you tell whether you've reached a state of "happy cows producing more milk"? In short, how do you assess the performance, productivity, and sense of self-fulfillment of your staff?

First, look at your turnover and retention statistics. The strongest and most successful companies benefit from long employee tenure. Where does your departmental or divisional turnover stand relative to the rest of your company and your broader industry? The general rules for most organizations in corporate America are as follows:

10 percent turnover is ideal.
20 percent turnover is average.
35 percent turnover or higher is excessive.

These numbers may vary with the industry and the types of positions, with sales typically seeing the highest turnover, and HR, accounting, and IT seeing the least. Next, compare your current turnover against last year's turnover and that of the year before. What trends and patterns do you see? How would you project this year's and next year's turnover in light of your company and department's current state of affairs? Are you happy with the trend or concerned?

Distinguish between voluntary and involuntary turnover. Voluntary turnover occurs when someone leaves the organization to join a competitor, return to school, or retire. Focus on the loss of employees to competitor companies. Conduct exit interviews to find out what their reasons are for leaving. If the main reasons are (1) lack of recognition, appreciation, or communication from management, (2) lack of career advancement opportunities, and (3) insufficient compensation, then you must prepare to address these areas to increase your retention rate.

Involuntary turnover stems from position eliminations (layoffs) and terminations for cause. Because layoffs and reductions in force are typically not within your control as a company leader, these numbers shouldn't play as significant a role in your turnover analysis. However, terminations for cause should be studied carefully. If you find that you're terminating more people than you'd otherwise expect, look closely at your interviewing, onboarding, and initial training programs to identify weaknesses or missed opportunities to select or train more effectively.

Remember as well that turnover is relative. High turnover could indicate that your employees have not been trained adequately, held to high expectations, or otherwise developed a healthy sense of engagement in their work or loyalty to the company. But low turnover could also be a problem as well if productivity of long-tenured workers fails to meet minimum expectations. Sometimes complacent teams need to have a fire lit underneath them to reinvigorate them and drive higher productivity. So while long-term tenure doesn't always spell success, the golden formula you'll be looking for is low turnover combined with high productivity and performance.

Finally, identify the human capital metrics that define your organizational priorities. For example, you might want to set up a simple scorecard or dashboard that looks something like this:

Average tenure (nonexempt):

Average tenure (leadership):

Number of corrective actions over the past quarter (distinguish among performance, attendance, and conduct):

Number of high potential ("HiPo") employees:

Number of individuals identified for succession planning who are ready to step up one or even two levels (your "bench strength"):

Number of cross-trained individuals who can cross seamlessly into other functional areas or roles:

Percentage of voluntary resignations versus terminations for cause (typically 70 to 80 percent voluntary and 20 to 30 percent involuntary):

Length of time to fill an open position (i.e., the amount of time an average position remains open):

Number of promotions/percentage of internal fills (especially from your HiPo population):

Average salary/wage per employee classification:

Average education level:

Average performance review score per team, department, or division:

Primary versus secondary reasons for leaving the company (according to exit interview data):

Reasons for progressive discipline and terminations for cause:

What gets measured gets managed, and determining your people statistics is a very important step in creating the checks and balances needed to ensure that you're on the right track. Once you create a profile of your "average" employee, you can then start to get more detailed in your approach. Books have been written on human capital metrics and analytics that link people performance to financial measures within the organization. The goal of such books is to replace the "widget" accounting standards of a hundred years ago that inform our generally accepted accounting principles and modernize them to reflect human capital input instead. While transitioning fully to a human capital–based measurement system may still be years away, the number of books on the topic shows the growing momentum in this new field of study.

64   *Lessons from the HR Trenches: Wisdom and Experience to Benefit Frontline Leaders*

After spending about two decades in the HR trenches, I've written this book from the vantage point of senior HR leadership, where I've watched well-intentioned managers step on land mines because of a simple lack of awareness. HR, when done right, demonstrates and models effective leadership, superior communication, and well-executed teamwork. Moreover, it's looked to as the department that fosters healthy morale, ethics, and career development. Many would argue that HR, more so than any other department, reflects the organization's heart and soul.

Most HR executives and practitioners want to help front-line leaders avoid the land mines that come with supervising workers on a daily basis. Many of the errors that managers make are avoidable, especially the ones that create a troublesome legal record for both the company and the manager. Hence the purpose of this book is to assist frontline leaders in strengthening their communication skills, awareness, and general approach to managing successfully.

Many leaders often fall prey to the common thinking that they have to be mean, tough, fierce, or otherwise feared to compete in the business world. Their reasoning? If people don't fear them to some degree, they won't be respected or otherwise effective in their role. The employees will take advantage of them if they're too nice.

Nonsense! Some of the most effective leaders in corporate America at all levels are loved and adored. They're seen as nurturers, good listeners, and empathetic and selfless human beings. The secret to their success doesn't lie in their ability to instill fear in others; it lies in their ability to make others better human beings. And people feel that sense of specialness when dealing with leaders like these. They sense their genuineness, their true love of people and their work, and their willingness to help others better themselves.

The purpose of this book is to inspire readers to become that very kind of leader—someone who engages and inspires others to become the best they can be. However, while you don't always see this type of leadership all around you throughout your career, you certainly know and appreciate it when you see it in others. The question you have to ask yourself is, What kind of leader do you choose to be? You can become an inspirational leader by simply changing your sponsoring thought about being so.

For those who doubt this approach because it sounds too Pollyanna-ish, simply think about the worst consequences that can come of this leadership style: people won't respect you and will take advantage of you. That may be true to a degree, at least initially. But selfless leaders put others' needs ahead of their own and *expect others to respond in kind*. And people typically do! They'll sense your genuineness and selflessness and put your needs (and the company's needs) ahead of their own. And they won't do it out of fear or a need to comply; they'll do it because they want to. They'll sense that you treat them with respect, hold them accountable like adults, and teach them so they can grow and develop in their own careers. And in feeling good about themselves because of your enlightened leadership style, they'll give more *discretionary effort* out of loyalty and pride. Greatness can be found at the margin of output in the form of additional energy, effort, and goodwill. That may sound like a small thing when you're looking at one worker, but think about the difference it could make when a department or an entire company has that orientation!

What about the occasional staffer who tries to take advantage of your good nature? It may go on for a little while, but before too long, peer pressure will fix the problem as peers "realign" that coworker's errant approach to your leadership style. "Hey, knock it off. Paul deserves better than that, and he'd never treat you or any of us that way. I see what you're doing and don't like it. So does everyone else, including Paul. This isn't going to work for you if you keep it up." And the beauty of this healthy and "self-repairing" ecosystem is that you'll have created an environment where even problematic employees can straighten themselves out because you'll have lifted up those around them. This isn't a fantasy. It's very real and practical, and it's working for thousands of leaders out there just like you.

Our goal, then, is to make this selfless leadership style more prevalent. To compete effectively in corporate America in the 21st century, companies and their leaders will have to make the employment experience more personal and intimate. It's the next step in our nation's commercial and psychosocial development and workplace history, and it's a long awaited and practical change that will help organizations compete by retaining the best and brightest talent.

65 *Putting Your Ethics "SOX" On: Your Reputation Is the Coin of the Realm*

When Congress passed the Sarbanes-Oxley Act of 2002, the new law unleashed an array of corporate obligations and responsibilities, not the least of which impacted the day-to-day conduct of employees of publicly traded companies. When most U.S. workers hear the name Sarbanes-Oxley, or SOX as it's often abbreviated, the first thing that comes to mind is financial and operational controls and disclosure requirements. And while financial measures and reforms in corporate governance standards make up a majority of SOX initiatives, documented codes of ethics are also a mainstay of the law. To comply, publicly traded companies must publish a code of conduct and ethics, often referred to as a business conduct statement, that must be proactively communicated to all employees.

That "proactive communication" typically comes in the form of live or online training, and here's why it's so critical. When SOX was passed, it had teeth. After the great stock market crash of 2000 to 2003 when millions of investors lost trillions of dollars in the equities market, having depended in good faith on falsified corporate financial statements, Congress made sure that any public companies that failed to comply with SOX reporting requirements would face stiff consequences. Specifically, CEOs and CFOs could face penalties of up to $1 million and/or imprisonment for up to ten years for something known as "defective certification." Defective certification means that the CEO either knew or should have known about the inaccuracy in the company's filed financial statement but failed to correct it. In addition, CEOs and CFOs could face penalties of up to $5 million and/or imprisonment for up to twenty years for "willful noncompliance," or fraud. Because the law made CEOs and CFOs criminally liable, American corporations took notice and rolled out ethics and compliance programs in all worldwide locations at an unprecedented pace.

Your Obligations: Disclose Potential Conflicts of Interest

Let's first look at your obligations to your company. SOX contains management certification requirements that confirm that no potential conflicts of interest exist that could threaten the validity of a corporate filing. To avoid defective certification, a CEO must certify that the information contained in a financial report like a 10Q or 10K is accurate and complete. And the only way your CEO can do that is to poll the workforce and ask employees to certify that they in turn have no conflicts of interest that could interfere with the larger corporate filing.

A conflict of interest exists when your outside business or personal interests adversely affect or have the appearance of adversely affecting your judgment at work. It's critical that you disclose in writing anything that could place your company at risk, and having an undisclosed family relationship with coworkers, customers, suppliers, or competitors of the company is typically the number one issue. Here are other examples of potential conflicts:

- Accepting a personal benefit that obligates you in any way to a customer, vendor, or competitor
- Accepting or offering cash under any circumstances

- Taking a business opportunity away from your company by doing personal business with a customer, supplier, or competitor of the company, except as a regular consumer
- Having a financial interest in a customer, supplier, or competitor, other than less than 1 percent ownership of a publicly traded company

How do you handle such situations? Simply report these potential conflicts on any employee certification form that your company asks you to complete. To be on the safe side, even if you're not given a formal disclosure form, when there is an issue, email it to your supervisor so that you have an electronic record of the disclosure to protect yourself.

Protect Company Time, Property, and Supplies

A critical obligation that you have to your company lies in your use of company property. Remember that your email and voicemail are company property. You have no reasonable expectation of privacy when it comes to email, voicemail, desks, or lockers, and you could expect your company to reiterate this point during SOX training. Company systems are for company use.

That doesn't mean that you can't surf the net for a few minutes to buy a book or schedule a flight. Most companies won't punish employees for limited and reasonable use of the Internet. However, you've got to be careful. If you visit a retail website and then minimize that site on your desktop (i.e., keep it running but out of site) rather than close it, it will still show up electronically as a continuous connection should you be audited by your company's IT department.

Here's how a "perception problem" could play out in the workplace: If your boss complains to HR that your performance is substandard because you're spending too much time on non-company activities, HR may ask IT to run a check on your Internet usage. The electronic record you will have made could come back to haunt you. If the retail site you were visiting was minimized for four hours even though you only accessed it for four minutes, it could end up being your word versus your boss's regarding the amount of *actual* work time that you spent making that retail purchase.

Bear in mind as well that if you purchase a screen saver for your home PC at a local retailer and later install it on your work computer, that could be a big problem. IT is obligated to conduct desktop audits on occasion, and if you've installed software that the company doesn't own a license for, you could be disciplined for violation of software licensing rules.

If you watch pornography on the Internet, even with your office door closed, you could be terminated even for a first offense. Many employees forget that their Internet activity is traceable. What do you do, however, if you accidentally connect to a website that contains inappropriate information like pornography? Disconnect the second you realize that you shouldn't be there. In fact, you may want to call HR or IT, explain the situation, and forward them the email link that you accidentally opened in order to make a record of the unintended site visit.

Your Rights Under SOX: Protection from Whistle Blower Retaliation

Section 806 of SOX prohibits retaliation against employees of a publicly traded company who make good-faith complaints and then are subject to retaliation for disclosing illegal activities by their employers that could ultimately constitute material fraud against shareholders. Here again SOX has teeth: employers will be subject to fines and up to ten years in prison for retaliating against informants.

For that reason, you can expect your company's code of conduct trainers to emphasize the importance of a flexible reporting chain when lodging a complaint. The whole thrust of SOX centers on disclosure and review. A company can only fix problems that it is made aware of, and if employees fear going to their immediate supervisors, they must be given the chance to speak with others in the company. That's why many publicly traded companies provide their worldwide employees with phone numbers and email addresses of senior corporate leaders and even audit committee board members. Employees may contact the board directly, either anonymously or by disclosing their names. Either way, employees have direct and immediate access right to the top of the corporation.

Antidiscrimination Provisions

Your company will no doubt take the opportunity to document and train all employees about its expectations regarding workplace behavior in terms of harassment and discrimination. SOX is, after all, a statement and confirmation about workplace ethics and behavior. Reminding everyone of their right to enjoy—and ensure—a workplace that is free from inappropriate workplace behavior consequently lies at the heart of SOX's ethics message.

First, understand that if you are a supervisor and develop a personal relationship with a subordinate, then that personal relationship must be disclosed. That's fairly logical; if you have the ability to impact a subordinate's performance review or merit increase, and you suddenly fall out of love, any negative work-related criticism could be viewed as retaliation. What would be a typical company response to disclosing a personal relationship with a subordinate? Transferring the subordinate to another unit or supervisor so that there is no immediate reporting relationship or threat of retaliation may provide a simple and fair solution. The key lies in disclosing the new relationship right away, before a perception of retaliation ever arises.

Second, remember that harassment can take place on duty or off, in the office or on the road. Therefore, you should expect coworkers to treat you with the same respect off-site as in the office. Likewise, you're under no obligation to put up with inappropriate comments or off-color jokes, physical contact (such as back rubs), or nonverbal conduct (such as leering or staring). Any such incidents should be reported immediately to a more senior member of management, including your supervisor, department head, HR, the labor relations department, or other company compliance officers (typically corporate counsel).

Be aware, however, that absolute confidentiality cannot be guaranteed if you make a claim that requires an investigation (and almost all claims do). Of course, all reports should be treated as confidential to the extent appropriate. However, HR or the individual conducting the investigation will very likely be obliged to expand that investigation on a "need to know" basis and ultimately bring your complaint to the individual charged. Such confrontation is never easy, but again, your company's antidiscrimination policies and practices should provide appropriate protections from retaliation.

The Sarbanes-Oxley Act certainly caught corporate America's attention. Any time a new law threatens criminal sanctions against a company's CEO and CFO, you can expect that law to garner lots of attention in the press as well as in the practice of company operations. SOX is a broad law that covers ethical business issues ranging from antitrust and insider information matters to political and charitable contributions and international antiboycott laws. Its most notable contribution lies in its emphasis on financial compliance and internal controls. But it also focuses on human behavior and ethics, and companies that undergo "best practices SOX training" will reemphasize the importance of maintaining a work environment that upholds the highest standards of business ethics and workplace behavior. Your rights and responsibilities are now more clearly outlined and defined than ever before, and for that you can be grateful, both as an employee and an investor.

66 *Educating Entry-Level Workers About Ethical Issues That May Derail an Otherwise Successful (Early) Career*

As with all things having to do with successful leadership, communication, and team building, it's the little things you do that count. If you're hiring recent high school or college graduates, take the time to teach them what they don't learn in school: the ethical rules of business. Far too many young adults have entered the workforce without the proper introduction and education, only to find themselves under investigation and terminated for cause—without realizing why until it was too late. Raise their accountability by heightening their awareness early on and engaging them in all matters relating to career growth and development. Teach them life lessons when they join your organization—arguably their first encounter with a full-time job and the sometimes harsh expectations of the workplace. More importantly, steer them clear of the mistaken assumptions that may have landed their predecessors in hot water for failing to understand that school and workplace expectations can differ significantly.

The following subsections give examples of the incorrect assumptions that young workers might make, and examples of how you might train them regarding these issues. Thus, in much of the following discussion, the "you" is not the reader of this book but rather the young worker.

Mistaken Assumption 1: "If I mess up, the company has to give me written notice before they can fire me."

Wrong! In most states, new hires are technically hired "at will," meaning that a company can terminate them with or without cause or notice. Further, most organizations have "introductory" or "probationary" periods, during which they can terminate a new hire at whim if that person isn't meeting performance or conduct standards. In fact, even if you're hired into a union job, most collective bargaining agreements give employers full latitude to terminate at whim within the probationary period (typically sixty to ninety days). So it's definitely not the case that you're entitled to some form of documented corrective action before a company will feel comfortable pulling the plug on your employment.

Mistaken Assumption 2: Companies treat performance problems similarly to how they treat conduct problems

Wrong again! Performance and conduct challenges are typically handled differently in most organizations. When you think of "progressive discipline" or "corrective action" in the form of a verbal, written, and ultimately final written warnings, you're usually referring to performance or attendance problems. However, conduct or behavior-based infractions often warrant what's known as "summary dismissal" (i.e., immediate termination), even for a first offense.

It's easy enough to understand why a company would terminate someone outright for theft, embezzlement, fraud, and the like, but employees don't realize that there are other types of infractions that typically result in immediate dismissal as well. Here are just a few:

Timecard Fraud. In the workplace, time is a proxy for money. If you steal time, it's the same as stealing money, because the end result is the same: The company is out the money that you took illegally. For example, if you put in for overtime that you didn't work, that's considered "timecard fraud." You may not have stolen $10 from the cash register, but the ultimate effect is the same: you're $10 richer at the company's expense. Likewise, if you arrive at work two hours late but falsify your timecard to show that you arrived on time, you'll be awarding yourself two hours of additional straight-time pay. Again, companies will likely view this as theft.

Further, employers don't have much wiggle room *not* to terminate in cases like these. After all, the new hire will have left them little choice: not terminating after an egregious act like theft (or timecard fraud, in this case) could create a bad precedent. And it would be difficult for a company not to terminate Employee A but then later terminate Employee B for the same offense. In short, when it comes to conduct infractions, the issue drives the outcome; no matter how much your supervisor likes your work, if you engage in egregious misconduct, the company will have no option but to terminate you for cause—even for a first occurrence. Think of it as a "third-rail" metaphor: if you step on the third rail of a train track, you're fried. So no matter how long someone has been with a company or how stellar the individual's record, with conduct infractions there may be no forgiveness or exceptions.

Casual Drug Use. What workers do in their private time is strictly up to them, but many companies have a "for cause" drug-testing standard that requires anyone involved in a slip-and-fall incident or auto accident to be tested for cause. Here's how it works: Say your general duties include driving a company vehicle and you're rear-ended at a stop sign across the street from the office. While it certainly wasn't your fault that someone rear-ended you while you were at a full stop, the fact that you were officially involved in an auto accident may require that you be tested for drug usage. Note that many companies' policies don't distinguish fault in situations like these—an employee's involvement is enough to trigger the drug test. Further, many employers count accidents as a "reasonable suspicion" that justifies for-cause drug testing.

Suppose you smoked marijuana or took some other drug about two weeks ago at your 22nd birthday party. Unfortunately, you didn't realize that pot and other drugs may remain in your bloodstream for 30 days or more, and lo and behold, you test positive for drugs. The end result? You're terminated for failing to abide by your company's drug and alcohol abuse policy, even though the effects of the pot have long since disappeared. No, life isn't always fair, but you're a working adult now, and you have to understand and be held accountable for the ramifications of your decisions and actions.

Employment Application Falsification. If you're four units short of your bachelor's degree, but show on your résumé and employment application that you already have a degree, you'll soon find yourself back on the unemployment line. Why? Because you falsified your pre-employment record to give yourself an unfair advantage that helped you land the job on false pretenses. The alternative: Create the proper record on your résumé showing that you're four units short of your bachelor's degree. Any falsification of your employment credentials may get you terminated even weeks or months after you start working if the company finds out. The company can't risk creating a bad precedent by not terminating you for material falsification of your employment application.

Companies terminate swiftly and consistently when it comes to ethics breaches and dishonesty. Put another way, conduct- and behavior-related infractions provide companies the discretion to skip any steps of written, corrective action and escalate immediately and directly to the termination stage. And the downside for you is two-fold: First, you will lose your job. Second, you will have a much more difficult time during a future interview when you're asked why you left your previous company. (Saying, "I was terminated for cause due to an ethical breach and violation of the company's code of conduct" isn't a great response when you're job hunting.)

So always tell the truth. Don't take shortcuts, especially when it comes to electronic records that can be easily traced in an audit (which companies do all the time). Avoid casual drug use. And most important, create a reputation for yourself early in your career as an ethical worker who demonstrates the highest level of integrity. It will help you avoid common pitfalls like the ones above and allow you to sleep better at night as you build your career and grow and develop in your role.

Mistaken Assumption 3: No One's Watching

As with most things in life, people watch you more than you know. That means you have a greater influence on others than you could ever dream of. How do you know that's so? When people come up to you years later and thank you for some small nicety that you did for them that you can't even remember, you begin to realize just how much you touch others' lives. That's just how the universe is designed, and that's always where your greatest opportunities lie.

Everyone's always watching you. That's not some Orwellian concept to make you nervous or paranoid. It's a grand insight and understanding about how important you are to everyone around you, both in the workplace and in your life overall. If you want to get ahead as you begin your career, follow these three very simple rules:

1. Create a welcoming environment so that others feel comfortable approaching you and feel drawn to you.
2. Go out of your way to provide outstanding customer service to everyone you come in contact with. Show that you care in everything you do. People respect competence, but they love even more dealing with someone who's passionate and excited about their work.
3. Look for opportunities to assume greater responsibilities. Everyone needs an additional set of hands and extra help from time to time. Be there for your coworkers. Develop a reputation for taking on more, assisting wherever and whenever you can, and become the "go to" person for anyone needing additional support.

These three simple rules will catapult your career to new heights. You'll make new friends and strong networking contacts. You'll gain exposure to opportunities you won't otherwise have known about. And you'll have fun doing it. Be the role model for others to follow. Go that extra mile to help. Then let your strategy pay off in spades as good things come your way for all the good energy you place into the universe. Always remember how special you are and what a gift your work offers you to define and re-brand yourself and give back to others.

67 Multigenerations at Work: Understanding Each Other's Perspectives

Millennials are becoming the majority in the workforce as we speak. More than one-in-three American workers today are Millennials (adults ages 18 to 34), and 2015 is the year they surpassed Generation X to become the largest share of the American workforce, according to new Pew Research Center analysis of U.S. Census Bureau data.

Further, for the first time in history, we have four generations in the workplace. In fairness, the workplace has never been a single-generation monopoly. Junior workers have always come in to gain experience and work toward advancement. Senior workers have always served as supervisors and mentors. And there's always been some tension between the two. And that's to be expected. However, workplaces generally employed Americans from two or (at maximum) three generations, not four. As one might expect, this phenomenon impacts the workforce in both subtle and overt ways.

Just a few decades ago, most workers retired at age sixty-five. But today, many are staying in the workforce well into their seventies. Young workers, meanwhile, continue to enter the job market at an unrelenting pace. This clash of multiple generations reveals differences in value systems that can lead to workplace clashes as members of different generations disagree about how to behave and perform at work. As they disagree, they can become frustrated by the very act of communicating with one another, a dangerous factor that can damage their ability to work together productively. A brief look at the four generations is important to understand just how they make up this multigenerational workforce.

The Stabilizing Traditionalists: The Veteran Generation

Demographers generally define this generation as born up to 1945. While they're currently in their early seventies or older, many members of the Veteran Generation remain in the workplace. Some enjoy highly paid leadership positions, while others are forced to continue working for low wages because they cannot afford to retire. Their parents lived through the Great Depression, and they consequently live modestly and view life and success as fragile. They believe in "toughing it out" through hard times and never complaining. The Veteran Generation believes in doing as you are told and respects a command and control structure that centralizes power at the leadership level. This generation views conformity as virtuous, an act of self-sacrifice and communal responsibility.

The Transformational Baby Boomers

This enormous generation—77 million in total—was born from 1946 to 1964. They were born to American soldiers who came home from World War II, purchased homes and happily created families. Their generational boom ended with the introduction of the birth control pill in the early 1960s. Baby Boomers were the first generation to watch television as they grew up. They had much greater access to higher education than their parents, and they found more financial success as a result. Baby Boomers are said to believe in the American Dream that their parents lived. They relish authority and seek out positions of power. They experienced a golden age of prosperity, although they would be challenged in their later years because of the Great Recession of 2008. Their parents had relied on pension funds, but Baby Boomers saw pensions vanish during their adulthood, and they failed to save adequately for retirement. As a result, Baby Boomers have largely stayed at work, and both Gen X and Gen Y can feel frustrated, unable to advance because Baby Boomers are not retiring on schedule.

"Entrepreneurial" Generation X

Demographers identify this generation as being born from 1965 to 1979. They're a small generation of only 46 million—the smallest of the four generations in the workplace, sometimes leading to problems with succession planning. Gen X-ers graduated from college just in time to face the jobless recovery that followed the mid-1990s recession. Many watched their parents get laid off or struggle financially, and upon graduation, experienced challenges obtaining meaningful employment and career paths themselves. As a result, Gen X's perspective on the business world is sometimes described as cynical and skeptical. As a generational force then, Gen X-ers prefer to work more independently, which can be interpreted as resistant to authority or even insubordinate. Like their Generation Y/Millennial brethren, Gen X-ers are described as having a slightly hedonist bent and don't necessarily live to work; they work to live and may not feel as inclined to sacrifice their own happiness for the good of the team.

Generation Y ("Millennials" or "The Net Generation")

Born roughly between 1980 and 2000, Gen Y is approximately 90 million strong and growing. Gen Y-ers are described as the most sophisticated consumers in history. Born with electronics all around them and the Internet an easily accessible tool, they know how to search for the products and opportunities well in advance of a sale or even a job interview. While some struggle to find employment in the shadow of the Great Recession of 2008, they nonetheless feel empowered by the information at their fingertips and the generous emotional support of their parents.

Gen Y's sense of empowerment (sometimes interpreted by the other generations as entitlement) spurs them to seek experiences that transcend the ideals of a traditional career path. They search for employment with the goal of finding experiences that satisfy them, and they can be peaceful about letting jobs go—whether they're laid off or leave on their own. Gen Y perceives lack of job security as normal, so they've chosen to be satisfied by opportunities that come their way for as long as they last. Gen Y's tech-infused upbringing created a generation that excels at multitasking. They're accustomed to juggling phone calls, emails, texts, and social media posts.

One in every three employees in the U.S. will be a Millennial by 2015, and by 2025 they will become 75 percent of the global workforce. They're confident in their abilities to change the world (like so many generations before them), but they look forward to making a positive difference both at work and in their world. Millennials are diverse, connected, and are activists for personal rights such as gay marriage and universal healthcare. They believe that business should focus on a societal purpose and the environment, not just be in business to make a profit. They strive to support causes that align with their values and personal belief system. In fact, they have forced companies to rethink flexibility, meetings, and the use of cubicles.

Solutions to Multigenerational Workforce Challenges

With such an eclectic mix of generations, worldviews, and experiences, how can any employer hope to create harmony and alignment in the workplace? Success in this realm, as in so many others, stems from open and honest communication, respect, and recognition. While differences will clearly exist in terms of views on authority, leadership and communication styles, and feelings about work–life balance, the following factors may foster a positive atmosphere in your workplace:

1. Cross-generational mentoring and coaching
2. Collaborative and rotational work assignments and projects
3. Flexible work schedules
4. Opportunities to cross-train on the latest technologies
5. Training workshops on leadership and communication
6. A social atmosphere of community at work, including environmental awareness and social causes that make the world a better place
7. Team building events that heighten awareness of others' backgrounds
8. Networks of cross-functional councils and boards that serve as a primary source of leadership and decision making
9. Social networking tools that build relationships, increase collaboration, and enhance employee engagement

Cross-generational mentoring helps acclimate older workers to new experiences and helps younger workers gain wisdom as they benefit from older workers' experience. Rotational work assignments and projects bring people together quite naturally and align them in a common cause. Flexible work schedules offer new alternatives to getting work done thanks to technology.

If a single project team spans several generations, communication could become a major stumbling block. Encourage team members to let one another know how they prefer to communicate. By sharing how—and how often—they plan to be in touch with one another, teams can anticipate and avoid communication gaps before they occur.

Despite their vast differences, it's important to remember that generations can work effectively together. Each brings a unique viewpoint and skill set to the table. And if they can be persuaded to communicate openly with one another and respect their differences, there is no workplace challenge that a diverse but united team can't master. To foster a more collaborative environment, embrace employees' differences, not from a sense of toleration but as a source of strength. Leverage the energy and creative enthusiasm that this newest generation of Millennials brings to the workplace. Support today's leaders by helping them understand and appreciate the many generations within their workforces, and prepare those leaders of tomorrow. Think carefully about succession planning, and coach up-and-coming supervisors and executives to work effectively with all the generations they lead.

68 *Integrating Newly Inherited Employees into Your Team*

Company or departmental restructurings may be minor or major, and they can result in your inheriting a new group of employees that need to be integrated into your existing team. In and of itself, that may pose no major problems; after all, having a larger staff provides extra "hands on deck" to keep the work flowing more smoothly in your area. And the bigger your staff, the greater the value it adds to your résumé.

There are career development advantages to showing how you've led dynamic teams through change in a post-merger integration.

But this process may also pose some significant challenges if the group you're used to managing has a different style than the one you're inheriting. And several questions are raised: Are you bound by the promises of raises and promotions that were made to your inherited employees by the prior management team? How do you reset your inherited employees' expectations? How do you appraise them at their annual review when you've been supervising them for only a few months? Finally, what happens if you inherit an employee who's known to be a troublemaker or who comes over to your group on final written warning status? Handling these problems needn't be all that perilous if you keep a few critical rules in mind.

Integrating Newcomers

When you learn that a new team is being reassigned to your unit, you may not be given the option of saying no, so think strategically about the move's benefits and plan proactively for its challenges. That all starts by doing your due diligence upfront and gathering the necessary data to determine the group's level of productivity and its style of working. Think of this as cultural integration because it's all about protecting and preserving the culture that you've created with your original group while welcoming the positive aspects of the new group's style. The catch, of course, lies in selecting those positive aspects while minimizing or eliminating the negative ones.

Your first step is to interview the prior management team, if it's still available. Ask about the team's overall strengths, achievements, cohesiveness, and areas for development. Ask the former management team to rank order from highest to lowest all the individuals involved regarding their productivity and performance as well as their personal styles. Here are some questions you might find useful:

- "If you had to hire any one of these individuals back into your group, who would be the first person you'd call?"
- "Who shows the most potential from a succession planning standpoint in terms of career progression?"

- "Who has the most needs or requires the highest maintenance?"
- "Are there any individuals who you'd advise me to be careful with or pay special attention to?"
- "Are there any special circumstances with any of these individuals that I should be aware of?"

Once that initial picture is painted for you verbally, it's time to review the paper trail for each individual involved in this crossover process. Review each individual's résumé, which may be updated or may be many years old. Even if you can access only the original résumés that the individuals presented at their interviews, they could still provide some important information:

- Does the résumé demonstrate straightforward, factual job responsibilities (e.g., typing, phones, filing), or does it structure itself around achievements and accomplishments, especially those linked to increased revenues, reduced costs, or saved time?
- Does the individual quantify results by quoting dollar amounts and percentages, or are job responsibilities in more of a "cut and paste" narrative style?
- How are companies described on the résumé: Do they get no mention beyond their name, or are they outlined according to gross revenues, number of employees, and corporate growth and achievements?
- How much commitment does the individual show toward education, certification, and professional networking?

Next, check each individual's personnel file, especially the performance evaluations and any written warnings. Performance evaluations are the sweet spot of the integration process, since they, more than anything else, can reveal clear documentation about an individual's performance, career progression potential, and areas for development. If performance appraisal is done correctly in the organization, those appraisals become an invaluable tool in picking up where the former management team left off.

If the transition to your team occurs just before the annual performance appraisal is due, then you will not have had enough time to accurately evaluate the individual's performance. But you may not be given the option of passing on this exercise by simply writing "too new to rate" on the appraisal form, so feel free to speak with prior supervisors within your company and find out how they would have rated the individual. Or try to split the review between yourself and the previous supervisors. Add narrative notes under both your names, outlining your respective roles and time frames and explain to the individual that the numerical score that you came up with reflects both supervisors' opinions.

But suppose the employee tells you that the previous supervisor unfairly disliked him. Explain to the individual that this shared review process is common within your company and that all the individuals in the transferred group are being handled in a similar and consistent way. You'll be able to form your own relationship with this individual over time, so both of you can have a clean start from this point forward.

The Challenge of Differing Management Styles

After you've interviewed the prior supervisors and reviewed the résumés and performance appraisals, you then need to integrate the transferred employees' different work styles into your group. For example, if your group enjoys open communication, an environment where their suggestions and recommendations are heard, and an overall culture of empowerment and shared decision making, how do you adopt a group that is used to "doing what it's told"? If you're used to eliciting feedback and suggestions from your team and enjoying a healthy sense of camaraderie, how do you integrate workers who lack trust in management and place doubt in even your most benevolent intentions?

You can't expect the inherited employees to take to your management style right away. They may be worried about their jobs and waiting to see what you're like and how you like to get things done. It may have taken a long time for them to get to the point where they are now; it may take as long for them to adjust to a new way of thinking.

Let your expectations err on the side of over-communicating. New relationships like this often require more support, structure, direction, and feedback. Once things are clearly coming together and you're comfortable with your newly merged team's interaction and productivity, then you can step back and take a more hands-off approach to managing them.

Inheriting Disciplinary and Other Challenges

Your new employees may present many new challenges to you, such as the following:

My boss promised me a 10 percent merit raise next year. Is that still on?

I've been told I'll be promoted on my anniversary, which happens to be next month. What will my new title to be?

Yes, it's true that I'm on final written warning for what my boss called substandard job performance, but she just didn't like me.

These challenges could be the most difficult part of the process of merging your old and new teams. Dedicate time to hearing the new individuals' side of the story and tending to his needs, but promise nothing until you've had a chance to research the situation thoroughly and through as many sources as possible.

What prior management promised in terms of promotions and salary increases might still hold because they were documented and were given final approval by the HR and Finance departments. But some of these claims may be based on incorrect assumptions on the employees' part, so be sure to temper their ambitions while you look into the matter further. Unfortunately, you may then have the unpleasant chore of telling your new employees that HR and Finance do not agree with former management, and that this was not a "done deal," so the promotion or equity adjustment won't be happening this go-around.

In cases like this, let the individuals know exactly whom you spoke with, what they said, and why there may have been confusion. Confirm that all parties are in agreement with the decision, and invite the employees to speak directly with those individuals if they so choose. Just emphasize that you weren't part of that decision; you're just conveying what was communicated to you, and you'll be open to evaluating the situation with a fresh set of eyes as you go forward.

Sometimes, though, it will be more than hurt feelings or disappointment that you'll be inheriting. Candidates who transfer to your group on final written warning for substandard job performance, attendance, or inappropriate workplace conduct may cause specific challenges. When that's the case, make copies of the written and final written warnings, and discuss them openly with the employee in a private meeting. But pretending that these warnings don't exist will be awkward and may cause drama down the road.

There may be two sides to every story, but the validity of the documents isn't in question. As far as you're concerned, they're valid because they're in the employee's file with the employee's signature (and possibly rebuttal). What you want to look for now is how the individual responds to those warnings. If she is very defensive and quick to blame others, she may be someone who feels victimized and who fails to take responsibility for her own actions. In comparison, if she readily admits that she's made mistakes, assumes responsibility for them, and is committed to avoiding those mistakes in the future, then she's demonstrating a high level of business maturity.

You may be reluctant to take on the added responsibility of integrating inherited employees into the close-knit environment that you've worked so hard to cultivate, but don't underestimate the value of this opportunity. You'll rarely be given such a chance to show your leadership development potential, and your résumé will have a new accomplishment—the ability to lead others through integration and demonstrate key leadership skills in a changing business environment. This becomes a strength that you can apply in any workplace situation that comes your way.

69 *Held Hostage by Underperformers: Strategic Group Turnarounds When a Team Is on the Brink of Failure*

Sometimes you have to pull out all the stops. The term *turnaround expert* typically refers to people who take a failing company and restore it to profitability. But it can also refer to a leader who develops a reputation for restoring a team of employees to success. The need for leadership turnaround experts is never higher than when a team or department appears to be on the brink of failure—in other words, when the entire functional area may be about to implode. As challenging as these situations may be, you'll rarely get an opportunity to affect change more than in situations where struggling teams need immediate performance turnarounds. Your ability to restore your team to high performance will speak volumes about the value that you bring to your company.

When teams appear ready to implode, look first to changes in circumstance. Crises typically occur when organizations ratchet up performance expectations, adjust sales commission formulas downward, or introduce new technologies that appear to limit workers' discretion or freedom of choice. Workers sometimes resist change vehemently and demonstrate their dissatisfaction by engaging in work slowdowns, undermining one another, or colluding to entrap their boss. Understanding what may be driving a sudden change in employee behavior will always be your first place to start.

Second, evaluate your front-line leadership team (typically supervisors and leads). Strong leaders can typically take change in stride, keeping their teams focused on achieving results—even when the immediate change at hand may be unsettling or otherwise disruptive to daily busy operations. More likely than not, however, when teams appear to be on the brink of failure, the immediate leaders may be at the core of the problem. Leaders who fail to provide an appropriate amount of structure, direction, and feedback or who otherwise avoid confrontation tend to suffer from excessive drama and meltdowns in their areas, leaving stronger subordinates to take the upper hand in terms of negatively influencing others.

Third, look to those strong voices on the team who exhibit a disproportionate influence over others at times like these. Departments in distress are often being overtaken by negative influencers who intimidate others and act as ringleaders of negativity—sometimes even intimidating their bosses, who avoid them at every turn. Let's take a look at a fairly common scenario where you, the department head, discover a multitude of problems with one individual who continues to bully others. The way you handle such a quagmire is critical in terms of maintaining a healthy environment for the rest of the team and creating the proper written record to protect your company from future legal challenges.

Creating an Appropriate Written Record for the Group

"Professional plaintiffs" become very adept at keeping others at bay, and what works in their favor is that people tend to avoid them—and the conflict inherent in challenging them—so they often act with impunity. As a result, they keep receiving "meets expectations" performance review scores and no progressive discipline is initiated, so their personnel records indicate no particular problem or concern with their performance. In fact, these problematic performers and workplace bullies may be the first to invoke the services of a lawyer, claiming that they themselves are being bullied and are the victim of a system run amok.

Here's what the plaintiff's attorney's argument typically sounds like: "Managers avoid her, and the company is clearly cutting a wide swath around her, withholding key responsibilities from her and otherwise not giving her a chance to excel in her role." Then comes the claim that this is all occurring because her supervisor harbors some animus against her because of her protected status (i.e., age, race, gender, or the like). This is the perfect formula for a discrimination claim from someone who's a lackluster performer with a negative attitude who's actually the cause—not the recipient—of the problematic conduct that's undermining the workplace.

The written record can only change, however, if you work with HR or with your department head to conduct an investigation into the team's allegations. Assuming everyone seems to get along fine with one another except for the one individual who aggressively confronts anyone who might challenge her, then you've got an excellent opportunity to hold a group meeting and share perceptions of what you've learned and also reset management's expectations.

Depending on what you learn during your investigational meetings, you then have the opportunity to issue letters of clarification to recap management's expectations for all members of the team. With everyone starting with a fresh beginning and with the appropriate written record in place, you'll be providing all individuals involved with an opportunity to reinvent themselves in light of management's new expectations. You'll have created a new line in the sand that outlines expectations and that allows the wound to heal. Any future transgressions should be reported directly to you, and you've now provided a simple solution that invites everyone on the team back to normalcy.

Resetting Management's Expectations for the Problematic Employee

Besides reestablishing group expectations, you also have the opportunity to follow up with the employee whom you find to be at the heart of the problem. Depending on what you learn during the investigation and group mediation, this individual may receive formal corrective action (in this case, a final written warning) in addition to the group letter of clarification, emphasizing the following:

> First, our findings show that you have demonstrated unprofessional conduct toward your coworkers. Specifically, several coworkers and even your immediate supervisor confirmed that you made inappropriate comments: "I'm in charge around here." "Management doesn't know its ass from a hole in the wall." "This company is just so f---ed up." Likewise, you tend to refer to members of leadership as "a---holes, idiots, and f---ups."

> Further, you were witnessed and admit to having shouted to an older coworker across the room, "Can I borrow your Depends [adult diapers]? I want to watch this Saturday's football game and don't want to have to get off the couch."

> You are not permitted to engage in such disparaging comments about the company, the leadership team, or your coworkers. Doing so will result in your immediate dismissal for cause. Further, you're not in charge of the team. You may be a senior member of the group tenure-wise, but that in no way implies that any kind of leadership, supervisory, or lead status has been conferred upon you. Therefore, no further comments along these lines will be permitted under any circumstances.

> Any further disparaging remarks about the company, your leadership team, or your coworkers' abilities will result in immediate dismissal. If you use the f-word again in public, you will be dismissed. If you make any other disparaging remarks relating to someone's age or slowness related to age, you'll be immediately dismissed.

> This is your last chance. Your job is now in immediate jeopardy of being lost. If you ever again violate these or other terms and conditions of employment or engage in similar misconduct, you will be immediately discharged for cause.

With a written record in place that addresses both group expectations and the individual's specific workplace conduct issues, you'll have furnished sufficient documentation to restore order to the team. The employee will have been notified in writing about the company's concerns, thereby according her workplace due process in the form of documented corrective action.

Management can now take back control and mitigate this employee's negative influence on the rest of the team. Thus, if she ultimately files a lawsuit, you will have a record that is written on your terms, not hers. At her next performance review, it should be noted that she does not meet minimum expectations for the entire review year due to this significant final written warning. This way, you'll have a final written warning on record, combined with a failed annual performance review, in addition to no merit increase or bonus. That's the kind of record you need to deal with this type of caustic behavior and remove it from your workplace.

The team can then begin to heal and regain its self-confidence. What typically becomes of these workplace bullies once they've been called out and their cases are appropriately documented is that they resign quietly within a few months. Why? First, they miss the self-imposed drama. Second, they realize that they've cut off their future prospects within the organization. And third, they perceive that they have been diminished in the eyes of their coworkers—the very people they chose to bully and intimidate. They leave without filing a lawsuit because that avenue will have been cut off for them via the paper trail that is now in place. And so the workplace is reinvigorated and set right again to return to productivity and profitability.

70 Dealing with Employees in Crisis: A Blueprint for Proactive Management Intervention

Preventing violence and enhancing workplace safety is important to all employers. However, instructing frontline leaders on how to deal with an employee crisis on a proactive basis sometimes gets short shrift. What do you do when you notice employees isolating themselves from the rest of the group? How do you deal with an employee who states that he's feeling suicidal? And what if your "suicidal" employee seems to go a step further and becomes potentially "homicidal"?

These extreme situations don't occur often in the workplace. Still, most HR practitioners have dealt with many employees in crisis, and now is the time to build a methodology for addressing such a critical problem.

Inviting the Isolated Employee Back into the Fold

Workers vulnerable to irrational acts typically appear as loners who are isolated from the rest of the group. These people often develop a "time clock" mentality where they go through the motions of doing their jobs but are otherwise disengaged. Extending a helping hand to them can sometimes be a daunting task, so managers avoid dealing with the issue.

However, left in a vacuum void of information and two-way communication, these employees create their own versions of reality. Generally speaking, such individuals may tend to demonstrate a low level of self-awareness and an entitlement mentality that makes it very difficult to approach them or gain their buy-in. As such, they may attribute negative intentions to others' actions where none are intended in order to justify their anger. What these loners may need is an opportunity to reconnect to the group and enjoy the social elements of work—recognition and appreciation for a job well done as well as a sense that they belong and can make a positive difference in the workplace.

Making it safe for solo players like this to engage with their coworkers is no easy task. It begins by strengthening your own personal relationship with the individual as the group leader. It's then followed by encouraging group activities where participation is required and you take the "outsider" under your wing and make it safer for everyone to interact more collaboratively. While there's no right or wrong way to do this, understand that players on all sides will naturally feel vulnerable if they need to engage more proactively with one another. Your job is to make it safe for them to feel vulnerable. And the best way to do that is to make yourself vulnerable and show everyone else that it's okay to feel that way. Your act of caring is enough, and it will speak volumes as to your character and compassion.

 A key step is to meet with your staff members one-on-one to learn how they view the situation. Ask questions like these:

> How would you grade our group in terms of camaraderie and teamwork? How do staff members get along with each other, and have you had any particular problems with other members of the group?
>
> Are you aware of any particular historical problems among the team members, and could you tell me how they were or weren't resolved? Did anyone "disengage" after any particular incidents or otherwise appear to be isolated or abandoned from the group?
>
> What would you recommend we do to better the situation?
>
> I've got to ask a favor of you. If I attempt to bring peace to both sides of this rift, would you support me and welcome the problem employee back into the fold?

More likely than not, you'll hear fairly consistent stories and explanations of the ongoing strife with each employee group, and you'll probably see both sides of the story objectively and have a better understanding of how the fallout came to be. With each individual's commitment to do her part in bettering the situation, it will then be time to hold a group meeting.

 The group meeting might open like this:

> Folks, life is too short. We spend more time with our coworkers than we do with our families and friends, and there's certainly more than enough work to go around. What can make this unbearable for us, however, is allowing a negative environment to fester. If there's a lack of communication, harbored unresolved resentments, and a lack of respect for one other, then not only is work not going to be any fun—it's also not going to be particularly productive.
>
> I've met individually with each of you to learn about issues historically affecting the group, and I want you to know that I'm holding each of you accountable for creating a work environment where everyone is treated with respect and dignity. I'm also holding you responsible for your own "perception management," meaning that it's not about being right or wrong. It's about ensuring that others understand your good intentions and are made to feel welcome in our department.
>
> I realize that this situation may have taken years to get to this point, and it may take just as long to get to a point where there's mutual trust and respect in your interactions. But people tend to respond in kind, and if you treat others

respectfully, they'll do the same for you. I'm here to ensure that that's the case, and I'll be here for each of you should you need me.

But I won't stand for any attempts to place blame on others. I also won't have any members of our staff feeling singled out or otherwise isolated from the rest of the team. If the problems continue, there will be disciplinary consequences. But if you support me in making this a more inclusive working environment, then we can discover new ways of adding value to our work. Can I count on your support?

Allowing people to feel safe will do more than anything to avert a potential crisis in the workplace.

Employee Assistance Programs

What happens if, despite your best intentions, the isolated individual tells you she's feeling suicidal? If your company has an employee assistance program (EAP), you can say to the employee:

Kristine, I want you to wait here with me while I call the EAP, because I'm not your best resource if you're feeling that way, and I know that Marilyn Jones at the EAP would certainly help. OK?

Making a "formal" referral to the EAP (as opposed to a "voluntary" referral where the employee self-refers) should almost always be done with the employee's consent. However, in extreme cases where a formal referral may be warranted, you must ensure that the employee has a job performance problem in addition to appearing to be mentally depressed, suicidal, or potentially hostile. In the case of formal referrals, you would discuss your perceptions of the work performance problems with the intake counselor on the front end (although not necessarily in front of the employee). With a signed release from the employee, the EAP will later be able to provide you with limited feedback about the individual's attendance, compliance, and prognosis.

In certain cases (for example, with potential workplace violence issues), you have the option of not permitting the individual back to work without a fitness-for-duty release from a licensed healthcare practitioner. Such leaves are typically paid through the initial period of evaluation. Beyond that, employees typically use accrued time off to be compensated while receiving further treatment.

Americans with Disabilities Act Limitations and Caveats

One caveat about "formal" EAP referrals: Although they may certainly be justified in cases of threats of employee suicide, recent case law shows that formal EAP referrals have created burdens on employers under the Americans with Disabilities Act (ADA). Specifically, plaintiffs' attorneys have argued that, on the basis of a mandatory EAP referral, the employer did indeed regard the client as disabled. (The ADA and some state disability discrimination laws protect individuals who either have or are perceived as having a disability, including a mental disability.) Such an interpretation could become legally problematic should you then decide to take some adverse action (especially termination) against the employee.

In addition, you shouldn't mandate that an employee attend treatment sessions by threatening termination for not doing so. Such a requirement could appear to make an EAP referral an extension of your disciplinary authority and give rise to claims of disability discrimination based on a perceived mental disability, invasion of privacy, or misuse of confidential medical information in certain states.

Put Safety First

An extreme worker reaction might also result in veiled threats of homicide rather than suicide. For example, what if an employee came to your office one morning, placed a live shell of ammunition on your desk, and stated that her coworkers better not bother her today "if they know what's good for them"? Veiled threats like these are not uncommon in extreme cases.

Your first reaction would probably be to fire this person and ensure that she has no further access to company property. And that may be the best decision for your organization in the end. Still, it's probably best to make a record that you didn't overreact or jump to unfair conclusions. In such cases, placing the employee on a paid

administrative leave might make the most sense. Explain your rationale to the employee this way:

> Kristine, I know you met with our EAP provider, and they gave us a written
> release for you to return to work. You also told me that you were feeling much
> better about work and about your relationship with your coworkers at that
> time. However, the feelings that you're sharing with me right now raise some
> concerns, as I'm sure you understand, and I think it's best to send you home
> with pay while I discuss with my superiors how to best handle this. We'll call it
> an administrative leave and continue to pay you as though you were working
> full time. I'll call you tomorrow at home.
>
> I've got to ask a favor, though. The way that our company normally handles
> these things is to ask the employee to go straight home. I can't have you here
> at work while I do my objective fact-finding. Having you wait at home is always
> part of an administrative leave. Is that reasonable to you, and will you support
> that request?
>
> [Yes.]

Gently escort the employee off the premises and alert Security or
take other reasonable steps to ensure your other workers' safety. Most
employment lawyers will recommend that you tell the others that
a threat, whether overt or veiled, was indeed made against them individually or as a group. You should likewise share the steps the company is taking to address the situation. However, in order to protect
the individual's privacy and to avoid later claims of defamation, you
should limit disclosure of specifics only to those individuals with a
need to know.

Bring these newfound threats to the attention of the EAP, and be
sure to seek the advice of qualified legal counsel before moving to
terminate. If you then choose to dismiss, do so over the phone within
24 to 48 hours. Send the employee's personal belongings and her final
check to her home via courier. Include a letter that states that she
may no longer enter company property for any reason without the
advance approval of the vice president of HR or similar designee. The
company attorney should approve the final draft of the letter. Finally,
remember that EAPs are also an excellent resource for your other employees should they need someone to talk to.

71   *Encouraging Employees to Leave Your Company: When It's Good for You and Good for Them*

Sometimes it becomes necessary to convince employees to leave your company because they are demonstrating serious performance or conduct problems. Some of these disenfranchised employees will insist on staying "on principle," that is, "I'll stay until *I'm* good and ready to leave. No one's forcing me out of my job until I'm ready to go—especially not that boss of mine!"

Unfortunately, the results can be very problematic, leading to stress claims for workers' compensation, leaves of absence, union grievances, or wrongful termination lawsuits. Reciprocally, months or years of feeling unappreciated and having their egos and self-esteem bashed await the employees. So your best solution from an employee relations standpoint may be to broker a peace where the employee may leave the job with her dignity and respect intact.

Some caveats: First, meetings such as this require a third-party mediator (typically HR or a senior member of management). If the immediate supervisors who are part of the problematic interpersonal relationship with disenfranchised employees attempt to encourage the employee to quit, their efforts may be seen as insincere or self-serving at best. They simply lack the credibility to be seen as objective.

Second, whatever is discussed with the employee in meetings like this may take on a different meaning if the company is later sued in a "constructive discharge claim," which is similar to a wrongful discharge claim except that the employee resigns instead of being terminated. Still, a plaintiff's attorney will typically argue that the conditions were so intolerable at work that any reasonable person would have resigned under similar circumstances. Consequently, the plaintiff's attorney will argue, "My client was forced into resigning her position, and the company had no right to create such an unfriendly environment. Her supervisor told her that she wasn't wanted there anymore and had no future with the company! Telling her that after two years of dedicated service and one full year of isolating her from the rest of the team, denying her a raise, withholding training, and holding her to a higher standard than everyone else was just too much. She had to quit, but it was *their* fault."

When it comes to job performance problems and termination, both sides are often in total disagreement about the situation; managers argue that the problematic employee is disrespectful, noncommunicative, and does not hold herself accountable for her own actions. As a result, managers complain, "I delegate as little to her as I can. Instead, I do the work myself or give it to the other members of the team. My other staff members resent that she doesn't do her own share of the work, and they're tired of my cutting a wide swath around this employee for fear of upsetting her or making matters worse."

The disenfranchised employee in this same scenario will argue the opposite, almost as if holding up a mirror: "My boss shows me no respect, never makes me feel like part of the team, and constantly holds me to a higher standard than everyone else. I'm never in the communication loop, and I'm never told when I do something right—only when I do something wrong. I'm sick and tired of being treated differently!"

In these situations there's enough blame to go around: the employees too often take the easy road out and justify their irresponsible behavior by arguing favoritism and blaming their bosses for their own unhappiness; managers have clearly failed in their responsibility to create a working environment where employees can motivate themselves and make a positive contribution to the department's goals. In essence, if the working relationship has deteriorated to this point, both the manager and worker have failed. Sometimes, however, trying to fix these problems just becomes an ongoing battle of wills where little good results.

Third-Party Intermediaries to the Rescue

Human Resources or senior management typically functions as the third-party mediator who attempts to fix the problem with the help of both the supervisor and the employee. When progressive discipline or an employee transfer isn't feasible, then the mediator/broker may attempt to gently inject respect, dignity, and professionalism into the working relationship by providing the employee with an exit strategy:

Mary, you've worked as Sue's secretary for the past two years, and I don't believe that you or Sue has felt that this was a good working relationship. Sometimes it's just not the right personality mix or the right timing in people's lives, and the working relationship suffers. Would you agree that it hasn't been ideal for you?

[Yes.]

Sue, you've shared your frustrations about Mary's substandard job performance and inappropriate workplace conduct with me privately. I've also recommended that you speak with Mary directly, and you've done that on multiple occasions. So you're frustrated too, right?

[Yes.]

Okay, then it may be time to lay down our shields and extend the proverbial olive branch. There's enough work around here to sink a battleship. When you add the interpersonal friction that you've been both experiencing for the past year or so, it becomes unbearable. I don't want to minimize the importance of your working relationship together, but with all due respect, it's *only* work. I mean, when you think about families who lose their health or parents who have to see their children through serious illnesses—that's important in life. If we're not suffering from that kind of illness, we're lucky. So let's keep that in perspective as we look at this workplace issue, okay?

Sometimes it's fair to say that it just isn't a good fit. What's important to me is that both parties feel that they're being supported and treated with dignity and respect. I don't want people feeling that their egos and self-esteem are being trashed. Life is simply too short for that.

Mary, you're an executive assistant, and Sue is a vice president with long-term tenure with the organization, so I need to tell you that Sue isn't going anywhere. Senior management believes she's doing an excellent job. That's an important point for you to keep in mind as you consider your options. As an objective third party, it appears to me that you're not happy here. You seem to be disappointed in the management team. You appear not to enjoy your work. And I'm sure you feel that you're not appreciated or part of the team, at least at certain times. Am I correct?

[Yes.]

Okay, so tell me your thoughts: Would leaving now on your own accord allow you an honorable exit strategy? Would exploring other opportunities outside the company while you're still employed make sense for you at this point in your career? We'd be willing to allow you to begin interviewing at other companies as long as you make sure that our work comes first and that we're given at least 24 hours' notice of an upcoming interview. I'm only mentioning this because I don't want you to feel that you need to feign illness or conjure up doctors' and dentists' appointments if you've got an interview coming up. I'd rather we all be above board and that you let us help you. More importantly, I want you to feel that you have options and choices in situations like this. You don't have to decide now, but please give some thought to how I may be able to help you with and through this.

One other thing, Mary. I want you to know that this is strictly up to you. If you'd like our support to either resign on your own terms now or to begin looking for other work, then we'll help you. If not, that's okay too. We'll do everything we can to help you reinvent your working relationship with Sue and to feel more appreciated for your efforts. I just want you and Sue to feel better about working with each other if you choose to stay. I also want to give you these additional options, Mary, because it's better that we discuss these things openly rather than leave them unsaid. What are your thoughts?

This gentle approach typically lowers the tension in the relationship immediately. The logic to this intervention is simply this: It's always better to let people know where they stand. When people are treated professionally and respectfully, they'll typically respond in kind. Although delivering a message like this can be confrontational, it's therapeutic. After all, most people would rather be told that their manager would prefer that they look for something else. That's a much better alternative than having to "divine" from their managers' actions that they're not wanted anymore.

There may be downsides to this intervention technique. You never know exactly how people will respond because principle can easily get in the way. As such, they may be looking to find fault in order to cause greater drama, such as a lawsuit. But as long as the third-party mediator is careful to ensure that the employee understands that this is *her* decision (thereby avoiding a constructive discharge claim later), this intervention should work well. People need to hear how others feel about them. Workers are responsible for their own "perception management," and perception is reality until proven otherwise. Most employees will appreciate the opportunity to hear about problems concerning them in an open and honest forum. Then the healing can begin.

Still, there's one additional hurdle that you have to bear in mind: If you "show your hand" as an employer, and then ultimately have to terminate the worker for cause, this could end up triggering a wrongful termination lawsuit. The record could be interpreted as follows: "My immediate supervisor and HR encouraged me to resign, and when I said no, they found a way to fire me." Okay, fair enough. But with HR and senior leadership working in tandem to offer the individual a respectful way out of the organization or at least the flexibility to interview elsewhere if she chooses, then most workers will respond in kind and not pursue a retaliation charge. But proceed with caution and consult with qualified legal counsel before initiating a meeting like this if you suspect that the individual may be inclined to litigate.

How often does this approach work? In my experience, it's an 80–20 game: 20 percent of the time employees choose to resign on the spot or agree to begin looking immediately for other work. That may not seem like a great track record, but if you look longer-term, you'll find that many employees will simply leave the company within a few months after a meeting like this. No matter how angry employees are at the company, they'll come to realize that fighting an uphill battle makes no sense. When angry people are treated respectfully, their anger dissipates. And when the anger and drama are removed from the equation, they often feel less inclined to keep the job "on principle." More importantly, they'll leave quietly on their own terms without all the histrionics and threats of lawsuits.

You can tell anybody anything but it's *how* you say it that counts. Both the involved supervisor and employee will appreciate your caring and objective approach to a difficult meeting like this. After all, involved management is all about getting to the truly human concerns at hand—issues that may have been left unaddressed for far too long. You'll simultaneously support your management team and allow your employees to take control back of their careers. That's what enlightened leadership is all about.

72   *Resignations: Properly Handling Employees Who Give Notice*

Employees who resign usually submit a letter and give two weeks' notice so that you have some lead-time to find a replacement. Usually there's little more to do than thank the person for his service and prepare your strategy for filling the position and distributing the individual's work to the remaining team members until a replacement can be found.

But what if the resigning individual refuses to provide a final termination date? What if she offers verbal notice, not written notice, and she's done this before, and now you're afraid she's going to change her mind again within the two-week notice period? And what if you prefer that a resigning employee leave immediately rather than in two weeks? As you can see, the exit process can get a bit complicated depending on the circumstances, so let's address some common scenarios.

First, if someone refuses to commit to a final separation date, that's not okay. They can't just walk in and tell you they're leaving without telling you when. Likewise, someone may walk into your office and tender notice 90 days from now (which just happens to coincide with the date she's getting married). Are you obligated to keep her through her wedding date? Bear in mind that once an employee places you on notice of her intentions to leave the organization, you have a legitimate business need to question her intentions and confirm the time lines. You're not obligated to employ an unexceptional worker who's buying time by remaining employed while she's waiting to get married, finish a bachelor's degree, or complete some other personal commitment. With calendar in hand, call the individual into your office in private and inform her that setting a specific date will help you plan for a successful transition. Agree on an end date that suits your needs—not hers.

As for the individual who graciously offers ninety days' notice, simply thank her for the generous offer but let her know that you plan on following the company's policy and past practice of accepting two weeks' notice. She'll be free to leave at that time and will be compensated for her work through that end date.

Then again, if you're in a situation where you'd rather send the employee home today rather than in two weeks, you have every right to do so. (This happens often with sales people, especially when they're going directly to a competitor.) However, it will likely make more sense for you to pay out the two-week notice period. Consider it a cheap insurance contract because if you, rather than the employee, determine the date that the worker is to leave your company (i.e., today rather than two weeks from now), you may be deemed the "moving party" under the Labor Department's definition. If that's the case, then technically you may have inadvertently transformed the "resignation" into a "discharge," and the individual may be entitled to unemployment insurance benefits. Further, sending resigning employees home the same day without paying them through their notice period could be viewed as a wrongful termination if your employee handbook states that you expect all terminating employees to provide your company with two weeks' notice. In such cases, the extra two weeks of pay function as a cheap insurance policy to ward off any potential wrongful termination claims.

But if an employee refuses to resign in writing and you suspect she may change her mind or is otherwise playing games, you have every right to confirm her verbal resignation in writing. A simple email or note might read something like this:

> Laura, I have accepted your verbal resignation today, January 30th, and I realize that February 15th will be your last day with our company. You will be relieved of your duties on that day, and I will appreciate your cooperation over the next two weeks in reassigning your current workload and helping with the job posting. Thank you for your contribution to our company over the past two years, and I wish you well in your future career.

Your written confirmation will serve as a proxy for hers, and it will make it more difficult for Laura to change her mind one week later and attempt to keep her job.

What about the employee who looks to rescind her resignation and demands that you allow her to keep her job? Does she have a right to insist that you retain her before her two-week notice period runs out? It depends. You have the right, as an employer, to rely on the individual's resignation in good faith and end her employment on the agreed upon date. But how you *act in reliance* on the notice becomes a key issue. Specifically, if you haven't truly taken action in reliance upon her resignation by posting her job, reassigning her work duties, and interviewing candidates, for example, then the employee may very well be free to rescind her resignation during the notice period. Or so will argue her lawyer, stating that your refusal to give her the job back—when you did nothing to act on her notice—amounts to nothing shy of wrongful termination. The lesson? When a problematic and under-performing employee tenders her notice, don't celebrate too quickly. Instead, demonstrate that you have accepted her resignation in good faith by posting the job, redistributing her work, and beginning interviewing as quickly as possible—especially within her two-week notice period. You'll have a much greater chance of warding off a wrongful termination claim if you can show that you responded appropriately to her notice.

73 *Terminations for Cause Versus Resignations by Mutual Consent*

Here's another common scenario: you're asked to allow someone to "resign by mutual consent" rather than being terminated for cause. While you're natural instinct may be to allow the individual to resign on his own terms, think carefully about this option before granting it.

Generally speaking, any ambiguity in the termination process could be held against you. If an employee fails to abide by the terms of a final written warning or exhibits egregious misconduct, then termination is appropriate. Lessening the blow by allowing the employee to resign, offering a separation package, or placing the individual on an inactive status while keeping him on the payroll could be interpreted as signs of weakness on the part of the employer, or worse, as a tacit acknowledgment that the employer was partly at fault. This falls under the heading of "no good deed goes unpunished," so be hesitant about granting employees the right to resign when all the termination paperwork and processing is in place.

Thus, it is important to avoid sugarcoating terminations. Assuming you've accorded the employee workplace due process in the form of progressive discipline, follow your company's policies and practices, and avoid exceptions. That's especially true in cases of "summary offenses" (i.e., immediate terminations without prior corrective action) for egregious misconduct, such as theft, forgery, fraud, record falsification, workplace violence, or severe cases of harassment or bullying. Termination for cause should be a straightforward management practice. Your good intentions may be distorted if a former employee tries to avert blame and may be capitalized on if a plaintiff's attorney seeks to attribute ulterior motives to your benevolent actions. When in doubt, always check with qualified legal counsel before agreeing to convert terminations for cause into employee resignations.

74 The Proper Care and Handling of Your Company's HR Team

As an HR leader, I've often heard company managers say, "I wouldn't want your job. How do you do this kind of work all the time?" Usually, these comments come up just as we're about to discipline, terminate, or lay off one of their employees. And I can't say that I always feel compelled to answer their question with an uplifting, optimistic response. Sure, sometimes I do ask myself, "Is this what I went to college for?" But then I think, "There's nothing I'd rather do and no place where I could make as great a difference for my company than in my HR role."

As a line manager in corporate America, you should maximize your relationship with the HR department, which can be an important resource and an ally—both for strategic partnering on business issues as well as for confidential, off-the-record discussions. If you do not develop a relationship with HR, you may feel that HR represents yet another barrier to getting things done the way you want. Here are some insights into understanding how HR wants to help you do a better job.

Many MBA programs devote a course to human resources (or organizational development or organizational behavior), so you may already know that the HR discipline, broadly speaking, is about leading and motivating people and maximizing employee productivity. As such, it's a portable skill that continually needs to be honed and strengthened throughout your career. People drawn to HR as a career often view it as a "calling" in the true sense of the word. Many HR practitioners feel a need to help others and to give back to the community. HR is the only discipline that allows for such workplace philanthropy.

That giveback often comes from one-on-one employee coaching, but more frequently it comes from interventions in which HR supports management in helping employees.

These interventions start with a line manager consulting HR for guidance on structuring a particular action (e.g., hiring, promoting, training, disciplining, or discharging). HR's key goal is to support management in making the best people decisions for the company, whether that be in staffing, retention, or performance management. But if a manager waits too long before consulting HR, then the problem requiring action may have reached a crisis level, which makes resolution that much harder. Following are some key areas where you'll want to develop strong relationships with your internal HR partners.

Recruitment

The HR department can help you avoid prematurely "giving away the farm" in terms of salary information. Salary offers are typically saved for the final rounds of interviewing, for several reasons. First, it's a matter of budgeting. As a hiring manager, you may not know exactly how much a particular position was budgeted for, and if you mention a dollar amount to candidates that is above the budget, then you'll be at a disadvantage in the salary negotiation. Once a candidate hears that a position pays up to $50,000 but the company only wants to offer $45,000, the likelihood of that candidate agreeing to the offer diminishes.

Second, there's the matter of internal equity. Regardless of what your budget will allow, you've got to slot the candidate into the existing employee population by reviewing similar employees' years of service, education, technical certification, skills, knowledge, and abilities. This sometimes extends even to staff members outside your immediate team or department. In practice, pay secrecy is often a fiction; employees share information about their salaries, and if your senior team members find out that you've paid more to an incoming recruit than they are paid, it could lead to frustration and angst and even to unwanted turnover. So be sure to allow HR to perform an internal equity analysis before discussing salaries or otherwise extending job offers, so that you don't end up hiring one person and losing three to premature resignations.

Also, consider allowing HR to extend all employment offers. First, you don't want to be haggling or negotiating over salary matters with someone who will be working for you. That's better done by a neutral third party like HR or a headhunter. Second, although most managers are very sensitive about what they say to candidates in the offer process, sometimes managers feel pressured or uncomfortable and begin offering the moon: "There'll be plenty opportunity for promotion. My guess is you'll be up and out of this job in six to nine months. And there's a lot of job security at our company; you really have screw up pretty badly to be fired around here." Such commitments can't always be fulfilled, of course, but the candidate might construe these comments as verbal commitments, which could create problems for you down the road. So let HR be the objective dealmaker and salary negotiator.

Employee Relations

One of the greatest benefits that HR can provide you is in the area of employee relations. Supervisors hate having to discipline or terminate staff members. Thus, many managers delay dealing with under-performing employees, hoping that the problem will fix itself so that they can avoid a confrontation. But the problems usually continue to build to the point that managers want the employee fired immediately. They rush over to HR with the demand, "I want this person fired now!"

The HR department doesn't want to be seen as an obstacle to management. Rather, HR exists to insulate the company from employee-related liability. So when HR first learns of a manager's desire to fire someone only at the crisis point, typically there will be no information in the employee's personnel file to warrant such a termination. Instead, HR often finds a series of acceptable annual performance reviews and no written progressive disciplines on file.

When that's the case, the only solution that HR can offer is to initiate the progressive discipline process by composing a first, second, or final written warning (depending on the circumstances). Unfortunately, that makes HR appear to be the "red tape" machine that stops you from taking the action steps that you feel are necessary to keep your operation running effectively. How much easier it would have been had HR been involved earlier in the process; with prior warnings documented and a substandard annual performance review on file, this most recent incident that "broke the camel's back" might have indeed justified a termination.

Also, as a manager, you should not take on too much liability yourself. The company doesn't pay you enough to shoulder the responsibility that could jeopardize your personal savings. In many states, managers found guilty of unlawful employment decisions can be personally penalized. So just make sure you're acting *within the course of scope of your employment* when making a decision to terminate or lay off an employee. The best way to do that is to have everything approved by HR first before taking any adverse action against an employee.

The HR department can help in more subtle ways, too. HR does more than extend employment offers or approve terminations for cause. HR can also help you address staff problems and get members of your team speaking to one another again. You've seen employees who have become mentally unemployed. They feel isolated from the group, develop a "time clock mentality," and do only enough work to get by. Correcting this problem can be a daunting challenge even for the most successful managers and supervisors, especially since they are often too close to the situation. Managers need a fresh set of eyes to assess the situation objectively—a neutral third party that is not involved in this particular group dynamic. HR can be that third party.

The HR representative might begin by saying, "We're here to open the lines of communication. This isn't about wrong or right. There's no attacking allowed, and no one has to defend himself. We're simply talking about differences in perception here. The goal is to get everything out in the open, and you also have to remember that whatever you say has to be said in a spirit of constructive criticism. We can fix this together; we just need to make ourselves a little vulnerable and to accept responsibility for our share of the problem."

Compensation

The last few years have been trying for everyone, what with minimal merit increases, frozen promotions and salary adjustments, mass layoffs due to corporate downsizing, and unforeseen corporate mergers and consolidations. To compensate, managers have been known to make quasi-promises to their staff members to motivate them and raise morale.

To be fair, most of these cases involve managers who truly believed at the time that they'd be able to give a higher merit increase or a promotion to a subordinate in the near future. Unfortunately, and to the manager's chagrin, those promises couldn't be fulfilled, for whatever reason. The result: lowered morale, heightened turnover, and more legal exposure than was necessary.

So any time you feel a need to discuss titles, merit increases, equity adjustments, or promotions with staff, first consult with the compensation experts from HR. They can provide you with some excellent tips on what to say and propose alternatives that you might not have thought of. You'll learn where your employees fit on the compensation scale for their positions, how their historical merit increases compare to those of their coworkers, and what the likely merit pool will be this year. This is critical information for you to have in hand before you begin your meetings with staff members.

Many line managers avoid dealing with HR, preferring to "keep it in the family" and go it alone; they feel that if they can't handle a problem themselves, they'll be perceived as weak. This is nonsense! As a line manager, you need support in resolving people issues and maximizing staff performance. If you're fortunate enough to have an HR resource on board, then be sure and use it to your advantage.

Indeed, in a business economy based on "intellectual capital," using all the tools available, including HR, to maximize your employees' productivity, add strong performers to your team, and handle employees who stubbornly fail to meet company standards is truly your key responsibility. Don't let pride or ignorance stand in the way of your developing the strongest team in your company. Instead, shift the balance of intellectual power your way by making use of HR as a "knowledge" resource for staffing, retention, and performance management issues.

75 *Inspirational Leadership: Some Final Thoughts*

We began this book with a simple premise: inspirational leadership is within your reach. It's not a far-off, idealistic fantasy. It's not about being a master communicator like Presidents Ronald Reagan or Bill Clinton. And it doesn't require extreme circumstances to reveal itself, like General George Patton in World War II. Instead, inspirational leadership reveals itself in many quiet ways, not only by what you do but, more importantly, by who you are.

We've discussed the concept that *beingness trumps doingness*, meaning that people respect you and are motivated and inspired by you primarily because of who you are as a leader, as a listener, and as a caring human being, not because of what you're doing at any given time. There's no need to try to figure out what to do, when in reality the simplest things, done in kindness and selflessness, help us stand out among our peers. Books on management offer hundreds or thousands of ways of motivating employees, but the truth is that workers motivate themselves. Your job is simply to create a work environment where they can do so. Discussions about motivation are typically called for at times of crisis: headhunters picking off our top performers or rumors regarding union organizing activities—"Quick, get that book on motivation!" But wouldn't it be easier to come from the wisdom that says that creating the right environment from the outset is all that's really needed?

"What you want for yourself, give to another" is an additional workplace wisdom that is sorely missing in corporate America. Unfortunately law firms, accounting firms, and physician rotation and training programs speak proudly of their working newcomers to the bone. TV shows document and dramatize the effects of those 24-hour shifts on young physicians' work lives and personal lives, while scientific and medical journals reflect the dangers of expecting young doctors to make life-altering decisions when sleep-deprived. "Track" career programs like these leave those who completed the program inflicting the

same pain on new hires as they themselves experienced. And neither this book nor any other will likely change that survival-of-the-fittest mindset.

It doesn't have to be that way in your company, in your office, or on your shop floor. No matter where you work or what you do, you can be the best boss that your staffers have ever had. You can be that person who influenced and supported them to become better people and stronger contributors. You can be that caring person who encourages, that experienced mentor who guides, and that engaged leader who motivates. In short, ask yourself, Would you want to work for you? If all leaders within your organization followed your lead, would your company be a better place to work as a result?

It's very easy to simply write off the idea of successful leadership. You may have not had very good bosses yourself throughout your own career. You may reason that you work in a cutthroat industry where everyone's out for him- or herself. And to a certain degree, this may be true. But that doesn't mean it has to be your reality or experience. Change your perspective and you'll change your perception. Look at the world through a different lens and, while the objective outcomes of the reality surrounding you may not change, your experience of them can actually change immensely. This doesn't mean sticking your head in the sand and refusing to recognize reality. It does mean, however, that despite the dog-eat-dog nature of your industry, the craziness of your own leaders throughout your career, or the constant pressure you face to produce greater volume at faster speeds, you can shield your people from those complexities. You can reason that the buck stops with you. You're the line of demarcation between the drama above you and what your team members get to experience under your leadership.

It all stems from simply changing your sponsoring thought about who you are as a leader, a motivator, and talent developer. Make it your goal to bring out the best in each of your subordinates—not to fix all their shortcomings but to harvest the best of the strengths that they have to offer. You know intuitively that successful leadership focuses on building on strengths rather than shoring up weaknesses, so find new ways of bringing out those strengths and inspiring employee engagement. Have fun. Consider lightening up just a bit. Understand that life is a gift, and for a significant portion of your lifetime, working with others will motivate you, frustrate you, engage you, and fascinate you. Work, like life itself, is meant to touch all those feelings and emotions through your various experiences. But know that at the end of it all, nothing will stick with you more than the people you've helped, the careers you've developed and built, and the people along the way who thanked you for all you did to help them excel and become their best. That's why leadership is the greatest gift that the workplace offers—because of its innate ability to help you touch lives and make the work world a better place.

That's the secret to all of this. That's the secret sauce of great leaders and inspirational leadership. It's not the end state—it's your trip along the way. Make the most of your career and your work life *through* people, not despite them. Teach what you choose to learn. Encourage others to take healthy risks. Be there when they make mistakes and offer support when they feel vulnerable. Understand that no one does anything wrong given their model of the world and, when in doubt, err on the side of compassion. You're the first domino in the row. You are the kind of leader you choose to be—the kind that can change people's lives and careers along the way. So go ahead and reinvent yourself. Make of your life a gift. The world is waiting to see—and receive—that gift of leadership, of personal and career development, and of selflessness that you're about to display. I hope this book helps you along the way.

Index

About the Author

AUTHOR AND HR EXECUTIVE PAUL FALCONE has twenty years of HR experience in the trenches and has held senior leadership positions at such organizations as Nickelodeon, Paramount Pictures, Time Warner, and City of Hope. He is the author of the bestselling *96 Great Interview Questions to Ask Before You Hire, 101 Tough Conversations to Have with Employees, 101 Sample Write-Ups for Documenting Employee Performance Problems,* and *2600 Phrases for Effective Performance Reviews.* He has also authored many articles on motivation and employee engagement for *HR Magazine,* as well as for the *AMA Playbook.* Paul is a top-rated international speaker and a long-term instructor in UCLA Extension's School of Business and Management, where he teaches courses on ethics for human resource professionals and legal aspects of human resource management. His website can be found at www. PaulFalconeHR.com.

39092 10112795 1